# Towards A View of Canadian Letters

A. J. M. Smith

# Towards a View
# of Canadian Letters

*Selected Critical Essays*
*1928-1971*

UNIVERSITY OF BRITISH COLUMBIA PRESS

TOWARDS A VIEW OF CANADIAN LETTERS
SELECTED CRITICAL ESSAYS 1928-1971

©The University of British Columbia 1973

This book has been published with the help of a grant from the Humanities Research Council of Canada using funds provided by the Canada Council.

International Standard Book Number 0-7748-0019-4(cloth)
0-7748-0020-8(paper)
Library of Congress Catalog Number 73-80448

Produced in Canada by
Evergreen Press Limited

To
George Woodcock
in friendship
and
admiration

# CONTENTS

## V. SOME POLEMICS: EARLY & LATE

## VI. A PERSONAL EPILOGUE

# ACKNOWLEDGEMENTS

The material in this book was published originally in other books or journals. The author and the publisher are grateful to the following publishers for permission to reprint the material cited. (Page numbers in parentheses refer to the present volume.)

*The Canadian Forum:* from issue of April 1928, "Wanted—Canadian Criticism," pp. 600-601, (p. 167).

*Canadian Literature:* from No. 9, 1961, "Eclectic Detachment: Aspects of Identity in Canadian Poetry," (p. 22); from No. 15, 1963, "A Self-Review," (p. 211); from No. 24, 1965, "A Rejected Preface to *New Provinces,* 1936," (p. 170); from No. 30, 1966, "A Unified Personality: Birney's Poems," (p. 125); from No. 31, 1967, "F. R. Scott and Some of His Poems," (p. 115); from No. 37, 1968, "The Canadian Poet I / To Confederation," (p. 55); from No. 38, 1968, "The Canadian Poet II / After Confederation," (p. 156); from No. 50, 1971, "The Poetry of P. K. Page," (p. 146).

Gage Educational Publishing Limited: from *The Book of Canadian Prose Volume I: Early Beginnings to Confederation,* 1965, "Introduction: Prose of the Colonial Period," pp. xii-xxii, (p. 47).

Université Laval: from *Etudes littéraires,* Volume 1, No. 3, Décembre 1968, for "Impromptu Remarks Spoken at the International Poetry Conference, Man & His World, 8 September 1967," (p. 206).

The Macmillan Company of Canada Limited: from *Writing in Canada,* ed. George Whalley, 1956, "Poet," pp. 13-24, (p. 186); from *The Collected Poems of Anne Wilkinson,* 1967, "A Reading of Anne Wilkinson," pp. xiii-xxi, (p. 134).

Memorial University, St. John's, Newfoundland: for "Some Poems of E. J. Pratt: Aspects of Imagery and Theme," the Second Annual Pratt Lecture, 1969, (p. 99).

Michigan State University: from *The Centennial Review of Arts and Science,* 1964, "The Poetic Process: On the Making of Poems," pp. 353-371, (p. 217).

University of New Brunswick: for "The Fredericton Poets," the Founders' Day Address, University of New Brunswick, 1946, (p. 65).

Oxford University Press: from *The Oxford Book of Canadian Verse,* 1960, "Introduction: A Brief History of Canadian Poetry,"pp. xxiii-xli, (p. 3).

*The Tamarack Review:* from No. 18, 1961, "Critical Improvisations on Margaret Avison's *Winter Sun,*" pp. 81-86, (p. 142).

University of Toronto Press: from *University of Toronto Quarterly,* "A Summing-up," from "Our Poets," 1942, pp. 92-93, (p. 77); "Canadian Poetry—A Minority Report," 1939, pp. 125-138, (p. 174); "A Survey of English-Canadian Letters—A Review," 1965, pp. 107-116, (p. 194); from *Proceedings of the Canadian Historical Association,* "Colonialism and Nationalism in Canadian Poetry Before Confederation," 1944, pp. 74-84, (p. 33); from *Our Living Tradition,* 2nd and 3rd series, 1959, "The Poetry of Duncan Campbell Scott," pp. 73-94, (published in association with Carleton University), (p. 79).

# AUTHOR'S NOTE

This book is a selection of essays on various aspects of Canadian literature, mainly poetry, contributed to various journals or written as introductions to anthologies over the past thirty-five years. I would ask the reader to pay special attention to the date of composition of each article. If he does, he will find, I think, what he may choose to consider either a remarkable consistency or a remarkable lack of development. Whichever view is right, I am content to let these pieces stand mainly as they were written. The editors have removed a few passages that were repetitious of material appearing elsewhere in the book, and this has necessitated a few slight changes in one or two places. Occasionally also I have improved a word or sentence or excised a comma.

I rather regret now that I did not include an essay on Northrop Frye's wonderful little book *The Well-Tempered Critic* I contributed to *Canadian Literature* in 1965 or the Introduction to *The Blasted Pine*, an anthology compiled in collaboration with F. R. Scott. But these are easily available.

To the publisher's acknowledgements I must add my personal expression of gratitude for his friendly encouragement to the great Canadian man of letters to whom this work is dedicated. And lastly, as always, to my wife.

A. J. M. S.

Drummond Point
Lake Memphremagog
Québec
June 28, 1973

# PART ONE

*Synoptic*

*A Brief History of Canadian Poetry*

## *Introduction,* The Oxford Book of Canadian Verse

Canadian poetry is a branch of English or French poetry and to some extent also, particularly in the work of contemporary writers, of American poetry. It arose about a century and a quarter ago—after the hard work of hacking a new home out of the wilderness had been accomplished, and there was time to catch one's breath before the task of consolidation and unification began. When it became possible for the pioneer to look beyond the harsh present and aspire to something more gratifying that colonialism, it became possible also—indeed, it became imperative—to cultivate the arts, and particularly poetry, the art that most directly and intimately expresses and evaluates the compulsions of life and its environment. The fact that Canadians were first Frenchmen or Englishmen or Americans and that their language, whether French or English, already contained a rich poetic inheritance can be regarded as an advantage or a handicap according as one looks for a continuation of the old tradition or hopes for something entirely new. There is in American poetry as well as Canadian a good deal more of the traditional and less of the original than modern critics like to admit. Except for *Leaves of Grass* and the unpublished lyrics of Emily Dickinson, American poetry in the nineteenth century is in the European tradition of the English romantics and the major Victorians, and so too is Canadian poetry. Canada, it is true, produced no poet of the stature of a Whitman, a Poe, or an Emerson; there are, however, a number of writers as interesting, each in his own way, as most of the other American poets, and there are traces of local peculiarity and national individualism worth considering as something special that could only have developed in the unique circumstances obtaining in the British North American colonies that remained loyal to England.

What was at first a wilderness, then a battleground, and then a group of isolated colonies became in 1867 a federated autonomous nation and in the twentieth century an independent member of the British Commonwealth, a state whose voice, like India's, is listened to with respect in the council of nations. Conditions of mind and ways of feeling characteristic of each of these three stages—the colonial, the national, and the cosmopolitan—can be examined with peculiar convenience in the poetry of each period, for whatever else it may be Canadian poetry is and always has been a record of life in the new circumstances of a northern transplantation. And the record takes on significance and attains a more than local relevance as technical proficiency makes possible a more intense and accurate expression of sensibility.

From earliest times Canadian poets, both French and English, have held, consciously or unconsciously, to one of two distinct and sometimes divergent aims. One group has made an effort to express whatever is unique or local in Canadian life, while the other has concentrated on what it has in common with life everywhere. The poets of the first group sought to discover something distinctively and essentially "Canadian" and thus come to terms with what was new in the natural, social, and political environment in which they found themselves or which they helped to create; the others made an effort to escape the limitations of provincialism or colonialism by entering into the universal civilizing culture of ideas. The first group was more homely, more natural, and sometimes more original, but it lacked, until the twentieth century, the technical proficiency necessary for real success. The danger for the second group was to be merely literary.

This is not a defect of the backwoods poets of the earliest period—perhaps because their model, when they had one, was Robert Burns or the popular broadsides of the eighteenth century. Their work has a solidity and tang that is emphasized and sharpened by the absence of polish and literary sophistication. Versifiers like Standish O'Grady and Alexander McLachlan, whose closeness to the soil and the forest clearing kept them from acquiring the smoothness and finish of the "serious" poet, interpreted their environment and society with sharper insights than the literary poets who followed two generations later. This they did by shunning the abstract and the grandiose and concentrating with a sympathetic or angry eye upon the familiar and the local. The backwoods poet who is to make anything worthwhile out of his restricted material does so by facing it squarely and looking at it not with the sentimental glance of the local colourist but with the strict and penetrating vision of the realist. It is the pioneer poets' chief claim to serious consideration that this is exactly what they did. They were colonial poets to the extent that they could not forget their sturdy and almost instinctive sense of hearty British rightness, but this, more often than not, made them independent and resentful of interference from the governing classes of the mother country and was one of the most powerful elements in the rise of Canadian national feeling. Indeed, it was the homesteader's vivid sense of the harsh necessities that confronted him in the wilderness which gave him the solid foundation on which to build a new national pride. This developed when he had at last conquered his environment and established himself in greater security and prosperity than he had ever known in the old country. When this was achieved his poetry—except as reminiscence—came to an end, and the literary poets of the Confederation period came into their own.

There were, of course, from the beginning a number of self-conscious literary poets, the earliest of whom, imitators of Lord Byron and Tom Moore, painted gaudy pictures of the noble red man and landscapes full of Alpine mountains and semi-tropical forests but produced nothing real enough to be of more than antiquarian interest. It is a curious and perhaps a significant fact that some of their volumes enjoyed a remarkable success among the colonists. W. F. Hawley's *Quebec, The Harp, and Other Poems* (1829) was awarded a gold medal by the Society for the Encouragement of the Arts and Sciences of Quebec, and Adam Kidd's *The Huron Chief* (1830) sold more than fifteen hundred copies within a year.

A quarter of a century later (after the rebellions of 1837, the establishment of responsible government, and the stimulation of a sense of national unity by the common fear of the American annexation movement) newspaper reviewers, magazine editors, and the public at large began to look for emotional and national inspiration from Canadian poets. As Standish O'Grady had written as early as 1842, "This expanded and noble continent will no doubt furnish fit matter for the Muse. The diversity of climate, the richness of soil, the endearing qualities of a genial atmosphere must no doubt furnish a just excitement to the poetic mind, and arouse the energy correspondent with a richness of scenery, which the contemplative mind will studiously portray." This enthusiasm is typical of the hopes and expectations that were held for the development of poetry in the new colonies. The Reverend Edward Hartley Dewart, who published a volume of selections from Canadian poets in 1864, wrote in his introduction that "A national literature is an essential element in the formation of national character," and while outlining with considerable perspicacity the difficulties hindering the rise of an indigenous poetry, he was able to single out a number of creditable achievements by Canadians, particularly the charming Spenserian stanzas of Sangster's *The St. Lawrence and the Saguenay* (1856), a somewhat Byronic sentimental journey down the two majestic rivers, and Heavysege's mammoth dramatic poem *Saul* (first edition 1857), both of which are actually more remarkable for their literary sophistication than for any native Canadian element. *Saul* particularly holds our attention—though not always in the way its author intended. The poem is a huge closet drama in blank verse, interspersed with lyrical interludes, a *tour de force* of linguistic adventures, an imitation of Webster and Tourneur by a self-taught, uncontrolled Beddoes. Heavysege is a strange "sport." There perhaps has never been in the poetry of the English-speaking peoples anywhere so curious a mixture of the grand and the grandiose, of the magnificent and the ridiculous as *Saul*. Both Sangster and Heavysege produced works of ambitious scope, and if there was actually little that was national in their poetry, there was a good deal—fragmentary and spasmodic though it was—that was poetry.

If, however, the claims of a national poetry can be satisfied by a minute and sometimes passionate delineation of landscape and of man's struggle to push into the heart of nature and make himself at home there, then two poets of a generation older than the famous Roberts-Lampman-Carman group of the nineties must be named as the creators of a new poetry in the seventies and eighties and the first distinguished members of a native Canadian school. These were Charles Mair and Isabella Valancy Crawford.

A good deal of Mair's verse is sentimental and verbose, but he has one claim to distinction—the sobriety and patience of his descriptions of the Canadian wilderness. In such poems as "The Fireflies" and in descriptive passages in his historical drama *Tecumseh* (1886), he bends a careful and almost microscopic glance upon the minutiae of the woods with their animals, birds, and insects, changing in the varying moods of the hours and the seasons. He watches the busy forms that ply about the underbrush in the heat of late midsummer and depicts their comings and goings with a loving care. His best descriptive poems have a Vergilian rectitude, though their diction and their rather stiff metrical regularity suggest a transplanted eighteenth-century "nature poet" like Cowper or Thomson. When he turned to the western plains or the vast stretches of unbroken forest, Mair's imagination caught fire and his writing took on an intensity and power that anticipate the more fervid spirit of the later poets. A few lines will show this heightened quality:

> Great prairies swept beyond our aching sight
> Into the measureless West; uncharted realms,
> Voiceless and calm, save when tempestuous wind
> Rolled the rank herbage into billows vast
> And rushing tides which never found a shore . . .
> Flushed with fresh blooms, deep perfumed by the rose,
> And murmurous with flower-fed bird and bee.
> The deep-grooved bison-paths like furrows lay,
> Turned by the cloven hoofs of thundering herds. . . .
> There vainly sprung the affrighted antelope,
> Beset by glittering eyes and hurrying feet.
> The dancing grouse, at their insensate sport,
> Heard not the stealthy footstep of the fox;
> The gopher on his little earthwork stood,
> With folded arms, unconscious of the fate
> That wheeled in narrowing circles overhead;
> And the poor mouse, on heedless nibbling bent,
> Marked not the silent coiling of the snake.

It is in verses like these, at once traditional and full of accurate observation, that Mair makes a genuine contribution to the development of poetry in Canada. It is to be regretted that so small a part of his work should have shown this solidity and directness, yet the few passages where he attains his fullest power have a rectitude and clarity that anticipate Lampman.

Good as such poetry may be, however, it was excelled by that of a younger contemporary of Mair, Isabella Valancy Crawford, who died in 1887 at the age of thirty-seven. If we place beside even the best lines of Mair the wonderful second part of "Malcolm's Katie" (1884), we shall see the difference between descriptive poetry which, though of a high order, is static and reflective, and impressionistic poetry that teems with energy and displays for the first time in Canadian writing an imaginative vitality commensurate with the western land itself and its challenge to the pioneer. "Malcolm's Katie," undoubtedly Miss Crawford's finest achievement, is the product of an imagination that is curiously geographical and geological. It bases itself on an exact observation of minute detail, but its characteristic operation is to expand, amplify, and generalize—and in the process to utilize the most concrete and precise appeals to the senses. The coming of winter in the north woods is seen—and heard—like this, through the heightened sensibility, imaginatively apprehended, of the red man:

> The South Wind laid his moccasins aside,
> Broke his gay calumet of flow'rs, and cast
> His useless wampum, beaded with cool dews,
> Far from him, northward; his long, ruddy spear
> Flung sunward, whence it came, and his soft locks
> Of warm, fine haze grew silver as the birch. . . .
>
> The late, last thunders of the summer crash'd,
> Where shrieked great eagles, lords of naked cliffs. . . .
>
> In this shrill moon the scouts of winter ran
> From the ice-belted north, and whistling shafts
> Struck maple and struck sumach—and a blaze
> Ran swift from leaf to leaf, from bough to bough,
> Till round the forest flash'd a belt of flame. . . .

Miss Crawford's "geographical animism" can be illustrated by many lines and images: "Ancient billows that have torn the roots of cliffs and bitten at the golden lips of firm sleek beaches"; "The round-eyed worlds that walk in the blank paths of space"; "Lesser seas tossed from their rocking cup"; and, finally, a perfect line, classic in its formal beauty and filled with the richest of implications:

Wrecks plunge, prow foremost, down still, solemn slopes.

For one reader this line has something of the magic of Rimbaud's "Bateau Ivre" or Hart Crane's "At Melville's Tomb."

"Malcolm's Katie" is the first, and not one of the least, of the few poems that can be really called Canadian, because its language and its imagery, the sensibility it reveals, and the vision it embodies are indigenously northern and western, a product not of England or the States but of Canada. We do not get this particular kind of success again until "The Cachalot" (1923) and *Towards the Last Spike* (1952) of E. J. Pratt. With Isabella Valancy Crawford the early period of Canadian poetry in English comes to an end. Maturity had been achieved.

The earliest French poetry in Canada was produced in the city of Quebec before the conquest. It was minor occasional poetry in the neo-classic tradition. From the beginning it went hand in hand with journalism and had a social and often political function. After the victory of the English, the political function became a national one, religious and even racial in its scope. The habitants, led by European- and American-inspired intellectuals, tried to win the struggle for survival by force of arms in 1837 and 1838, and lost. They were to win it instead, as the century developed, by industry and the arts of peace. The study of the heroic past in the work of a national historian, François-Xavier Garneau, and a national poet, Octave Crémazie, gave an impetus to French-Canadian patriotism at the very moment it had become essential to survival. The national pride of the defeated and, as they felt, abandoned colonists of New France was stimulated and their wounds to some extent salved by the glowing pages of Garneau and the impassioned verse of Crémazie.

Crémazie is acknowledged to be the father of French-Canadian poetry. He was a man of wide culture, and though the theme of faithfulness to the court-ly and Catholic ideals of pre-Revolutionary France was his chief inspiration, he was not himself provincial or even only national. He was well read in Eng-lish and French, and like some later poets he studied Sanskrit. His first verses, published in 1854, hailed the partnership of Britain and France in the Cri-mean War. The immense enthusiasm aroused in Quebec, and indeed throughout the whole of Canada, by the visit of the French corvette *La Ca-pricieuse* in 1856, marking the first time the flag of France had appeared in the St. Lawrence since the fall of New France, was shared also by Crémazie, and he wrote the first of a series of ambitious patriotic poems of which "Le Drapeau de Carillon" is the most famous and the best.

Crémazie, however, was too intelligent a critic and too modest a man not to recognize the limitations and weaknesses of purely patriotic poetry, where rhetoric and hyperbole are the most effective instruments, and in his later years which he spent as a kind of Canadian exile in France, whence he had fled in 1862 from the financial catastrophe that had overtaken his efforts as a bookseller, he analysed with considerable acumen the difficulties, chiefly economic, of the writer in a colony and was able to make fun of his own popular and in French Canada very influential verses. "Il faut bien le dire," he wrote to his friend Abbé Casgrain, literary critic and editor, in 1867,

> Il faut bien le dire, dans notre pays on n'a pas le goût très délicat en matière de poésie. Faites rimer un certain nombre de fois *gloire* avec *victoire, aïeux* avec *glorieux, France* avec *espérance,* entremêlez ces rimes de quelques mots sonores comme notre *religion,* notre *patrie,* notre *langue,* nos *lois,* le *sang de nos pères;* faites chauffer le tout à la flamme du patriotisme, et servez chaud. Tout le monde vous dira que c'est magnifique.

Crémazie outlined here not only his own worst defects, but those of one long-lived school of French-Canadian poetry. Only a very good poet can make something permanently valuable out of such material, and though it was his patriotic poetry that gave Crémazie his fame and his influence it is the melancholy "Les Morts," in spite of echoes of Hugo and Lamartine, that testifies best to his poetic power. Perhaps the most satisfying example of early French-Canadian nationalism in poetry is the briefest and the simplest, the folk-song-like lyric by the novelist Antoine Gérin-Lajoie, "Un Canadien errant," which celebrates the devotion of the exiled *patriotes* of 1837.

The mantle of Crémazie, who died in Le Havre in 1879, descended upon Louis Fréchette, a young law student of Lévis, across the river from Quebec. Fréchette associated with the older poet in his bookshop in Quebec City and published his first volume *Mes Loisirs* in 1865, poems emphasizing, as Crémazie had, the glorious past of French Canada. For three years in the late sixties Fréchette sought his fortune in Chicago and in *Voix d'un exilé* he published some bitter attacks on the conditions that forced a young Canadian to leave his home for the more prosperous United States. Later, after his return to Quebec, his participation in Canadian politics, and the acceptance of his poetry by his compatriots, he bought up and destroyed this volume. His poems published in Canada and in Paris during the late seventies were crowned by the French Academy, and it seemed at last as if something done in the North American Dominion was meritorious enough to place beside the masterpieces of the old world. Fréchette acquired enormous prestige among his countrymen—English as well as French. He was winning recognition outside the narrow confines of his own province at the very moment that English-speaking poets in the Maritimes and Ontario—Roberts, Carman, Lampman, and Duncan Campbell Scott—were about to achieve something of the same sort of success in London and Boston. Fréchette's finest work was his *Légende d'un peuple* (1887), which utilized the method of Victor Hugo to depict the heroic passages in the history of French Canada.

It is clear that both Crémazie and Fréchette had a divided aim and were attempting to do two somewhat incompatible things at once. They wished to express and interpret their native French-Canadian scene and to write a kind of Genesis and book of heroes; at the same time, they wished to demonstrate that poetry as good as, and therefore like, that produced in France could come out of the lost colony. It was this objective that prevented them from achieving a genuinely contemporary expression of the individual life of the province and limited their work, as so much of the thought and feeling of Quebec has been limited, to a nostalgic and static evocation of an idealized past. Nearly all of the contemporaries, rivals, and successors of Fréchette continued, as he did, the patriotic tradition of Crémazie, but all of them, in part of their work, developed a school of sober realism devoted to the minute delineation of the hard and homely life of the farmer and of the virtues of integrity and endurance that were really a part of the make-up of the *habitant*. Among these were Pamphile LeMay, the founder of the *terroir* school, William Chapman, and Nérée Beauchemin. Beauchemin had written in the vein of Crémazie in the nineties, but his best work was reserved for a volume of sonnets and lyrics of the soil published as late as 1928 and demonstrating the continuing vitality of the *terroir* poetry.

The success of Crémazie and Fréchette in the last thirty years of the nineteenth century was paralleled in English Canada by a group of remarkable poets born in the early sixties who produced a series of ambitious and successful volumes in the eighties and nineties. The acknowledged leader of the group was the New Brunswick poet Charles G. D. Roberts; closely associated with him were his cousin Bliss Carman and the Ontario poets Archibald Lampman, Wilfred Campbell, and Duncan Campbell Scott. These men were all classically educated, were lovers of nature (in the Wordsworthian sense), were filled with something of the same local and national pride that animated their French confrères, and were stimulated by such contemporary English poets as Arnold, the Pre-Raphaelites, and Swinburne. Though the romantic spirit which animates their classical forms is out of fashion just now, it cannot be denied that they established a national school of reflective nature poetry and achieved a standard of technical excellence unattained in Canada before and only rarely equalled since.

The work of these poets was stimulated by the spirit of rather blatant national sentiment that preceded and followed Confederation, but it served to humanize and refine that spirit. It was Roberts, quite consciously, and

Campbell, Lampman, and Scott implicitly, who demonstrated for the benefit of those who wished to see the new Dominion unified and strengthened by the rise of a national literature that the poets at least were willing to try. Yet only Roberts was openly and obviously a patriotic poet dedicated to the national theme (as Crémazie and Fréchette had been dedicated to *their* national theme). But patriotic enthusiasm did not provide him with his finest poetry. This is to be found in what is really a close equivalent to the poetry of the *terroir*, the homely sonnets and lyrics collected in *Songs of the Common Day* (1893) and *The Book of the Native* (1896). It was the local scene and nature treated realistically or with classical restraint that gave him his most enduring subjects. His finest poetry is not to be found in his ambitious odes on Confederation or in his pseudo-mystical transcendental pieces but in the verses that most faithfully and soberly present the life of the farmer, the fisherman, and the woodsman going about their eternal tasks under the changing skies of the four seasons.

In his best work Roberts kept his feet solidly on earth, but Carman soared, or tried to soar, into the "intense inane." His gift was purely lyrical, and though it achieved some beautiful successes, it proved dangerous and eventually enervating. Carman reflected in his own special way the glow of Swinburnian lyricism and at the same time a good deal of the heartiness of the cult of the open road that stemmed from Whitman through Stevenson, Henley, and the American poet Richard Hovey, with whom Carman collaborated in the well-known series of *Songs from Vagabondia* in the early years of the new century. Carman's gift of song was an ambiguous one. It is impossible not to see him as a kind of sorcerer's apprentice. He has the power to burst forth in song but not the taste or intelligence to know when to stop. There are few of his poems that are not too long, and too many of them trail away after a fine beginning into a glib and tenuous vacuity. Yet in his small number of perfectly successful lyrics and in many scattered lines and occasional stanzas there is an unforgettable quality that makes itself felt as a strange and troubling mixture of the beautiful and the sinister. It is the product of an acute and quivering sensibility, and it testifies to the presence of a genuine and original emotion. "Low Tide on Grand Pré" and "Daphne" express an awareness of the mystery and beauty of life and at the same time of its frustrations and disillusionments. It is unfortunate that so pure a lyricist should, in his later career, have fallen under influences that diluted and distorted the spirit of his work and caused him to fritter away much of his talent in the pursuit of an attentuated transcendentalism that was neither very new nor, intellectually speaking, very reputable.

Associated with these two New Brunswick poets were three men in Ontario: Archibald Lampman, Duncan Campbell Scott, and Wilfred Campbell. They were born within a year or two of one another and all began their careers in the late eighties and early nineties. All were inheritors of the Eng-

lish romantic movement, but its influence on them was modified and tempered by a classical education and, at least in Lampman and Scott, by an
enthusiasm for Matthew Arnold and Robert Bridges and for Keats and William Morris rather than for Shelley or Swinburne. While they learned their
craft from their predecessors and contemporaries among the English poets,
they did not cease to keep the immediate Canadian scene before their eyes,
and they continued, with more art than Mair if not with more intensity than
Miss Crawford, to interpret nature and the impingement of nature upon the
sensitive mind in ways that were peculiar to their northern locale.

Lampman, like Roberts and Carman, was of loyalist descent and the son of
an Anglican clergyman. He was educated at Trinity College, Toronto, and
after a brief spell of schoolmastering he went into the civil service in Ottawa
where he remained until his early death in 1899. In such finely etched pictures as the delicate and perfect "Heat" and in such very different, but again
perfect sonnets as "Solitude," "A Sunset at Les Éboulements," or "Winter
Evening" Lampman displays his fine painter's eye for significant detail and
his poet's power of striking the unforgettable phrase or cadence, and demonstrates that a recognizably distinct eastern Canadian landscape can be presented with the artistry of a Keats or a Bridges. It is in his nature poems and
poems of pure landscape that Lampman is generally most himself; when he
attempted to philosophize or moralize he became dull and unoriginal, and he
had little gift for narrative. In one poem, however, the remarkable "City of
the End of Things," Lampman transcended his usual themes and became for
once a poet of vision and prophecy.

Duncan Campbell Scott, the friend of Lampman and editor of his *Collected Poems*, served in the Department of Indian Affairs at Ottawa and was
brought into close contact with the wilderness and the life of the red man. It
was this that gave him one of his most characteristic themes—the conflict
between the heroic or the primitive and the new commercial world with its
superior arms and its superior cunning. But Scott in his poems of the forest
settlements and the Indian is far from being a romantic primitivist. His evocations of the cruelty and magic power of the wild, whether in man or nature,
were unsentimental and accurately observed. As a result, some of his tragic
narratives of Indian life—"The Forsaken" and "At Gull Lake, August 1810"
are the best—are among the most original and valid of Canadian poems. But
this was not the only theme of Scott's poetry, and his manner was more varied
than that of any other poet of his generation except Roberts. His first volume
had been published in London in 1893, and it showed in about equal proportions the somewhat feverish emotionalism of the aesthetic movement and the
formal fastidiousness of classicism. Such a fusion appears too in the strange,
intense evocations of night and storm that introduce a note of cruelty at the
heart of beauty into many of his descriptive and narrative poems—a troubling perception that is found also, perhaps only half consciously, in his early

love poems. In his best work Scott is as sensitive as Carman, and as accurate as Lampman or Roberts.

The last poet of the group, Wilfred Campbell, sought to make himself a kind of unofficial laureate of the Dominion and the Empire, but he is interesting and significant in only one volume, *Lake Lyrics,* his first, which appeared in 1889. Here, in poems like "How One Winter Came in the Lake Region" and "The Winter Lakes," he caught the spirit of the Georgian Bay region of northern Ontario in a way that anticipated the starkness of the Group of Seven painters of some thirty years later. A close attention to details of landscape and weather, an insistent rhythm, and a relevant and powerful emotion that rises in some of the winter pieces to terror and hysteria give Campbell's best lyrics their special claim to distinction.

The influence of this school of poets had a dazzling and, it must be admitted, rather stupefying effect on their successors for two generations. In the sincere and often competent work of Theodore Goodridge Roberts, the younger brother of Charles, Francis Sherman, and, more recently, Audrey Alexandra Brown, the tradition of romantic nature poetry tended to lose its grip on the immediate and the local, and much of its energy was dissipated in rather attenuated reflections of various European movements such as Pre-Raphaelitism and the Celtic Twilight. An exception must be made, however, for the best of Theodore Roberts' pieces and for a handful of the lyrics of Marjorie Pickthall, which sound a note of singular purity that lifts them above the work of any of her contemporaries, at least among the English-Canadian poets. A sharp perceptiveness of the beauty and transience of life and a passionate longing for escape into God give to her poems "Resurgam" and "Quiet" a quality not much inferior, if at all, to that of Christina Rossetti. In striking contrast to the delicacy of feeling and suavity of expression in the work of Marjorie Pickthall is the hearty Bohemianism in the Villonesque ballades and rondeaus of the West Coast poet, Tom MacInnes, who developed the cult of the open road and dramatized the figure of the happy vagabond, which had been one of the most energetic aspects of Carman before him. At about the same time also, Robert W. Service, who can be considered only as a visiting Englishman, produced his immensely popular synthetic ballads. The fame of these was to be equalled a little later, during the First World War, by John McCrae with his widely quoted lyric "In Flanders Fields," published originally in *Punch.*

In French poetry also the decade of the nineties was a sort of "golden age," and here its influence was to extend fruitfully into the two first decades of the new century. Beginning with the establishment in 1895 of the *École Littéraire de Montréal* the patriotic themes of the Quebec masters Crémazie and Fréchette were replaced by a more cosmopolitan emphasis on craftsmanship, personal emotion, and variety. The Montreal School was established by two young law students, Jean Charbonneau and Paul de Martigny, and regular meetings of poets, critics, scholars, and journalists were soon being held in the Château de Ramezay, the old headquarters of the French governors of Montreal. The proceedings of some of the meetings and new work by the poets belonging to the group were published in 1900, including also a contribution by Fréchette, who was honoured if not imitated by the succeeding generation. The new poets were inspired in their experiments with form and in their more emotional and original themes by the various poetic movements in France, particularly Parnassianism and Symbolism. Among these poets must be named Gonzalve Désaulniers, one of the oldest, who much later, in 1930, turned back to the homely task of depicting in brief realistic descriptions the scenes of his native province; Charles Gill, the painter poet who planned a series of ambitious descriptive and historical tableaux of the River St. Lawrence; the critical and sceptical Charles Dantin; the invalid Albert Lozeau; and the tragic figure of Émile Nelligan. The last two made the most impressive and enduring contribution to Canadian poetry.

From the age of eighteen Lozeau had been confined to his bed with a form of spinal paralysis. Forced to relinquish any attempt to interpret the life of his *beau pays Canadien,* which he confessed he did not and could not know, he became instead the poet of the closed-in life. With great elegance, charm, and modesty—"Je suis resté neuf ans les pieds à la hauteur de la tête," he wrote once, "cela m'a enseigné l'humilité"—he developed a narrow but pure talent for the inner life of sensibility and reverie, which provided him with material for three volumes of verse between 1907 and 1916.

The career of Émile Nelligan was briefer and more brilliant. His poetry, which introduced Baudelairism and Verlainism into the opening circles of the French-Canadian literary consciousness, was hailed with enthusiasm by the poets and critics of the Montreal School, and the reciting by the young poet of his "Romance du vin" at one of the *soirées* of the Château de Ramezay was a memorable event. Technical virtuosity, aspirations of more than local scope, and a passionate, if feverish, sensibility combined to produce some of the finest poems ever written in Canada. A new, surprising, and, for French Canada, extremely salutary movement was being inaugurated at the moment it could be most useful, a movement that was at once aesthetic, passionate, cosmopolitan, and exotic, and that gave an immense impetus to the *other,* the non-native tradition in Canadian literature. It was later poets, however, Paul Morin and René Chopin particularly, who were to carry on the movement. Nelligan, like Chatterton or Rimbaud, was a marvellous boy, whose work was done before he reached twenty. In 1899 his mind collapsed, and though he did not die until 1941 he remained hopelessly insane, one of the most tragic figures in the history of North American letters.

One or two poets of lesser stature belonging to the Montreal School indicate almost as clearly as Lozeau and Nelligan the new winds that were blowing into the closed garden of Quebec culture. Louis Dantin, in such ambiguous poems as "Noël intime," sounds the familiar note of religious scepticism, a scepticism, however, which is actually a painful, if inescapable, shadow of faith. Albert Ferland, who later, however, was to become a poet of the French-Canadian soil, wrote with bitter irony in "La Patrie au poète" what amounts to a repudiation of the earlier school of patriotic poetry:

> Va, Barde primitif des vierges Laurentides,
> Va-t'en pleurer ton coeur comme un fou dans les bois,
> Fidèle au souvenir des héros d'autrefois,
> Tandis que l'or vainqueur fait les hommes avides!
>
> Poète, mon enfant, tu me chantes en vain.
> Je suis la Terre ingrate où rêva Crémazie;
> Célèbre si tu veux ma grave poésie;
> Mais pour toi, mon enfant, je n'aurai pas de pain!

Joseph-Arthur Lapointe, at one time president of l'École de Montréal, produced in the twelve lines of "Les Pauvres" a poem of social indignation and pity worthy of Thomas Hardy. Paul Morin, who published two volumes, *Le Pâon d'émail* in 1911 *Poèmes de cendre et d'or* in 1922, was a leader of the aesthetic and exotic school. He had frequented the salon of la Comtesse de Noailles in Paris and had travelled in Greece, the Levant, and North Africa. His poetry was polished, brightly coloured, heavily jewelled, and with a Byzantine glitter that was in itself something of a criticism of the provincialism and piety of so much French-Canadian poetry. Morin was accused of dilettantism and coldness, of exoticism and paganism; but the perfection of his forms and the dedicated spirit of his devotion to art answered for him even more effectively than his own humble reply in the poem "A ceux de mon pays."

The modern movement in Canada began a little later in English poetry than in French, perhaps because it began in France before it did in England. The significant dates are the publication of E. J. Pratt's "little epics," *The Witches' Brew* in 1925 and "The Cachalot" and "The Great Feud" in 1926. There was a great flurry of new poetry also in the magazines, particularly in the undergraduate journal the *McGill Fortnightly Review* (1925-27), which introduced the work of some of the poets who were later to become influential. Among them were Leo Kennedy, F. R. Scott, and A. J. M. Smith.

These joined with A. M. Klein and the Toronto poets E. J. Pratt and Robert Finch to produce a group anthology, *New Provinces,* which did not appear, however, until 1936. With the exception of Pratt these poets did not publish volumes until the early forties, when certain Toronto publishing houses suddenly became receptive to work in the modern manner, and the poetic revival which was to distinguish the forties and fifties was at last under way.

Of contemporary poets, the oldest and the first to be established, E. J. Pratt, has been the most ambitious, the most self-confident, and in some ways the most adventurous; and he has reached the widest audience. He is, with the exception of the younger West-Coast poet, Earle Birney, the only English-Canadian poet whose gift is mainly for narrative and who has created on a large scale. His main contribution has been a series of dynamic narrative poems, some fabulous, some heroic, some humorous, some historical, and some (during the war) topical, but all filled with vitality and power. Pratt was born in Newfoundland, and the sea and the rocky coast are in his blood. The poems of 1925 and 1926 are fantastic, fabulous, and humorous—miniature epics that dramatize man's struggle with nature or, as in "The Great Feud," tell of the suicidal war to extinction between monsters of the primeval slime. These narratives present a philosophical or quasi-religious attitude toward the problem of man's survival and of man's significance. They are essentially parables, but their success is due to the fact that the poet never stoops to moralize or allows his action to bog down in exposition: everything is concrete and active. During the thirties Pratt wrote two soberly realistic narratives, *The Roosevelt and the Antinoe* and *The Titanic,* and a compassionate "novel in verse," *Brébeuf and His Brethren* (1940). Pratt's most recent work, *Towards the Last Spike,* is sub-titled "a verse panorama of the building of the Canadian Pacific Railway." The poem is a brilliantly original treatment of the theme that recurs frequently in Pratt's poetry—the theme of power and its analysis into factors of good and evil. The ironic solution to the conflict is that man triumphs over his antagonist, the Laurentian Shield and the Rocky Mountains, by a fusion with it or a merging into it. Here, as in other poems, Pratt's attitude towards Power, whether natural, human, or demonic, is complex and ambiguous, and the emotions it arouses in him are ambiguous also—exaltation, terror, and ultimately compassion. The irony implicit in this attitude gives Pratt's poetry its intellectual tang; compassion humanizes it and gives it its final calm.

In his poems of the sea and the war Pratt has an affinity with Masefield and in his fantastic imaginative pieces with Roy Campbell. Although he is not well known outside Canada, in neither case need he fear the comparison. His very virtues, however, have tended to separate him from his younger contemporaries of the thirties and forties. His energy, enthusiasm, and faith, and the expansiveness of his good humour, are all somewhat alien to the divided and disillusioned spirit of the new generation.

Only one modern Canadian poet has shown a similar boldness and a similar ability to create on a large scale. He is Robert Choquette, who was born in 1905 and who launched his first volume *A travers les vents* in 1925 when Pratt was producing his earliest original work. Choquette repudiated the aestheticism of Nelligan and the exoticism of Paul Morin and cultivated instead, not a poetry of the soil or the village but a universal and emotional poetry that was to be at once national and filled with energy and thought.

> Nous avons grandi [he wrote] parmi la nature la plus virile, la plus âpre, la plus pathétiquement sauvage que porte la terre; nos plaines, nos lacs, nos fleuves, nos forêts donnent le vertige aux imaginations européennes: nous sentons remuer dans nos corps la vigueur d'une race pleine de sève et vierge et neuve comme nos sapins verts; et voici qu'au lieu de chanter à pleins poumons des hymnes d'amour et d'enthousiasme, voici que nous apportons au peuple de petites soies fines ou des barres de métal poli.

Expressed thus rhetorically this enthusiasm does not sound very convincing. These are sentiments that might have been heard from the earliest of the patriotic and romantic Canadian poets and reviewers, English and French alike. Parallel thoughts can be found in Standish O'Grady, Sangster, and Dr. Dewart, as well as in Garneau and Crémazie. But there is a difference. Choquette, a romantic though he may be, whose rhythms recall those of Hugo and Lamartine, is a child of the twentieth century, and it is a modern consciousness that expresses itself in his best and most ambitious poems *Metropolitan Museum* (1933) and the long and beautifully sustained *Suite marine* (1953).

The modern spirit in Canadian poetry, indeed, has developed, as it has in Europe and the United States, in a progressive and orderly revolution. There was first a widening of the subject matter of poetry to include all aspects of contemporary life, especially the homely, the familiar, and the urban, treated realistically or with irony. At the same time there was a simplification of poetic language and an expansion of its scope to include the colloquial and the ordinary. This was part of the world-wide reaction against the rhetoric of the nineteenth century and academic doctrines of poetic diction. The free-verse movement in France and imagism in England and America were part of this technical revolution. Influences which made for simplicity and inclusiveness were felt by all the serious Canadian poets after the First World War, and particularly by the writers of the native tradition. These were mainly poets who experienced the left-wing political impulses of the post-depression years and, among the French, young revivalists of the school of *le terroir*. Dorothy

Livesay, Anne Marriott, and Earle Birney in the west, and Raymond Souster and Louis Dudek in Toronto and Montreal are representative of the poets of this school writing in English; Alfred DesRochers, particularly in the final edition of *A l'ombre d'Orford* (1948), is the best of its French adherents. Two poets somewhat older than any of these, W. W. E. Ross and Raymond Knister, who was drowned in 1932, represent this realistic and imagistic aspect of modernism more purely and with a narrower but possibly sharper vision. In any case, the accurately pinpointed and rigidly objective "laconics" of Ross and the brief vivid farm poems of Knister have an originality and native flavour that is lacking in the work of more ambitious poets. Some of Knister's earliest poems and stories were published in *transition* under the editorship of Eugene Jolas, and Ross's work was admired by Marianne Moore and printed in *The Dial.*

The metaphysical revolution effected by Eliot was reflected as early as the mid-twenties by the English-speaking poets of a new Montreal School, Scott, Klein, Kennedy, and Smith, while the theories of T. E. Hulme and Ezra Pound had an invigorating effect on the whole community of new poets. The Jewish poet, Abraham Klein, has a unique and special interest that derives from more than the energy and spirited bravura of his technical achievements. He throws a surprising and penetrating light on the problem of nationalism—a problem that has remained unsolved from the beginning of Canadian literature. Klein is the most successful and intensely dedicated of national poets, but the nationalism that stirs him is not a Canadian but a Jewish nationalism. Steeped in the ancient lore and ritual of Judaism, he is a Jewish poet in the sense that Claudel was a Catholic poet, and while his first two volumes, *Hath not a Jew...* (1940) and *Poems* (1944), concern themselves with the traditions and aspirations of his own people, his last book, *The Rocking Chair* (1948), is a brilliant and sympathetic interpretation of the province of Quebec. The patriarchal, ecclesiastical, and conservative structure of the French-speaking province, with its own language, its own laws, and its own religion, is something that his Hebraic conservatism envies and understands, though he has a bitter awareness also of the folly and racial intolerance that sometimes corrupt it.

The other poets of the group were more firmly committed to a cosmopolitan tradition, and sometimes with irony and sometimes with more uncomplicated emotions they assimilated the methods of the symbolists and the modern metaphysicals. During the war years of the forties poetry centred on little magazines in Montreal and on the West Coast, and the editors, the late John Sutherland, of *First Statement* and *Northern Review,* and Alan Crawley, of *Contemporary Verse,* deserve great credit for their part in the contemporary revival. Among the poets themselves, an Englishman, Patrick Anderson, was a dynamic and inspiring source of energy. He had come to Canada on a Commonwealth Fellowship from Oxford and became a Canadian citizen, working first as a schoolmaster in Montreal and later as a lecturer at McGill University. From 1940 to 1950 he remained in Montreal and in association with F. R. Scott, P. K. Page, Neufville Shaw, Bruce Ruddick, and others edited the experimental literary journal *Preview.* Anderson is a gifted and fluent writer. Adopting the manner now of Auden, now of Macneice, and now of Barker or Dylan Thomas, and inspired both by Marx and Freud, he turned his attention with refreshing gusto to the problem of Canadian identity. His "Poem on Canada" (1946) has much that is individual and penetrating, while lyrics like "Sleighride" and "Camp" indicate the influence of nature in Canada upon a sophisticated European sensibility. The most brilliant poet of the group, however, is Miss P. K. Page, whose sympathies are warmer than Anderson's and whose flair is psychological rather than political. Her style is characterized by subjective but exceedingly concrete images and witty conceits that sometimes are both verbal and visual. In "The Stenographers," for instance, she looks into the harassed eyes of her fellow workers in a government office under war-time pressure and expresses her sense of horror and breakdown in a characteristic conceit:

> In their eyes I have seen
> the pin-men of madness in marathon trim
> race round the track of the stadium pupil.

"I lie in the long *parenthesis* of arms," she writes in another poem, and achieves a conciseness and ambiguity that would please Mr. Empson, while in such poems as "Man with One Small Hand" and "Arras," strangeness and terror grow naturally out of the familiar, as they do in dreams.

There is a good deal of psychological subtlety in the work of all these English-Canadian poets of the forties and fifties, but for spiritual insight we must turn to two of their French compatriots, Saint-Denys-Garneau, a descendant of Canada's first historian, and his cousin, Anne Hébert. Saint-Denys-Garneau, who was born in 1916 and died in 1943, was the master of an abstract and symbolic poetry that mirrors a metaphysical anguish. The poems in his *Régards et jeux dans l'espace* (1938), though they have an affinity with the *method* of Rimbaud and recall sometimes the *subject* of Rilke or Kafka, are nevertheless quite individual and original. Their unifying theme is the problem of responsibility and guilt. The perceptions of childhood, of nature, and finally of death and nothingness are explored in an effort to recover lost innocence. Anne Hébert is perhaps less adventurous, but her sensibility and her style are even purer, if that is possible. Her poems collected in *Les Songes en équilibre* (1942) and *Le Tombeau des rois* (1953) deal also with childhood, loneliness, memory, and death. They show an awareness that sometimes approaches mysticism. Solitude, reverie, and the enclosed life are valued in their personal aspect. In some of her poems, however, notably "Vie de Château," she expresses a sense of the stifling atmosphere created by the enclosed, backward-looking, ancestor-worshipping, earthbound spirit of French-Canadian nationalism. It is a new and more critical attitude that is replacing the patriotic and religious poetry of the school of *le terroir* in the work of the French poets of the forties and fifties. Sometimes the transcending of provincial limitations is found in the cosmopolitan modernism of the technique rather than explicitly in the subject-matter—Pierre Trottier's "Femme aux couleurs de mon pays" is a good illustration of this—and certain poets, notably Alain Grandbois, have introduced the methods of surrealism into Canadian poetry. His "Fermons l'armoire" is explicit enough in its rejection of the óld spirit, and so are the later poems of François Hertel, a Jesuit priest who, having for a number of years in the late thirties and forties exercised a considerable influence as poet, critic, and editor, underwent a spiritual crisis, came to doubt his vocation and even his faith, and exiled himself to France, a colonial, a hopeless outsider, proclaiming himself in his prose memoirs a new *Canadien errant,* "porc parmi les porcs." Of the many young French poets of the new cosmopolitanism Gilles Hénault, Roland Giguère, and Jean-Guy Pilon may be allowed to represent the adventurousness of style and the resolute seeking for a new faith to replace the old, no longer satisfying, objects of respect.

A somewhat similar progression can be seen in the poetry of the English Canadians, though the story is less one of definable literary movements than the simultaneous emergence of a number of brilliant and independent talents. The poetic revival of the forties was continued throughout the fifties without diminution. Perhaps the most striking figure of the new decade was Irving Layton. A holdover from the early days of *First Statement* and *Northern Review,* Layton had written a series of shrill and strident volumes of left-wing poetry and had had some success in shocking the bourgeoisie with the verbal frankness of his love poems and social satires. But with the publication in 1954 of *In the Midst of my Fever,* and of *The Cold Green Element* in 1955, he suddenly revealed himself as one of the most original poets of his generation in North America. The self-confidence that looked like arrogance in the early verse and the savage indignation that had looked like mere contempt had here ripened and grown sharp and relevant. The qualities that distinguish the later poems — and that won the praise of Williams Carlos Williams, whom along with Whitman, Blake, Lawrence, and the Hebrew prophets Layton looks upon as a master—are both technical and what one must not be afraid to call spiritual. Our pleasure in such a poem as "The Cold Green Element," for instance, depends on many things: the elegance of the writing, the neatness of the stanza pattern, the emotional variety and energy, and the myth-making creativeness that draws its materials as easily from drugstore shelves as from the myth of Orpheus.

It is the fusion of the modern world with the archetypal patterns of myth and psychology rather than with Christianity or patriotism that gives a characteristic cosmopolitan flavour to much of the poetry of the fifties in Canada. We find various aspects of such a fusion in the exotic and deceptively innocent infantilism of James Reaney, in the metaphysical intensity of Anne Wilkinson's revitalization of ballad and pastoral, in the gnomic suggestiveness of Jay Macpherson's finely chiselled lyrics, and in the toughness of mind and tenderness of spirit revealed in Margaret Avison's difficult poetry.

The themes that engage these writers are not local or even national; they are cosmopolitan and, indeed, universal. The bewildering multiplicity of scientific, moral, and metaphysical data with which the poet must now come to terms, and the burden of guilt, fancied or real, which the disintegration of values in religion, politics, and morals places on his unsupported shoulders, make it very difficult, if not impossible, for him to be anything but complex, divided, erudite, allusive, and sometimes obscure. These of course, are the characteristics of modernity in the poetry of Europe and the United States as well as of Canada. But the Canadian poet has one advantage—an advantage that derives from his position of separateness and semi-isolation. He can draw upon French, British, and American sources in language and literary convention; at the same time he enjoys a measure of detachment that enables him to select and adapt what is relevant and useful. This gives to contemporary Canadian poetry in either language a distinctive quality—its eclectic detachment. This can be, and has been, a defect of timidity and mediocrity; but it can also be a virtue of intelligence and discrimination.

# 1961    *Eclectic Detachment*

## Aspects of Identity in Canadian Poetry

*from* Canadian Literature, *No. 9*

In the closing paragraphs of the Introduction to *The Oxford Book of Canadian Verse* I made an effort to suggest in a phrase that I hoped might be memorable a peculiar advantage that Canadian poets, when they were successful or admirable, seemed to possess and make use of. This, of course, is a risky thing to do, for what one gains in brevity and point may very well be lost in inconclusiveness or in possibilities of misunderstanding. A thesis needs to be demonstrated as well as stated. In this particular case I think the thesis is implicit in the poems assembled in the last third of the book—and here and there in earlier places too. Nevertheless, I would like to develop more fully a point of view that exigencies of space confined me merely to stating previously.

The statement itself is derived from a consideration of the characteristics of Canadian poetry in the last decade. The cosmopolitan flavour of much of the poetry of the fifties in Canada derives from the infusion into the modern world of the archetypal patterns of myth and psychology rather than (as in the past) from Christianity or nationalism. After mentioning the names of James Reaney, Anne Wilkinson, Jay Macpherson, and Margaret Avison— those of the Jewish poets Eli Mandel, Irving Layton, and Leonard Cohen might have been added—I went on to comment that the preoccupation of these poets is with themes that are "cosmopolitan and, indeed, universal."[1] In this sense, Canadian poets are writing about the same themes that engage their counterparts in Europe and the United States.

So far there is no room for misunderstanding and little, I imagine, for disagreement. But the core of my argument was—and is—that the Canadian poet possesses one great advantage, "an advantage that derives from his separate-

---

[1]A. J. M. Smith, Introduction, *The Oxford Book of Canadian Verse* (Toronto: Oxford University Press, 1960), pp. xlix-li.

ness and semi-isolation,"[2] his ability to draw from British, French and American sources in both language and literary conventions while maintaining a detachment that permits him to select what will best work in his own special circumstances. "This gives to contemporary Canadian poetry ... a distinctive quality—its *eclectic detachment*. . . [which] can be ... a defect of timidity and mediocrity; but it can also be ... a virtue of intelligence and discrimination."[3]

My purpose here is to examine the phrase *eclectic detachment* in the light of its applications, to clarify it if necessary, and to defend its validity. This is a useful undertaking, for even if it should fall short of its full purpose it cannot fail to stir up some lively controversy and stimulate thinking about the quality of Canadian poetry that might be exciting and helpful, and that might even ultimately lead us to discard a point of view that sees the Canadian poet as in a predicament, plight, or fix.


I first used the phrase *eclectic detachment* in an effort to define concisely the essential quality of the best modern Canadian poetry in 1955 in a paper read at the Canadian Writers' Conference held at Queen's University in the summer of that year, and the poets then cited as exhibiting this quality were Scott, Klein, Anderson, and Page, as well as Reaney, who, of course, had not yet published *A Suit of Nettles*. Nobody took much notice of the expression at the time; but some comments in recent reviews have suggested the need for amplification and explicit illustration. Professor John Bilsland in the course of a detailed review of the new *Oxford Book* in *Canadian Literature* questions the validity of the phrase in a paragraph I will quote:

> The expression *eclectic detachment* sounds well: it seems to suggest a learned objectivity, the capacity in our poets to draw freely on diverse cultures and traditions.

I interpolate briefly here. It does not *seem to suggest:* it does suggest; as a matter of fact it states. I believe that one of the greatest advantages that a poet like Frank Scott or Reaney or Klein or Gustafson really possesses is the fact that he is immersed both in the European and the North American cultural tradition—I use "cultural" in the widest possible sense to include the sociological and political aspects of environment and inheritance as well as the literary and the artistic—but he is not *of* it. He stands apart and, as all Canadian writers must do, he selects and rejects. He selects those elements from varied and often disparate sources that are useful to him and rejects

2Ibid.
3Ibid.

those that are not. Useful *to him.* This brings in the personal. Detachment surely does not imply in this context detachment from the self or from personality. This is where Professor Bilsland, it seems to me, goes wrong. He continues:

> One wonders if the very attractiveness of the fine expression has not misled Professor Smith. Surely a very marked quality of much of the best Canadian poetry is its intensely personal note. Many of our poets are highly derivative, but writers like A. M. Klein, Anne Wilkinson, and Irving Layton have achieved a decidedly personal utterance, not particularly eclectic, and not at all detached. . . .

The question at issue is: What is the Canadian poet detached from? *Eclectic* detachment would suggest that he is not detached from everything, but only from what he chooses to be detached from. This implies also that there are some things he chooses to attach himself to. I emphasize *himself.* It is someone, a person, a poet, who is attached or detached. The term *detachment* in this context has nothing to do with objectivity or impersonality. It is actually an affirmation of personality. Certainly in poets like Klein and Wilkinson and Layton it is.

The function of personality in the poet is to create a thing, a persona, a poem; and in Canada the problem of the critic, if not of the poet, has been to relate this thing to its place and to its time. For the scholar watching the critic as the critic watches the poet, the Canadian literary scene offers an almost classic instance of an easily isolable phenomenon: the quick and almost forced development of a compact and self-contained literary tradition—arising from the practice of the poets—and of an orthodoxy (rather rapidly changing)—arising from the sensibility of readers and the cogitations of critics.

The task that the Canadian establishers of a literary orthodoxy addressed themselves to with the greatest enthusiasm was the effort to isolate and describe some peculiar quality that might be felt to distinguish Canadian poetry. W. D. Lighthall in his Introduction to *Canadian Songs and Poems* published in London and Toronto in 1892 was quick to recognize that there are two main streams of Canadian poetry, which for convenience I have called the cosmopolitan and the native.

> The present is an imperfect representation of Canadian poetry from a purely literary point of view, on account of the limitation of treatment; for it is obvious that if only what illustrates the country and its life *in a distinctive way* be chosen, the subjective and unlocal literature must necessarily be passed over, entraining the omission of most of the poems whose merit lies in perfection of finish.

The anthologist himself italicizes for emphasis the phrase *in a distinctive way;* and it is interesting to note the assumptions implicit in his point of view: that what is distinctively Canadian (or perhaps merely local) will tend to be (a) technically crude and (b) impersonal or objective. This second condition is not, however, meant to imply coldness or insensitivity but is an early perception of a view that later critics, looking back, were able to substantiate. This is the conception of Canadian poetry as being in its essence heroic and mythological rather than personal and lyrical which Northrop Frye developed in his *Canadian Forum* review of the first edition of *The Book of Canadian Poetry* (December 1943) and his paper on "La Tradition narrative dans la poésie canadienne-anglaise" in *Gants du ciel* (Spring 1946), and which is behind much of the thinking in James Reaney's "The Canadian Poet's Predicament" in the *University of Toronto Quarterly* (April 1957).

Lighthall's critical introduction is not all forward-looking and perceptive. It has (inevitably) the defects of its time. The book was just able to include some of the early poems of Roberts, Carman, Lampman, Campbell, and Scott; it illustrates the spirit of rather blatant nationalism characteristic of the post-Confederation period and prepares the way for the Maple Leaf school of versifiers and critics that was dominant until the late twenties. . . . Nevertheless Lighthall's essay makes the significant assertion that the characteristic note of Canadian poetry is the heroic. And to foresee so early a tradition that was to include *David* and *The Wind Our Enemy* as well as *At the Long Sault, Brébeuf and His Brethren,* and *Towards the Last Spike,* with nothing more than the somewhat tentative efforts of Heavysege, Mair, and Crawford to guide him, is not a negligible achievement.

The effort to isolate a peculiar Canadian quality in the poetry of the Dominion has since Lighthall's time become a kind of occupational hazard of the Canadian critic and anthologist. Lighthall's point of view is a little naive, and it is certainly too narrow, but it marks a beginning.

The modern critic has had not only a much larger but a much more varied and complex body of work to consider. In the last twenty years a new and incomparably more vital and sophisticated poetry has arisen in Canada; and it has made imperative an effort to assimilate it and evaluate it, which has called forth the talents of a remarkable school of new scholarly critics.

The new poetry and the new criticism have had their effect on the poetry of the past. The critics have had to raise their sights as it were and have imposed an increasingly severe standard of judgment, not only on the early pre-Confederation versifiers but upon the poets of our rather glibly or perhaps ironically named "golden age"—the Roberts-Carman-Lampman group. This is much better than adulation, but there is a danger too that something valuable may be lost.

Reading the serious reviews of *The Oxford Book of Canadian Verse* I have been surprised to see how far the revulsion of feeling has gone and how sud-

den has been the reversal of fortune. Everyone seems ready to discard the
colonial pioneer poets to the junk pile. "Victorian versifiers like Heavysege
and Sangster and Mair," wrote George Woodcock, "were dead before they
reached the grave." And this critic's praise of Lampman, Roberts, and Carman is distinctly unenthusiastic. "One should not over-disparage Lampman," he warns I suppose himself, and goes on, in an obvious effort to be fair,
to say *something,* however vague, in praise of the group. His praise, however,
is pretty much nullified by the qualifications that precede it." [Lamp-
man] and Roberts may have been minor Victorians, colonials in their
dependence on English models, and almost completely derivative, but they
did bring to Canadian poetry what it needed before it could even start—a
sense of the image and a high craftsmanship. . . ." Nevertheless the critic
found it laborious "except perhaps in nostalgia for the Edwardian afternoon,
to read through as much of the Confederation poets as [the] anthologists . . .
give us." Millar MacLure in the *Tamarack Review* No. 17 agrees. He con-
fesses a long-standing inability to assume a scholarly stance before the verses
of the Confederation poets. "Lampman," he declares in a rather self-conscious effort to be unscholarly, "is a good old cheese, but Roberts and Carman belong on captions in the New Brunswick Museum (Carman's verse is to
poetic speech what Baird's Lemon Extract used to be to Demerara rum)." On
the earlier poets he is considerably more severe. "I can see no reason for taking either Heavysege (lie heavy on him, earth!) or Mair more seriously than
John Hunter Duvar. . . ." Norman Levine, reviewing the Oxford book in
England, speaks of "the dead wood of the nineteenth century" and of "the
much overvalued output of the poets of the 1860s." Donald A. Davie, an
unprejudiced outsider, finds only one *poet* before Pratt—Lampman, of
course.

I cite these opinions not mainly because they come from intelligent,
responsible, and serious critics but because nothing like this emphatic and
widespread denigration of the past found its voice when the three editions of
*The Book of Canadian Poetry* appeared in 1943, 1948, and 1957 or when
Ralph Gustafson's Penguin anthologies came out in 1942 and 1958. I myself
would not wish to discard and do not think it necessary to scorn our older
poetry. It is worth preserving because it shows us what our ancestors were
able to do when they tried to do their best. They do not and could not provide
us with a tradition, but neither do they offer us horrible examples and furnish
us with something consciously to reject. They simply show us what it felt like
to live here in 1840 or 1860 or 1890. These earlier poets did not have what the
modern reviewer might call advantages. They had not read Hulme or Eliot or
Dylan Thomas, but we must not condemn them entirely for having read
Wordsworth, Shelley, Keats, or Matthew Arnold — as most of them, and I
think fruitfully, had. Do we condemn the Bartlett prints because they are not
like the paintings of the Group of Seven or later abstractionists?

The more tolerant point of view I have been outlining has never of course been without its exponents, and if I call one or two of these as witnesses it will bring us back to where we started—to the question of our sense of identity and to some illustrations of our *eclectic detachment.*

Northrop Frye, who has the catholicity of the true scholar, is able to see the always changing and always developing kaleidoscope of our literary history as a single pattern, and thus can see also the characteristic virtues and defects of the Confederation poets in the new perspective that modern poetry places them in. Frye excels in the art of making just discriminations. Speaking of Roberts, Carman, Lampman, and D. C. Scott he says:

> All four are romantic and subjective poets, at their best when confronting nature in solitude, in moods of nostalgia, reverie, observation or extra-sensory awareness. Their sensibility is emotional in origin, and they obtain conceptual precision by means of emotional precision. . . .

After speaking of the greater frequency of Lampman's successes and of the common tendency for Roberts and Carman to "let their sensibility get out of focus," he ventures some more general assertions, which bring us closer to the question of a Canadian tradition—though I am not sure whether *habit* might not be a better word.

> This subjective and lyrical sensibility, sharp and clear in its emotional foreground but inclined to get vague around its conceptual fringes, is deeply rooted in the Canadian tradition. Most of its characteristics reappear in the Group of Seven painters, in Tom Thomson and Emily Carr, with their odd mixture of *art nouveau* and cosmic consciousness.

This is followed by a statement that every Canadian writer and reader should take to heart: "The Canadianism of Canadian poetry is of course not a merit in it, but only a quality in it; it may be revealed as clearly in false notes as in true ones, and may be a source of bad taste as well as of inspiration."

These sentences from Northrop Frye's general survey of poetry in Malcolm Ross's *The Arts in Canada* (1958) bring us back to the idea of *eclectic detachment.* For the person living in Canada, there are two things he cannot be detached from—his personality and his Canadianism. These are both invisible and often unconscious attachments, and they condition the inevitable way in which emotion and thought rise out of sensibility. Where freedom of choice comes in is in the intellectual effort of the artist as maker who seeks to eliminate bad taste and encourage good, who chooses the true note and rejects the false. In Canada this task is made easier by the absence of conventional bonds that fasten us to an oppressively superior tradition such as that of English poetry and leaves us free to pick and choose just those poets (or just those aspects of those poets) that can satisfy our needs. The most exciting poets of the present revival have found refreshment and nourishment in the most widely varied and often surprising sources—James Reaney in Chaucer and Spenser; Irving Layton in Nietzsche, Catullus, the Hebrew prophets, and William Carlos Williams; Jay Macpherson in Blake and Northrop Frye; Ralph Gustafson in Job, Hopkins, and Melville; Margaret Avison in Tycho Brahe, George Herbert, and Marianne Moore.

Professor Malcolm Ross in the Introduction to his paperback selection from the Confederation poets sees this eclecticism in them also—and sees it, I think, as a kind of limitation or brake on a too obvious nationalism:

> Our leap from colony to nation was accomplished without revolution, without a sharp cultural and ideological break from Europe, without the fission and fusion of Civil War. Roberts and Carman learn as happily from Emerson and Royce as from Browning, Rossetti, and Verlaine. And Darwin is made to take on the look of a Miramichi backwoodsman! True, Lampman and Roberts suddenly find they are Canadians. But they are also (and at the same time) thoroughgoing provincials (with a feeling for place), and thoroughgoing citizens of the world (with a feeling for time).

The terms *provincialism, regionalism,* and *colonialism* are not generally o.k. words, and a good deal of Canadian criticism has been a wasted effort either to deny or excuse these appellations. Professor Ross sees, however, that these local applications do not rule out but in Canadian poetry go along with cosmopolitan ones. "Our group of Confederation Poets is important for us— among other reasons—because already it shows forth the peculiar and inevitable 'openness' of the Canadian culture." It is in an "open" culture that an eclectic detachment becomes possible. Milton Wilson, literary editor of the *Canadian Forum,* and perhaps the most receptive to advanced trends of all Canadian literary critics, had already developed this idea in some brilliant paradoxes in a paper read before the Association of Canadian University Teachers of English at Edmonton in June 1958 and easily available in the *Tamarack Review* No. 9. Part of his purpose was to reconsider "that doubtful quantity, our 'sense of identity.' " He does so by dealing with the problem first in relation to space—the effect of the vastness and the emptiness of the country into which a small number of quite divergent regions have been placed at intervals—and then in terms of time. "When we speak," he says, "of a recognizably Canadian poet we usually mean a regional poet who uses the distinctive objects and actions of his locality as poetic material. . . ." After mentioning some of the regions where an active poetry seems to be flourishing particularly at the present time—Montreal, New Brunswick, southern Ontario and Toronto, and the West Coast—Wilson goes on to point out that labels do not always stick, that the regionalists hop about a good deal, and that "our regionalism is perhaps more a way of looking at things than a rooted stance."

> Perhaps our identity is to be one of Miss [P. K.] Page's "Permanent Tourists," and our larger sense of place is best expressed by the kind of hopping regionalism exemplified in [Earle] Birney's "North-Star West"—[or F. R. Scott's "Trans-Canada"]—with its transcontinental series of scenes joined by compressed air, and its rapid shifts of perspective.

The effect of this is named by the critic, accurately enough but hardly I think discriminatingly enough, as "a kind of continental discontinuity." Not discriminatingly enough because I discern the very same phenomenon in the contemporary poetry of the United States. It is a continental one, North American, not merely Canadian.

Mr. Wilson, admitting that all discussions of the Canadian poet's sense of space tend to be fanciful and arbitrary, says that "something more substantial can be said about his sense of poetic time." What he goes on to say is something quite new and at first seems startling, if not bizarre; but through paradox I believe he has hit on the truth, and like the poor brother of the fairy tale discovers in our very limitations the source of our special good luck:

> We have often been told [he writes] of our necessary dullness because we had no Revolutionary War, no French Revolution, no War Between the States. In poetry likewise we had no Renaissance, no neo-Classicism, no Romanticism. But one of the advantages of a poetry less than a hundred years old is that all the things that couldn't happen when they should have happened keep happening all the time.... The Canadian poet can be *avant-garde* with whatever material he chooses.... I even wonder whether colonialism may not be, in theory at least, the most desirable poetic state. It gives you a catholic sense of all the things poetry can do without embarrassing you by telling you what at this particular moment it can't.... The Canadian poet has all the models in the language (not to mention other languages) at his disposal, but lacks the deadening awareness that he is competing with them.

This brings us round full circle to freedom of choice and eclectic detachment. There is only one flaw, as I see it, in this provincial paradise. There is a serpent lurking in the phrase "lacks the deadening awareness that he is competing with them." It seems to suggest a double standard—which I am sure is far from Mr. Wilson's intention. The Canadian poet, like every poet, is in competition with every other poet, past and present, or, more precisely, he knows he must be judged by as severe standards as any. And I believe that it is an informed freedom of choice that comes from being Canadian that has made it possible for our best poets to sustain this test—and perhaps more easily than if they had been English or American.

# PART TWO

*Before Confederation*

*Colonialism & Nationalism
In Canadian Poetry
Before Confederation*

*from* Proceedings of the Canadian Historical
Association

In a former essay I referred to the Reverend Edward Hartley Dewart's statement of 1864 that "A national literature is an essential element in the formation of national character."[1] An ardent advocate of Confederation, the critic doubted whether a people could be "firmly united politically, without the subtle but powerful cement of a patriotic literature."[2] Such a literature, he felt, and particularly a poetic literature, would be a counterpoise to the sectionalism which was the political weakness of Canada. Dewart did not deny that such a literature was then only in its infancy and that it had many obstacles to overcome. Among these was a general absence of interest and faith in all indigenous literature that led him to the melancholy conclusion that "there is probably no country in the world, making equal pretensions to intelligence and progress, where the claims of native literature are so little felt, and where every effort in poetry has been met with so much coldness and indifference, as in Canada."[3]

The anthologist brought forward a number of reasons to account for this state of affairs. First was the obvious one that in Canada then few people possessed wealth or leisure, while the large majority were engaged in the hard task of subduing the wilderness. But the most interesting of Dr. Dewart's reasons was the stifling effect of the colonial habit of mind.

Our colonial position, whatever may be its political advantages, is not favorable to the growth of an indigenous literature. Not only are our mental wants supplied by the brain of the Mother Country, under circumstances that utterly preclude competition; but the majority of per-

---

[1] *Selections from Canadian Poets; with Occasional Critical and Biographical Notes and an Introductory Essay on Canadian Poetry* (Montreal: John Lovell, 1864), p. xiv.
[2] Ibid.
[3] Ibid., p. x.

sons of taste and education in Canada are emigrants from the Old
Country, whose tenderest affections cling around the land they have left.
The memory of the associations of youth, and of the honored names that
have won distinction in every department of human activity, throws a
charm around everything that comes from their native land, to which the
productions of our young and unromantic country can put forth no
claim.[4]

Here then at the beginning of Canadian literary criticism the issue is clearly
stated. The value of independence is asserted and the dangers of an imitative
colonialism boldly faced.

Colonialism is a spirit that gratefully accepts a place of subordination, that
looks elsewhere for its standards of excellence and is content to imitate with a
modest and timid conservatism the products of a parent tradition. If we
examine the poetry of the pioneer and emigrant in the days when the Canadian provinces were struggling for constitutional self-government, we shall
find, I believe, that such colonialism reveals itself most surely in the abstract
and conventional patriotic poetry, the ostensible subject of which might be
devotion to the Empire — or even to Canada—while true nationalism rises out
of the local realism of the pioneer. Indeed, poetry that was colonial in its conventionality and correctness makes up the bulk of the verse in Dewart's
anthology that was consecrated to the description of "Canadian" scenery and
the expression of nationalist sentiment. This sort of poetry, certainly, com-
prises most of the verse on "Canadian" themes written by such poets as Mrs.
Moodie, who belonged to the class of "persons of respectable connections" to
whom, as she says, emigration was "an act of severe duty, performed at the
expense of personal enjoyment." Such, too, was the poetry of the Maritimes,
where a Tory gentry was anxious to create a little local autonomy that was
colonial in its fervent imitation of England. *The Rising Village* of Goldsmith
and the *Acadia* of Joseph Howe were also an expression of colonialism,
though there are touches of realism in these poems and a sympathetic fidelity
to nature; but the form, style, and technique, and the sensibility expressed
are reflections of eighteenth-century England.

One of the most damaging of the results of pure colonialism is the feeling
of inferiority and doubt it engenders and the remoteness it encourages. The
colonial attitude of mind, as Professor E. K. Brown has well said, "sets the
great good place not in its present, nor in its past nor in its future, but some-

[4]Ibid., p. xiv.

where outside its own borders, somewhere beyond its possibilities."[5] Thus a direct result of colonialism may be a turning away from the despised local present not towards the mother country but towards an exotic idealized crystallization of impossible hopes and "noble" dreams. The romantic spirit, indeed, is encouraged by a colonial sense of inferiority. This is illustrated by the preface to a book of poems by a New Brunswick author, Peter John Allan, which was published in London in 1853. The verse showed strong influences of Byron, Moore, and Shelley. "My lot," wrote the poet, "having been cast on the wrong side of the Atlantic in a colony where the Muse cannot find a resting place for the sole of her foot—in its very little capital, whose politics would be a mere private scandal to a European ear, and where society is strangely limited—can it be a matter of surprise that I should have sought for relaxation from more severe studies in the amiable foible of verse making?"[6]

To consider the realities of the life around him as too modest or too coarse for the attention of poetry is a temptation that faces the poet in a colony, particularly if he thinks of himself as an inheritor of the elaborate tradition of the poetry of the Motherland, and he makes poetry an escape from reality.

Mrs. Catherine Parr Traill, whose *Backwoods of Canada* anticipated by some sixteen years her sister Mrs. Moodie's classic *Roughing It in the Bush,* agreed that Canada was not romantic enough to provide rich material for poetry, and she quotes with approval the "lamentation of a poet." " 'It is the most unpoetical of all lands,' this person said; 'there is no scope for imagination; here all is new—the very soil seems newly formed; there is no hoary ancient grandeur in these woods; no recollections of former deeds connected with the country.' "[7]

This is an example of pure colonialism, before the slightest feeling of veneration for the new land had a chance to arise. Mrs. Traill complains that poetic feeling is quite alien to the sort of people who are likely to succeed in Canada. "The class of people to whom this country is so admirably adapted are formed of the unlettered and industrious labourers and artisans. They feel no regret that the land they labour on has not been celebrated by the pen of the historian or the lay of the poet. . . . They would not spare the ancient oak from feelings of veneration, nor look upon it with regard for anything but its use as timber. They have no time, even if they possessed the taste, to gaze abroad on the beauties of nature."[8] We hear in these words the disillusioned voice of an English gentlewoman, the wife of a half-pay army officer, submitting to the painful drudgery of the unbroken wilderness. The English pub-

---

[5]*On Canadian Poetry* (Toronto: Ryerson, 1943), p.14.
[6]*The Poetical Remains of Peter John Allan, Esq., late of Fredericton, New Brunswick.* Edited by the Rev. Henry Christmas (London: Smith, Elder, 1853), Preface by the author, p. xx.
[7]Catherine P. Traill, *Backwoods of Canada* (London: Natalli & Bond, 1836), p. 154.
[8]Ibid.

lisher of Mrs. Traill's book was able to take a more romantic view of things, and he wrote in the Introduction of a special compensation that the colony might afford the better-class settler's wife: "To the person who is capable of looking abroad into the beauties of nature, and adoring the Creator through his glorious works, are opened stores of unmixed pleasure, which will not permit her to be dull or unhappy in the loneliest part of our Western Wilderness."[9]

This latter opinion is the orthodox one. It was held by Dr. Dewart and others like the emigrant poet, Standish O'Grady, and the encyclopedist, Henry J. Morgan, whose testimony I have quoted elsewhere.[10] The first person who arose with a sufficient command of language and feeling to treat what were felt to be the particularly "Canadian" aspects of scenery with the enthusiasm expected of a genuine romantic poet was Charles Sangster.

Sangster (1822 to 1893) was born in Upper Canada—in the navy yard at Kingston—and though he knew poverty he did not experience the hard lot of a pioneer settler. He became a journalist in Kingston, and later a civil servant in Ottawa. He published *The St. Lawrence and the Saguenay* in 1856 in Kingston and New York, and at once he was hailed as a national poet. "A Canadian Poet, whose poems are far above mediocrity—whose songs are of Canada—her mountains, maidens, manners, morals, lakes, rivers, valleys, seasons, woods, forests, and aborigines, her faith and hope"—so he was described by a contemporary reviewer.[11] Dr. Dewart proclaimed him first among native poets. "Many other Canadian poets," wrote the anthologist, "having spent their youth in some other land, though cherishing a strong regard for the country of their adoption, keep their tenderest affection for the land of their birth; selecting their principal imagery from its scenery and associations, somewhat to the neglect of the materials, which nature so profusely lavishes on the scenery of this country. But Mr. S., while cherishing a loyal attachment to the motherland, gives Canada the chief place in his heart."[12]

Yet we cannot feel that Sangster succeeded in becoming a national poet; and the reason is, I believe, that he was not first a local poet. Romantic enthusiasm and literary polish kept his work vague and general. He was steeped in the romantic tradition of Byron and Shelley, and his diction and imagery were much less national than his early critics wished to think. It is

[9]Ibid., Intro., p.4.
[10]In *The Book of Canadian Poetry* (Chicago: University of Chicago Press 1943), pp. 12-13.
[11]In *McKenzie's Message,* quoted in "Opinions of the Press" at end of Sangster's *Hesperus and Other Poems and Lyrics* (Montreal: J. Lovell, Kingston: J. Creighton, 1860).
[12]*Selections from Canadian Poets,* p. 150.

true that he chose to describe Canadian scenery, but the sensibility that interpreted what he saw and the language in which he expressed his feeling were the common heritage of European romanticism. "His whole soul seems steeped in love and poesy," wrote another reviewer. "He is thoroughly sentimental, teeming with ideas of the sublime and beautiful. . . ."[13] His diction and imagery are indistinguishable from those of a minor romantic poet in England or the United States, and he suggests comparison with Campbell, Moore, or Longfellow—occasionally with Byron, Shelley, or Tennyson. The real source of the enthusiasm with which Sangster was hailed as a national bard was pride in the fact that here was a poet who was *not* different from English poets but good enough to be named in the same company with some of the most firmly established of them.

This, I think, is the heart of the problem of nationalism in Canadian poetry (and in the other arts as well). Is a Canadian poet one who is indubitably a *poet* because he has, in sufficient strength, qualities which are recognizably the same in kind as those of the standard poets of the English tongue, and a *Canadian poet* because he happens to live and write in Canada, to use Canadian place-names, and to mention the flora and fauna of Canada? Or is he a poet as original and indigenous as Thoreau or Whitman?

I put these questions; and I shall not try to answer them here. I shall content myself with two remarks. The first is that Canada need feel no sense of humiliation that a poet who is Canadian as Whitman is American should not have arisen among us. America only produced one Whitman and one Thoreau. The rest of the American poets are no more and no less American than our poets are Canadian. My second observation is that we have called our poets (Carman and Roberts, if not Sangster) *national* because they were recognizably *poets*, judged by the standards of the accepted English masters, and then have pretended to ourselves that they were *Canadian*. The late Professor James Cappon, of Queen's University, perhaps the best literary critic this country has produced, was right when he remarked, "Perhaps our best Canadian poets have devoted themselves too much to an almost abstract form of nature poetry which has too little savour of the national life . . . and is more dependent on literary tradition than they seem to be aware of."[14]

Professor Cappon's observation is as true of Sangster as it is of Roberts. But there were men in Canada whose closeness to the soil and the back-breaking labour of clearing the wilderness kept them from acquiring the smoothness and glossy finish that was expected of the "serious" poet, and it was these,

[13]In the *Huron Signal*, quoted in "Opinions of the Press" at end of *Hesperus*.
[14]J. Cappon, *Roberts and the Influences of his Time* (Toronto: Ryerson, 1905), p. 84.

more than the literary poets, who prepared the way for the expression of a genuine nationalism. This they did by avoiding the abstract and grandiose and concentrating with sympathetic insight upon the familiar and the local. The result was a poetry less poetic than Sangster's but native enough, and *tangy*—the necessary prelude to a realistic nationalism.

The best known of these poets was Alexander McLachlan, who came to Canada to escape the hard lot of a poor tailor's apprentice in Glasgow. He told the story of his voyage to Canada and the opening up of a pioneer settlement in the wilderness near Guelph, Ontario, in a spirited little epic called *The Emigrant* (published 1861). On the ship bound for Canada, one of the emigrants sings a song that states the feelings of McLachlan towards the country he is leaving. It has a humour and heartiness that suggest no one more certainly than Cobbet. The middle stanzas will show the radical independence and economic bias of McLachlan's thinking.

> I love my own country and race,
>   Nor lightly I fled from them both,
> Yet who would remain in a place
>   Where there's too many spoons for the broth.
>
> The squire's preserving his game.
>   He says that God gave it to him,
> And he'll banish the poor without shame,
>   For touching a feather or limb.
>
> The Justice he feels very big,
>   And boasts what the law can secure,
> But has two different laws in his wig,
>   Which he keeps for the rich and the poor.
>
> The Bishop he preaches and prays,
>   And talks of a heavenly birth,
> But somehow, for all that he says,
>   He grabs a good share of the earth.[15]

An equally spirited poem and one that gives a good picture of the agrarian distress that prompted the emigration can be found among the verses of a fellow-countryman of McLachlan, Alexander Glendinning. This author described himself on the title page of a volume simply called *Rhymes,* published in London, Ontario, in 1871, as "sometime in Eskdalemuir, Dumfriesshire, Scotland." He appears to have come out to Canada in the late thirties,

---

[15] *The Emigrant and Other Poems* (Toronto: Rollo and Adam, 1861), pp. 27-8.

via New York, and settled in Upper Canada, near Scarborough. Glendinning's name is not mentioned in any book on Canadian literature, but his work, homely and unpretentious in the extreme, has a directness and personal tang which give it a value that mere literary polish could never have imparted to it.

Glendinning tells of the hardships of "Annandale Farming" in a poem that unites humour and social significance.[16] The ills are a compost of "dead sheep, daft bargains, a tea-drinking wife;/Dull markets, partial payments, a long rent." His description of his stock is a fine bit of country realism—precise, disillusioned, and humorous:

> Four or five horses, leaning 'gainst their stalls,
>     Eight calvers, high of bone and hard of skin;
> Some forty porkers, making hideous squawls,
>     Through lack of murphies, pitifully thin,
> With savage snouts they undermine the walls;
>     Soon shall the half-rotten roof-tree tumble in
> And crack their rigbones, pound their hams and flitches,
>     And put a finisher upon the wretches.

The poem continues with an ironic address to

> Ye happy few, ye owners of the soil,
>     Who feed upon the fat and drink the sweet,
> Just look and see how your poor tenants toil,
>     And, after a', have hardly bread to eat;
> Let down your rents, live and let live the while,
>     And we will be your servants, as 'tis meet;
> We'll gang and buy oursels new coats and breeks,
>     And never speak a word on politicks.

Glendinning gives us an excellent account of his journey to Canada and of the opening up of a new home in the wilderness. He describes the discomforts of the ocean voyage in feeling terms. He was battened down with other "luckless wretches"

> In a ship's hold and under hatches
> 'Mang twa three hunder lowsie bitches,
>     Brood of blue ruin!
> These, as the vessel rolls and pitches,
>     Cursin' and spuein'.[17]

---

[16]*Rhymes* (London, Ont.: Free Press Printing Co., 1871), pp. 72-4.
[17]Ibid., p.46.

Glendinning landed at New York and travelled in a steam boat up the Hudson to Albany. From there he journeyed westward by stage (rather than by Erie Canal) and crossed Lake Ontario to settle for a time at Scarborough. Then came the hardships, the new kind of back-breaking labour, the discouragements, and the loneliness. The years during which all these disadvantages are slowly overcome and a new feeling of pride and independence gained gave Glendinning the subjects of his spirited rhymes. It is the same story we read in Mrs. Traill, Mrs. Moodie, and Alexander McLachlan, but the accents are harder, the tone richer and more realistic.

Sincerity, simplicity, and directness distinguish the verse of the best of the pioneer poets. They were not, most of them, distracted by any self-conscious literary awareness. They did respond to one literary influence—that of Burns: but this influence was on the side of reality, homeliness, good sense, and humour; it was not a distracting or sentimental one like that of Shelley or Byron, Poe or Tennyson, upon Sangster.

This poetry is full of realistic and vividly humorous pictures of life in the bush. Glendinning describes

> A band o' loggers at a bee—
> Smart chiels wi' handspakes working free
>   In shirt and breeches,
> And teamsters, loud wi' ha and gee,
>   Twirling blue beeches.[18]

One of Glendinning's compatriots—Robert Boyd, who came to Upper Canada in 1830 from Ayrshire and died at Guelph in 1880, at the age of eighty-three—painted the hardships of a settler's life in a vivid descriptive poem called "The Bachelor in His Shanty."[19] Here humour and realism are united in a characteristic manner. Why, he wonders, did he leave his native country and "freens of social glee"

> To come to this strange land o' trees,
> The vile abode o' frogs and fleas
> Wi' no ane near to sympatheese,
>   Or yet to hate us;
> Devour'd alive by slow degrees
>   By curs'd mosquitoes.

Roasted by summer's heat, frozen by the winter breeze, his sheep and lambs

---

18Ibid., p.52.
19In *Selections from Scottish-Canadian Poets. . . . With an Introduction by Dr. Daniel Clark* (Toronto, 1900), pp.61-8.

carried off by wolves, the poor shanty man tells of his other troubles:

> A grumphy, too, I fed with care,
> Till he might weigh Twal' stane or mair;
> And when about to scrape his hair,
>     Though no' that able,
> A muckle black and ugly bear
>     Saved me the trouble. . . .

> A farmer too I'm called by name,
> Nay—even a Laird—so much for fame,
> Which makes me blush wi' burnin' shame
>     The truth to tell,
> For a' my craps scarce fill my wame
>     And nane to sell.

> Twa-three bits o' potato hills,
> For stumps are sworn foes to drills,
> Some pumpkins big as cadger's creels,
>     Is a' my crop;
> For aught I raise, markets and mills
>     Might a' gie up.

But the significance of the story that all unite in telling is that a real source of pride, at first local but later becoming national, grows out of the sense of accomplishment when the fruits of strenuous labour are made the foundation of independence, if not of wealth. "Canada, say what they will on't," declared Glendinning:

> There's mony a gude-gaun' busy mill in't,
>     And weel-fill'd ark,
> And every man gets bread and yill in't
>     That likes to wark.[20]

And one of the finest passages in Isabella Valancy Crawford's masterpiece, "Malcolm's Katie," tells how the "axe-stirr'd waste" is filled with eager crowds:

> Upheav'd by throbs of angry poverty,
> And driven by keen blasts of hunger, from
> Their native strands—

[20]Glendinning, *Rhymes,* p.52.

who found new vigour as they found new hope.

> The lab'rer with train'd muscles, grim and grave,
> Look'd at the ground and wonder'd in his soul,
> What joyous anguish stirr'd his darken'd heart,
> At the mere look of the familiar soil,
> And found his answers in the words— *"Mine own!"* [21]

It was this independent spirit more than anything else that prompted, sustained, and rewarded the emigrant, and eventually motivated his patriotism. At first it may have been limited by colonial loyalties, but it eventually and almost inevitably became a national one. This can be traced in the verse of Alexander McLachlan, though McLachlan's background made him a little different. His youthful experiences as a poor weaver in Glasgow had given him the humanitarian and political tenets of the Chartist movement. He writes of the horrors of poverty in an industrial metropolis,

> Where bloated luxury lies,
> And Want as she prowls the streets
> Looks on with her wolfish eyes,[22]

and his verse is nowhere keener than in his description of the modern city with

> Its palaces raised to gin,
>     And its temples reared to God;
> Its cellars dark and dank,
>     Where never a sunbeam falls,
> Amid faces lean and lank
>     As the hungry-looking walls.[23]

One of the liveliest of the sketches in McLachlan's *Lyrics* is a reminiscence of old country radicalism. It is called "The Glasgow Chap's Story; or, Confessions Over a Bottle"[24] and describes a Chartist meeting with a clearsighted irony that must not be mistaken for antipathy. The speech of "bloody Tom" is rendered with fidelity and humour:

> Odd man! how nicely he set aff
> The guid that's in puir folk,

---

[21]Crawford. *Old Spookses' Pass, Malcolm's Katie, and Other Poems* (Toronto, 1884), pp.51-2.
[22]*The Emigrant*, p.34.
[23]Ibid., p.35.
[24]Alexander McLachlan, *Lyrics* (Toronto: A. H. Armour, 1858), pp.54-9.

> And o' their rights and virtues lang
>     And tenderly he spoke. . . .
>
> Says he, we a' came naked here
>     The best get but a grave,
> Then why should ane be made a lord,
>     Anither made a slave.
>
> How ane should drive a coach and six,
>     While millions drive the shuttle,
> How ane should waste while thousands want
>     Were questions rather kittle;
> And thus he argued lang to prove
>     That things are ill divided,
> Then put it to a show o' hands
>     And it was soon decided.

Finally, catching the enthusiasm, the Glasgow chap jumped to his feet and essayed to make a speech. But his tongue and knees failed him, and in mortification at his lamentable exhibition he slunk away and emigrated to America.

McLachlan himself brought such ideas into Upper Canada. In his early poetry the prevailing note is one of radical idealism. A characteristic expression of it may be found in *The Emigrant*, chapter IV, "Cutting the First Tree." This describes the celebration at the end of the logging bee, during which one of the settlers addressed his "fellowmen." The orator outlined a mythical age of gold, when "a simple honest race" lived in communal anarchy which recognized only the individual conscience as its law.

> They gave power and place to no man,
> And had everything in common;
> No one said this is mine own—
> Money was a thing unknown;
> No lawgiver and no pelf,
> Each a law was to himself. . . .[25]

Peace and plenty blessed this innocent classless society. The contrast with the present is obvious—now

> Every man is for himself . . .
> Hunting for the root of evil,
> Restless as the very devil—[26]

[25] *The Emigrant*, pp.48-9.
[26] Ibid., p.49.

and it provokes a passage of biting satire upon the hypocrisy and double-dealing that lead to modern success. The modern gospel is "get cash if ye can come at it by fair means, but be sure and get it." The moral of the speech is Utopian co-operation. Let us unite to redeem the world from gold.

> Each for all, and all for each,
> Is the doctrine that I preach;
> Mind the fable of the wands,
> 'Tis a fact that always stands;
> Singly, we are poor and weak,
> But united, who can break. . . .[27]

It was the hope of establishing in Canada a classless society, where energy and merit would be unhampered by the unfair competition of birth and privilege that inspired McLachlan with an independent national zeal. In one of his later poems, "Young Canada, or Jack's as Good as His Master,"[28] his patriotic enthusiasm is kindled for "The Land where Labour's free." "Rank and cast are of the past,/They'll never flourish here," he exults, and praises the new artistocracy of labour, "the nobles of the forge and soil,/With ne'er a pedigree."

McLachlan's patriotic poetry is sometimes both radical and national in tone. This can be seen in a little song called "The Genius of Canada" in the volume of 1858.[29] The Spirit speaks:

> Though bleak the skies may be,
>    The maple dells
>    Where freedom dwells
> Have a special charm for me.

She avows a determination to "rear a race to shed a grace/On the mighty page of time." The arts shall flourish and the palm of peace shall wave over a home of rest for the oppressed; and if at the end of the poem the shamrock, rose, and thistle entwine in the land of lake and pine, at the beginning there is a clear indication of sympathy with the abolitionist cause of the north which was in sharp contrast with the attitude of the British government. From the point of view of the mother country, indeed, Canada's apathy in the face of a possible attack from the United States as a result of Britain's encouragement of the Confederacy was one of the most distressing aspects of Canadian nationalism. McLachlan went so far as to write an "American War Ode" in

---

[27]Ibid., p.51.
[28]Alexander McLachlan, *Poems and Songs* (Toronto: Hunter, Rose, & Company, 1888), p.119.
[29]*Lyrics*, pp. 16-17.

which his republican radicalism found expression in a hymn that was neither Canadian nor imperialist.

> The spirit of Washington
> Stalks from the grave,
> And calls on his children
> Their country to save. . . .

> Where backwoodsmen triumphed,
>   O'er tyrant and King;
> There still the long rifle,
>   For freedom can ring.[30]

But such ideas, we must remind ourselves, are exceptional, and even in McLachlan they were found along with others that were impeccably and almost fulsomely loyal to Britain. The Crimean War, the birthday of the Queen, the visit of the Prince of Wales, the Fenian raids—these and like subjects inspired the Scottish emigrant poets as often, and about as effectively, as they did Sangster.

It would be unjust to deny, however, that the patriotic nationalism so earnestly fostered by Dr. Dewart—and by most of his successors among critics and anthologists—found expression in an occasional lyric of precision and power. Indeed, it would have been surprising if it had not; for that spirit was the one in which the political and economic life of the provinces was developing in the crucial years between 1840 and 1867, when the poetry we have been discussing was written. The causes are well known: they were long ago summarized by J. L. Morison. "With reciprocity had come prosperity; with prosperity had come independence, and a great increase in the number of colonists. . . . Education in the energetic hands of Egerton Ryerson was playing its part; every addition to the travelling convenience of the provinces meant additional political cohesion. . . . The strong imperial note in John A. Macdonald's speeches bears witness to the popular movement by its underlying nationalism—it is Canada, no mean national unit, which begins to offer filial assistance to the mother country."[31]

This note is heard in the poetry of the times. It is sounded often in Dr. Dewart's anthology, but it rarely takes on an accent of power and beauty. Sangster's "Brock" perhaps comes closest.

[30]*The Emigrant*, pp.234-5.
[31]*Canada and Its Provinces* (Toronto: Publishers Association of Canada, Edinburgh: Edinburgh University Press, 1914), v. p.79.

> One voice, one people, one in heart
> And soul, and feeling, and desire![32]

This is the sentiment that all the poets and versifiers express and return to. Nowhere does the idea of annexation or of independence find expression in our early poetry, but the ideal of Confederation and of a Canadian nationalism that will contribute strength to imperialism because of the free participation of a strong, self-reliant, and unified nation: that ideal we can watch growing in the quarter of a century before Confederation. But before this feeling could find adequate expression, it had to be nourished in the very earth of the new land. It is the pioneer realism and humour of the backwoods poets that show the solid base of experience out of which national pride and self-confidence alone could grow.

[32]Sangster, *Hesperus*, p.84.

## *Introduction,* The Book of Canadian Prose

The purpose of *The Book of Canadian Prose* is to make available a representative selection of texts which illustrate the special character that geography, climate, and politics have imposed upon the sensibility and thought of the Canadian people. The inevitable, often unconscious, and sometimes artistic expression of this character in writing is what we mean by Canadian literature.

Canadian literature, when it has not been neglected entirely, has either been contemptuously dismissed or extravagantly praised—the latter by well-meaning enthusiasts whose interest is mainly bellelettristic and sentimental; the former by historians and social scientists, who have not been impressed by the imitative and artificial quality of the examples (usually limited to romantic fiction, literary essays, and lyric verse) commonly cited as masterpieces. There has indeed, in spite of the recent work of a handful of scholars and critics, been a general failure to recognize that the historical development of Canada "from colony to nation" has imposed an individuality upon Canadian literature that is missed if one limits it to belles lettres. Just after Confederation, it is true, and in the period from about 1870 to 1910, few Canadian writers seemed able to escape from a genteel English tradition that was unmistakably literary, and for this reason their work, often technically quite accomplished, seems weak, derivative, and, in spite of a national assertiveness, actually thoroughly colonial.

Surprisingly perhaps, these are not the faults we shall find in the work of the practical, amateur writers among the pioneers and settlers, the United Empire Loyalists, the explorers and fur-traders, and the politicians engaged in the struggle for responsible government whose writings make up this volume. These people created a literature simply by minding their own business and writing out of the immediate experience of the world around them and their struggle to master it.

Looking back from the vantage point of the mid-twentieth century we see that here we are concerned with the first of three clearly marked periods of Canadian development, the products of each of which are sharply distinguished in tone, attitude, and purpose from those of the others. It is the period of roughly a hundred years from the conquest of New France in 1763 to Confederation in 1867, the period of settlement and exploration, of the struggle for responsible government, and of the gradual drawing together of the colonies into a federal union to resist absorption by the expanding United States. Its main events were the Loyalist settlement, the English, Irish, and Scottish immigrations, the replacement of the fur-trader by the permanent colonist, the war of 1812, the rebellions of 1837, the long struggle for responsible government in the Maritimes, in Lower Canada, and in Upper Canada, and finally Confederation itself. All of these events and the conditions they produced gave a peculiar stamp to the literature of the period and set it off sharply from the more self-conscious and less immediate writing of the later periods.

Most of the work included in the volume is closely identified with the various regional interests, geographical, social, and political, which conditioned the new hard life of the settlements. The characteristic literature of the colonial period is practical and utilitarian. It is the knowledgeable product of men and women whose main business is not letters as a profession or writing as a fine art. Their writing is an instrument or a tool to be used in the main task of subduing the wilderness, achieving an emotional adjustment to the new environment, and securing their kind of social or political organization. At its best it has a native tang and a craftsmanlike goodness that more than compensates for any lack of polish or sophistication. This applies especially to the work of the fur-traders and explorers in the north and west. Samuel Hearne, Alexander Henry, and David Thompson write with a steady downright competence akin to the skill with which they used the sextant or wielded the paddle. These are the writers of our heroic age, as are the Jesuit missionaries of that of our French-Canadian brothers. They found, each in his own way, a style, rough and ready though it often was, which was commensurate with the great story they had to tell, or rather the great work they had to do.

No personal narrative of hairbreadth escapes is more vivid than Alexander Henry's account of the massacre at Michilimackinac, and no true adventure story was ever more packed with pity and terror than Hearne's account of the slaughter of the Esquimaux. The patriarchal David Thompson writes like a figure out of the Old Testament in his portrayal of the two races of being, Man and Beaver, who contested the supremacy of forest and stream. At other times he impresses us as a sort of primitive and northern Gilbert White: "The Rivers and Lakes have Pike (the Water Wolf). He preys on every fish he can master, even on his own species; he seizes his prey by the middle of the back, and keeps his hold until it is dead: when he swallows it. He catches readily at any bait, even a bit of red rag. It is a bold active fish, and in summer is often found with a mouse in its stomach. Its jaws are strong, set with sharp teeth, somewhat curved; it is of all sizes from one to fifteen pounds. . . ."

Perhaps the greatest stylistic achievement of all is Alexander Mackenzie's, and not written with ink or inscribed on paper. Alexander Mackenzie, servant of the Northwest Company, accompanied by a little band of *voyageurs* whose names he recorded in his book like an Homeric list of heroes—Alexander Mackay, Joseph Landry, Charles Ducette, François Beaulieu, Baptiste Bisson, François Courtois, and Jacques Beauchamp, with two Indians as hunters and interpreters—set out in a twenty-five foot canoe to penetrate the Rockies and reach the Pacific Ocean. By mid-summer of 1793 (they had started early in May) the little party reached salt water near Bella Coola, British Columbia, the first to cross the continent by a dozen years. It was then that Mackenzie achieved his greatest stylistic success, a success inseparably bound up with his heroic exploit. It is a single sentence of monumental grandeur: "I now mixed up some vermilion in melted grease, and inscribed, in large characters, on the South-east face of the rock on which we had slept last night, this brief memorial: *Alexander Mackenzie, from Canada by land, the twenty-second of July, 1793.*"

But the fur-traders and explorers were not the only heroes, and they were not the only writers of good solid clear vivid prose. Travellers like Patrick Campbell, writers of memoirs like Dr. William Dunlop, and historians like Major Richardson wrote well because they too were dealing simply and directly with what was immediately before them. Mrs. Moodie, wife of a forest settler in Upper Canada, though she could never forget she was an English gentlewoman, brought to her narrative of colonization the same sturdy doggedness that had enabled her and her kind to survive and conquer. This is the quality too, though in this instance quite divorced from morality or good will, found in the half-savage self-reliant Indian-killer David Ramsay, whose story is recorded by Patrick Campbell. Ramsay is a frontier type, absolutely irresponsible, and with a courage like Robinson Crusoe's, born of lack of imagination. He was a settler, not really a trader, a sworn foe of the Indian, and thus actually more an American than a Canadian, a great contrast to a Hearne, a Mackenzie, or a Thompson, whose remarks on the red man are of value because they are based on close observation and genuine respect.[1]

Within the colonial period, of course, there is plenty of variety, as the regional and temporal divisions of the material should suggest, and there are some sharp contrasts too. Strikingly different not only from the writing of the fur-traders but from that of women of her own class like Mrs. Moodie and her

[1]"Fur traders and Indians were inseparable partners who cherished the same hope of stopping the advance of American settlement and the same ambition of preserving the fur-trading commercial empire of the west." Donald Creighton, *Dominion of the North* (Boston: Houghton Mifflin, 1944), p.185.

sister, Mrs. Traill, were the novels of Mrs. Frances Brooke several generations earlier. One of them, *The History of Emily Montague* (1769), can claim the distinction of being the first Canadian novel. Mrs. Brooke was the wife of a regimental chaplain in the garrison of Quebec immediately after the fall of New France. She utilized the material afforded by the society around her, English and French, military and civil, to depict the manners and foibles and the political aspirations of the new British colony of Lower Canada. Mrs. Brooke was an English blue-stocking, and on her return to England she moved in the circles of Fanny Burney and Dr. Johnson. She cast her witty and accurate observations of Quebec into the form of the fashionable epistolary novel. Yet in spite of the wit and the keen observation, the book in many respects is conventional and romantic. Everything in Canada—the scenery, the climate, the redskins, the habitants, the seigneurs, the pretty ladies and charming nuns, and the gallant officers, Wolfe's or Montcalm's, are seen in a heightened and sentimental haze that reveals them as quaint or grand or exquisite or fierce. The Indian is the Noble Savage of the eighteenth century *philosophe*, and the attitude towards nature sometimes suggests Rousseau and sometimes Pope. Mrs. Brooke is most refreshing (to a Canadian reader at least) when she is in her neo-classic vein: "The scenery is to be sure divine," writes her heroine, "but one grows weary of meer scenery."

This is what might be called the literature of preconceived ideas, at the opposite pole from the solid practical inductive observation of a David Thompson or a Mrs. Moodie. It is second rate perhaps, but at least the writer was on the spot at the time, and her book is closer to reality than the romantic historical novels or even the painstakingly "got-up" period pieces such as *The Golden Dog* or *The Seats of the Mighty* of later novelists. It has a genuine social and historical interest. It shows, for instance, how closely the British governing party after 1763 identified its own interests with those of the seig-neurs and the land-owning aristocracy of the old regime. Sometimes, as in her unflattering account of the habitant, Mrs. Brooke anticipates Lord Dur-ham. In her remarks on the adverse effect of the northern climate on the growth of a native literature she says: "I no longer wonder the elegant arts are unknown here; the rigour of the climate suspends the very powers of the understanding; what then must become of those of the imagination ...? Genius will never mount high where the faculties of the mind are benumbed half the year."

Mrs. Brooke was a sophisticated English gentlewoman. Her work is bright and amusing. It is also prejudiced and conventional, but it is not superficial, and it affords us a clearer picture of the social life of Quebec immediately after the conquest than any of the sober histories. It is superior, however, and condescending, and thus it is not in the mainstream of native Canadian let-ters. Such doubts as those just quoted should not be allowed to enter a Cana-dian breast. The United Empire Loyalists, with whom the headwaters of

Canadian literature may be said to rise, certainly never entertained such doubts of themselves or of their new home.

Actually their new home was not so different from their old one as we might think. British North America began, as the New England colonies did, by settlement from the mother country, though there were not only the Indians but the French as well to subdue. From the first there had been the closest ties between Nova Scotia and New England. Halifax was much closer in every way to Boston than to Quebec or Montreal. Even before the American Revolution—and more certainly *after* the American Revolution, when between fifty and sixty thousand Loyalist refugees crowded into the British maritime colonies—these eastern seaboard colonies were not entirely alien to New England. The easy sea passage to Boston, a common background of tradition and religion, and the enterprise of the Massachusetts merchants all combined to prolong a kind of relationship between the old colonies and the new ones to the north. The Loyalist settlers were mostly Congregationalists, and their pastors and schoolmasters were Harvard men.

Nevertheless the Loyalists had suffered heavily for their stand during the war, and they were outraged and bitter. By birth and education they were confirmed Tories and looked on the triumph of the American mob pretty much as Edmund Burke was to look on the excesses of the French Revolution. Besides, they had been hurt where they were most sensitive. Their property had been confiscated, and it was to re-establish themselves as landowners and capitalists that prominent men such as Jonathan Odell, Jacob Bailey, or the Winslows came into the maritime colonies.

Yet many of them still thought of themselves as Americans. When the Puritan Jacob Bailey left his parish in Maine and sailed in a chartered schooner across the Bay of Fundy to Halifax, his vessel was pursued by an American privateer—and to make matters worse, on a Sunday. He speaks of the Americans as "my countrymen" and writes of them as follows:

> I am persuaded that my countrymen exceed all mankind in a daring and enterprising disposition. Their bold and adventurous spirit, more especially, appears with distinguishing *éclat* when they are engaged in any unjust and vicious undertaking, and their courage commonly increases in proportion to the badness and villainy of the cause they endeavour to support. Let a New England man once throw off the restraints of education, he becomes a hero in wickedness, and the more strict and religious he has been in his former behaviour, the greater will be his impiety in his present situation. It has often been remarked by foreigners who have engaged in commerce with our Puritans that when they first come abroad no people alive have such a prevailing aversion to profane swearing, and yet they quickly become the most docile scholars in the school of vice, and make the greatest proficiency in every species of

profanity. They openly ridicule their former attachment to devotion, and are very ingenious in framing new and spirited oaths, and when they have an extraordinary mischief to perform they always choose to perpetrate it on a Sunday.

The close affinity between the Maritime Provinces and the New England States was to have a curious consequence as late as 1812 when the world war between Britain and the Napoleonic empire resulted in an unnecessary inconclusive conflict between Canada and the United States. The New England States were strongly opposed to the war. The mercantile communities of the American tidewater from Chesapeake Bay to New Brunswick were doing too well in contraband trade with Halifax and Quebec. They voted against the war in Congress; and when war came they did their best to thwart it by trading with the enemy; indeed for a little while in 1814 they seriously discussed secession.

The results of the war of 1812, some of the events of which are recorded in the writings of Dr. William Dunlop and Major John Richardson, were merely to establish a *status quo ante.* But it did leave in Canada a vague and long-abiding uneasiness about the United States coupled with a certain pride in having achieved the seemingly impossible in avoiding being overrun and conquered by a nation immensely more wealthy and with nearly eight million inhabitants as against fewer than one-half million, of whom only one-hundred thousand lived in Upper Canada, where the bulk of the fighting took place.

The war did more to unite the Canadas and turn the thoughts of the people towards an eventual union of all the British North American colonies than any other event before the American Civil War, when the complex relations between the Canadian colonies, the warring powers in the United States, and Great Britain were seen by Canadians as a threat to the very existence of the colonies. The British government was talking of withdrawing its garrisons and its financial support from the colony, and at the same time its warlike acts at sea on behalf of Southern blockade runners and privateers seemed likely to bring about a war with the North that Canada did not want, feared intensely, and had done nothing to provoke. Canada's sympathies, indeed, were almost entirely with her immediate neighbour, particularly, of course, on the Abolition question.

What Canadians thought about the American Civil War and the dangers of being drawn into it and overrun by the vastly more powerful Northern states is very effectively illustrated in the writings of two remarkable Nova Scotian men of letters. One of these, the Honourable Joseph Howe, was a statesman and orator of the calibre of Daniel Webster, and the other, Judge Haliburton, was a political humourist, whose series of Pickwick-like volumes devoted to the lucubrations of Sam Slick, the Yankee clockmaker, written during the late thirties and forties, gives him a substantial claim to be considered one of the most potent of the putative fathers of American humour. Haliburton's sketches and tales, full of broad characterization and horseplay, are even more remarkable for their politics and their social satire.

Here now is Mr. Sam Slick, the sharp, sharp-tongued, clever, humorous, boastful, loquacious, hard-headed, and somehow immensely likable Connecticut Yankee—not at the court of King Arthur but in the little capital of Nova Scotia talking to the Tory country squire, the John-Bullish Judge Haliburton. It is night:

> "Jist look out of the door," said the Clockmaker, "and see what a beautiful night it is—beant it lovely? I like to look up at them 'are stars when I am away from home; they put me in mind of our national flag, and it is generally allowed to be the first flag in the univarse now. The British can whup all the world, and we can whup the British. It's near about the prettiest sight I know on is one of our first class frigates, manned with our free and enlightened citizens, all ready for sea; it is like the Great American Eagle on its perch, balancing itself for a start on the broad expanse of blue sky, afeard o' nuthin' of its kind, and president of all it surveys. It was a good emblem that we chose, warn't it?"

A little later Mr. Slick contrasts the lethargic Nova Scotians with the up-and-coming Yankees. "An owl should be their emblem, and their motto 'He sleeps all the days of his life.' The whole country is like this night; beautiful to look at, but silent as the grave—still as death, asleep, becalmed."

Haliburton's attitude towards slavery may be seen in a piece of savage social satire entitled "The White Nigger," which is concerned not so much with the evils of slavery in the United States as with the hypocrisy of Canadians in denouncing the South while enjoying the fruits of unconscious slavery in their own rural communities.

Yet it was not the question of slavery that really stirred the Canadians but the fear that England, without consulting her colonies and indeed against their will, would provoke a war with the Northern states in which the Canadians would be overrun and destroyed. Here is the way that Joseph Howe, the other great man of letters in pre-Confederation Nova Scotia, saw the situation. He is writing an open letter to a British member of parliament interested in colonial affairs. The time is December 1862.

> When you ask us to defend ourselves against thirty or even against twenty millions of people of our own race, whose settlement and civilization precedes our own by a hundred years—who, forty years ago, were sufficiently numerous to maintain war on land and sea for three years against the whole power of Great Britain, you ask us to do that

which is simply unreasonable and unjust. If this be expected or asked, it is quite clear that the Queen's Government abdicates dominion in North America. Shall it be said that the diplomacy of England is to involve us in foreign quarrels, and that the arms of England are not to be employed in our defence?

Howe works up to a magnificently rhetorical peroration:

But is it not apparent that what has happened to the Virginians would happen to us? Our cities would be captured, our fields laid waste, our bridges would be blown up, our railways destroyed. The women of British North America, as remarkable for their beauty as for their purity of thought, would become a prey to a soldiery drawn from the refuse of society in the old world and the new. Our commerce would be destroyed, our improvements stopped, our whole society disorganized. But, whatever its issue, trust me that that portion of the British family who had sought our subjugation, who had shed our blood, traversed our country and outraged our women would stand higher in our estimation than that other branch of the family who, from craven fear or calculating selfishness, had left us to contend with such fearful odds. . . .

Far better would it be, if this were to be the result of the amended relations you propose, that England should at once say to British North America: Assume the management of your own foreign relations. Send your own ministers to London, to Washington, or wherever else you please. We will admit you to the status of the most favored nation, but we can no longer burden our treasury with your defence.

Howe's is a proud and independent point of view. Its self-reliance is not diminished because it goes along with love and respect for the mother country. Self-consciousness and self-confidence give a special quality to the literature of the British North American colonies in the two or three decades before Confederation. But the confidence has to be won with difficulty, so that what we have is actually a literature of stress and tension. The pull of opposing forces—from south of the border and from across the Atlantic—had to be resolved. And this was done not by opposing the one or submitting to the other but by utilizing both in order to attain, and then maintain, a balance. When that could be achieved, as it was with Confederation, the literature of colonialism ceased to have validity, and a new era, in letters as in life, opened before the Dominion.

To Confederation

*from* Canadian Literature, *No. 37*

Before Confederation there could have been no poet to reflect a national identity because there was as yet no political framework to link the various widely separated regions together and no economic or social factors in common. . . . The *idea* of something in common, the *aspiration* towards union, and the *hope* of an eventual federation found expression in the writings of versifiers and essayists long before social and economic conditions made Confederation at first a possibility and eventually a necessity. The ideal of a national—or rather, perhaps, a continental—identity was found thrilling by poets, or would-be poets, who hoped that a national bard would arise to hymn the glories of a new nation in the north. Thus, Standish O'Grady wrote in 1842 in the Preface to *The Emigrant, A Poem:* "This expanded and noble continent will no doubt furnish fit matter for the Muse. The diversity of climate, the richness of soil, the endearing qualities of a genial atmosphere must no doubt furnish a just excitement to the poetic mind, and arouse that energy correspondent with a richness of scenery, which the contemplative mind will studiously portray."

In spite of these natural advantages, however, a poet of commensurate greatness was slow in appearing. Twenty-three years later Henry J. Morgan, writing in his valuable *Sketches of Celebrated Canadians,* had to admit that "We in Canada are unfortunate enough not to have had many persons entitled to the distinction of being marked as poets, though possessing every facility that a grand and scenic country possesses, capable of exciting the proper inspiration and spirit of poetry."

We are tempted to feel such remarks—especially a phrase like "the *proper* inspiration . . . of poetry"—to be incredibly naive. Yet the idea that the Canadian poet or often, rather, *the Canadian*, that mythical figure, is a product of his natural environment and at once in both a regional and a continental sense expresses and is formed by his surroundings appeared early and is with us still. The question has always been, of course, whether the ubiquitous wilderness and the northern climate in a mainly empty semi-continent was to stimulate or intimidate. On the whole, our poets—(and here I mean all of them, modern as well as ancient)—have written out of the conviction that the challenge creates its response; and while the terror, that Professor Northrop Frye sees as providing the great tragic theme of our poetry, is real and intense, our poets have fought it.

Occasionally, the wilderness triumphs, as in Earle Birney's "Bushed," where a stoic endurance becomes the only response; but usually it is man's courage and resourcefulness in subduing the wilderness that is stressed, as in Isabella Crawford's "Malcolm's Katie" of 1884 or Pratt's "Towards the Last Spike" of 1952.

The idea that the rigorous climate and the many natural obstacles to be encountered in the north and west preclude the development of intellectual life and the creation of art and poetry had found expression very early and may be taken as presenting a diametrically opposite but equally sentimental point of view from that of Standish O'Grady or Dr. Morgan. . . .

The notion that a land gripped for six months of every twelve in wintry winds cannot produce writing of consequence is still to be heard in English reviews of Canadian, or rather, "colonial" books, even occasionally in such capable publications as the *TLS* and the *New Statesman*. This view has the authority of Professor Arnold Toynbee, who notes in his *Study of History* that a line drawn somewhere—just a few miles, one gathers—north of Boston marks the boundary beyond which no intellectual maturity or artistic excellence can be expected.

Another problem that poets and men of letters in pre-Confederation British North America saw confronting them was their belief that this was a country without a mythology. Mrs. Traill, in her account of pioneer life in Otonabee County, *The Backwoods of Canada* (1836) laments the fact that this is a new country, unsanctified by myth or legend, settled by matter-of-fact folk who have neither time nor inclination to people the forests with deities or the mountains with nymphs. This state of affairs was thought of as denying to the poet an audience interested in what a poet (even in the wilderness settlement) is interested in by definition—the traditional classical myths of European culture.

This attitude persisted a long time, and is responsible for much of the imitative "literary" poetry of the eighties and the nineties. The so-called Confederation poets, in one aspect of their work, sought to import from English romantic poetry a mythology they might well have found elsewhere in the tales and beliefs of the Indian. Both Charles G. D. Roberts and Duncan Campbell Scott made the attempt; but only the latter was successful—and that in a surprisingly small proportion of his total work.

Only very late—after the work of anthropologists and scholars like Sapir, Barbeau, and Alfred Bailey—has it become possible to make genuine poetry out of the native mythology of Canada, as for example in the translations of Haida poems by Hermia Harris Fraser or a few of the poems of Alfred Bailey, or to deal dramatically and sympathetically with the Indian, as in John New-love's moving poem "The Pride." An exception must be made, of course, for "The Forsaken" and "At Gull Lake" by D. C. Scott, the first dating from 1905 and the second from 1935, both of them products of Scott's lifework in the Department of Indian Affairs.

One myth, however, did seize the imagination of Canadian poets, and that is the *myth of the machine,* especially the machine that becomes a means of transportation and serves to draw us together. Lighthall speaks of the poetry in his anthology of 1889 as a poetry of the canoe; with Pratt it becomes a poetry of steamship and transcontinental railway; with F. R. Scott and Bir-ney it is the airplane—"Trans-Canada" and "North Star West."

"In Canada," Northrop Frye has written, "the enormous difficulties and the central importance of communication and transport, the tremendous energy that developed the fur trade routes, the empire of the St. Lawrence, the transcontinental railways, and the northwest police patrols have given it the dominating role in the Canadian imagination." It is Pratt certainly, as Frye affirms, who has most fully and most dynamically grasped this fact, but it is not Frye alone, *nor the modern poet alone,* who has seen the machine as monster or genie. Sangster, the best of the versifiers that James Reaney calls the "dear bad poets/Who wrote/Early in Canada," has a good descriptive piece, written in dashing couplets, on the noise and excited astonishment as the Iron Horse bursts for the first time into the forest clearing and its sparse settlement. In some of the spirited Spenserian stanzas of his long Byronic poem, *The St. Lawrence and the Saguenay,* he describes an excursion steamer winding its way through the channels of the Thousand Islands. He passes eas-ily from the myth of the red man to the myth of the ship as fiery dragon, a *living* monster:

> Many a tale of legendary lore
> Is told of these romantic Isles. The feet
> Of the Red Man have pressed each wave-zoned shore,
> And many an eye of beauty oft did greet
> The painted warriors and their birchen fleet
> As they returned with trophies of the slain.

That was the past. And now all has returned to primeval loneliness once again ... "Save where some vessel snaps the isle-enwoven chain," and the poet watches with an animating eye "the strong steamer, through the watery glade,/Ploughing, like a huge serpent from its ambuscade."

This was in 1856. But already Sangster, and therefore, it is certain, others along the northern shores of Lake Ontario, were thinking of a unification of the Canadian colonies. When the monument to Brock was dedicated at

Queenston Heights on 13 October 1859 Sangster wrote a poem for the occasion—a clarion call to Canadians to unite again as they had been united when they repelled the invader in 1812.

> One voice, one people, one in heart
> And soul and feeling, and desire!
> Re-light the smouldering martial fire,
> Sound the mute trumpet, strike the lyre,
> The hero deed can not expire,
> The dead still play their part.
>
> Raise high the monumental stone!
> A nation's fealty is theirs....

A *nation's fealty*. In 1859? This, of course, is not fact, not even at the time it was written a certain feasibility. It was aspiration, hope, an ideal desideratum — not politics but poetry (and, ironically, when compared with Emerson's great "Concord Hymn," written for a similar occasion, pretty hollow poetry). But it demonstrated the birth of a feeling in the hearts and minds of the people of Upper Canada at least that a regional isolation was not enough. Those like Sangster, and others I shall turn to in a moment, who were concerned with the development of poetry and letters in the new country were particularly anxious that a nation should be created that might produce, and be worthy of, a national poetry. The idea of a distinctively national poetry was born at the same time as the idea of a distinctive nation.

This is quite explicit in Edward Hartley Dewart's introduction to his *Selections from Canadian Poets* of 1864. In spite of his enthusiasm, however, Dewart was realistic enough to recognize that Canada and Canadians treated their authors with an "almost universal absence of interest."

The cause of this lamentable indifference, the critic went on to affirm, was in part the wide prevalence of low and false conceptions as to the nature and influence of poetry itself, but in Canada a more important reason was to be found in the inferior status of a colony. This curse of colonialism, it can be added a hundred years later, did not leave us after Confederation; E. K. Brown, writing in *On Canadian Poetry* (1943), puts his finger on the colonial spirit as the chief diluter of our poetry just as Dewart did—and so many years and so many political changes later!

Dewart's anthology appeared three years before Confederation. Its chief interest today is its Introduction. The only poems in it that are worth preserving are one or two by Sangster, a couple of rhymes by Alexander McLachlan, and one or two passages from Heavysege's *Saul*. Canadians had to wait until thirteen years after the first Dominion Day for the appearance of a second survey of Canadian poetry. This was *Songs of the Great Dominion,* published in London and Toronto in 1889.

Here the cautious and rather gloomy sobriety of Dewart has been replaced by a full-fledged patriotic enthusiasm. It would seem that Dewart's faith in the efficacy of a national federation to bring a national poetry into being had already been amply justified by an abundance of good works. "The poets whose songs fill this book," wrote the anthologist Lighthall,

> are voices cheerful with the consciousness of young might, public wealth, and heroism. . . . The tone of them is *courage:*—for to hunt, to fight, to hew out a farm, one must be a man! . . . Canadians are for the most part descendants of armies . . . and every generation of them has stood up to battle. . . . The delight of a clear atmosphere runs through it too. . . . Canada, Eldest Daughter of the Empire, is the Empire's completest type! She is the full-grown of the family—the one first come of age and gone out into life as a nation. . . .

A good many summers ago I was conducting a seminar in Canadian literature and history at the University of Toronto with Professor Donald Creighton, and I remember his bewildered amusement when we read this passage. That this should have been written in the year of Canada's most serious and almost disastrous economic depression was not beyond comprehension perhaps, but it was almost beyond justification.

Yet I must make the attempt. To begin with, Lighthall could certainly look with pardonable pride at the poetry available for his anthology when compared with that of his pre-Confederation rival. Here now were poems of Isabella Crawford, Mair, Roberts, Lampman, Wilfred Campbell, and Duncan Campbell Scott—the earliest, and some of the best, pieces by the poets who were later to be known as the Confederation Poets or the poets of our "golden age." Secondly, when you read the poems collected in Lighthall's anthology— it is by far the best of the early anthologies—you will find that the poems *are* filled with a spirit of cheerfulness and wonder, delight in the beauty of nature, and confidence in man's power to conquer. What actually the appreciative critic is expressing—and so are the poets—is a general spiritual sense of euphoria induced by Confederation—a certain indefinable spirit of confidence that economic difficulties and political differences could not destroy. Its best expression is the least explicit—in the mythopoeic passages of Crawford's "Malcolm's Katie," in Roberts' sonnets of the New Brunswick landscape, and in Lampman's painterly evocations of the woods and hills around Ottawa in winter or midsummer. These are Canadian *poetry.*

Let us look, however, at some of the more explicit treatments of the Confederation theme. In some of the pieces by Mair that came out of the Canada

First movement and in the very explicit Confederation odes of Roberts we shall see what people felt they ought to feel. (It is in the true poems of Roberts, Lampman, and Scott that we find what they really felt—and in some cases, to the justification of Lighthall, the two are not always very far apart.)

Charles Mair was the poet who most clearly and consciously set himself to advocate and celebrate Canadian autonomy. Like Sangster before him, he had been hailed as a national poet, and he *thought* of himself as one. In addition, he took an active part in politics, being one of the five original members of the Canada First movement when it was organized by William Foster and George Denison in 1868, and later he had the distinction of being held a prisoner by Riel during the first Red River insurrection. As to the "Canadianism" of Mair's poetry, Professor Norman Shrive in his biography of the poet, tells us how two of the earliest effusions of Mair, "The Pines" and "Summer," were read in 1862 before the Botanical Society of Canada at Kingston and elicited the praise of the Reverend Leitch, principal of Queen's. Of one, he said, "it is a truly Canadian production, inspired by an acquaintance with and love of the forest"; of the other, that it "has more of the old world stamp." For many of the critics of Canadian verse in the nineteenth century and the first three decades of the twentieth these were the comments oftenest made. And they were intended as high compliment. If the Canadian poet could be uniquely and yet vaguely and generally "Canadian" and yet at the same time write like an English poet he was to be given the highest praise. Colonel Denison knew better what was wanted of a poet, particularly a practical poet, and after the publication of Mair's first book of poems, significantly entitled *Dreamland,* he wrote in a letter to his friend:

> For God's sake drop the old style. You're living in a new world and you must write in the language of the living to living men. . . .

And the good soldier continued:

> Most Canadian poems should be published with mild Eau Sucrée style of names—such as "Midnight Musings" or, what is more to the point, "Nocturnal Emissions."

Mair did occasionally speak out, and the lines he wrote to commemorate the leading spirit in the Canada First movement, William Foster, who died in 1887, are a clear manifesto of the aims and hopes he held for the future of the young Dominion.

> . . . Throw sickly thoughts aside—
> Let's build on native fields our fame;

Nor seek to blend our patriot's pride
With alien worth or alien shame!

First feel throughout the throbbing land
A nation's pulse, a nation's pride—
And independent life—then stand
Erect, unbound, at Britain's side.

This, one feels, is a piece of classical verse in which each word and phrase has a precise significance, explicit or implied. What these are we cannot be certain from the poem alone—and this is a defect it shares with a good many other political or patriotic poems—but from the writings, letters, and speeches of the members of the Canada First movement we can learn enough about their views to interpret "alien worth" as British worth and "alien shame" as American shame—an implication in the word "alien" found as late as the Massey Report, by the way—and that "Erect, unbound, at Britain's side" means "courageous, free, equal and ready and able to come to Britain's aid, not timidly depending on her aid." A more independent statement than Kipling's much later famous phrase about Mother and Daughter.

Yet the limitations of Canada First and Mair's views about Canadian unity are very clear. Professor Shrive speaks of the movement's self-destructive weakness. "Decrying provincialism, it was itself provincial, even parochial. Culturally it was militantly anti-Ultramontane and anti-French. Socially its members represented the 'respectable,' even, as in Denison's case, the upper classes." The national unity, in other words, to be advocated and stimulated, was an English, genteel, and Christian one. It was a union embracing only Upper Canada, the dominant English minority of Lower Canada, and the Maritimes.

This dream of a limited union was shared also by the so-called Confederation poets, particularly Roberts and Wilfred Campbell, and the anthologist Lighthall, but it has been revealed for what it is—only a dream—by the two great events in the history of Canada since the end of the Second World War—the influx of European immigrants into our rapidly expanding cities and the awakening of Quebec. Roberts' finely phrased and classically modulated lines beginning "O Child of Nations, giant-limbed" are perfectly turned and present a truly inspiring picture of an ideal, strong, free, independent, and unified nation—but it was only a dream, a dream made unreal by the fact that it was dreamed by only half the nation.

# PART THREE

*Poets of a Golden Age?*

| *The Fredericton Poets*

*from* Founders' Day Address, *University of New Brunswick*

Among the founders of the university was Jonathan Odell, the Loyalist poet of the American Revolution, one of the most spirited and the bitterest of the Tory satirists who lent their pens to the cause of England. "When," as the American literary historian Moses Coit Tyler has written, "the contemptuous wrath of England gave way, and she forced her reluctant king to make terms with the late American rebels, Odell would not make terms with them ... he abandoned the land of his birth and his ancestry and settled himself in Nova Scotia [New Brunswick], where he sustained a distinguished civil career, and where at last, in extreme old age, he died, without ever taking back a word, or uttering an apology, or flinching from an opinion—a proud, gritty member of a political party that had been defeated, but never conquered or convinced."

Odell's town house still stands in Fredericton, but his poetry is almost forgotten. Perhaps this is as it should be, for his rhymes and satires have long ago served the purpose they were written to serve—to encourage the Tories in their struggle against rebellious faction and to relieve the feelings of a little group of unfortunate Loyalists in the days of adversity. Yet it may be useful to consider for a moment the fundamental difference between the verses of Odell (and later on of Joseph Howe in Nova Scotia) and the poetry of Roberts and Carman at the end of the nineteenth century. Odell's verses are social and practical. They are not the expression of a peculiar sensibility; they are the feelings and opinions of a party; and their purpose is a very practical one—to hearten and band together those engaged in fighting an actual battle. Odell is so much at one with the particular audience he is writing for that much of his best poetry consists of sociable verse—political and patriotic drinking songs, written for a special occasion and often performed by the whole convivial group, toasting the king and calling down confusion on his enemies.

Here is an example of Odell's poetry that will show you something of the spirit of the gentlemen, who not so long after this was written were to help

found a college in New Brunswick. The poem was composed on 4 June 1777
in honour of the birthday of George III.

> Time was when America hallowed the morn
> On which the loved monarch of Britain was born,
>      Hallowed the day, and joyfully chanted
>           God Save the King!
> Then flourished the blessings of freedom and peace,
> And plenty flowed in with a yearly increase.
>      Proud of our lot we chanted merrily
>           Glory and joy crown the King!
> But see! how rebellion has lifted her head!
> How honour and truth are with loyalty fled!
>      Few are there now who join us in chanting
>           God save the King!
> And see! how deluded the multitude fly
> To arm in a cause that is built on a lie!
>      Yet are we proud to chant thus merrily
>           Glory and joy crown the King! ...
> Though faction by falsehood awhile may prevail,
> And loyalty suffers a captive in jail,
>      Britain is roused, rebellion is falling:
>           God save the King!
> The captive shall soon be released from his chain;
> And conquest restore us to Britain again,
>      Ever to join in chanting merrily
>           Glory and joy crown the King!

What cheerful high spirits and faith doomed never to be justified there was
in this jolly poetry! And also (one who is interested in the craft of verse cannot
help noticing) what a remarkable metrical skill is shown in the sudden surprising shift from the anapests of the first two lines of each stanza to the dac-
tyls of the next two—a device that is repeated in the second half of each
stanza. This was written by a man who had a good classical education, a
clergyman of the Church of England, and the inheritor of a culture that the
Loyalists from New York, New Jersey, Pennsylvania, and the New England
states were to bring with them into the Maritime provinces. It was to endure
many vicissitudes and suffer many losses before the means of its preservation
and transmission were finally assured. ...

It was in the seventies and eighties, and in a culture that was ripe and
apparently fixed in its ripeness, that a group of young men of Loyalist stock,
most of them close kinsmen, came under the influence of a great teacher in
the Fredericton Collegiate School and then passed into the University of

New Brunswick. The most notable of these were Charles G. D. Roberts, who graduated in 1879, and Bliss Carman, who graduated in 1881. Two men who were to achieve a measure of success as poets not much less than that of Roberts and Carman were Francis Sherman, who attended the university but did not graduate; and Charles' younger brother, Theodore Goodridge Roberts, war-correspondent, story writer, and poet, who was at the university in the nineties, though the lure of adventure called him to sea, to Newfoundland, and the West Indies before he could be capped and hooded. Nevertheless, it was the culture of the best in English literature which he had imbibed in the rectory library and at the Fredericton Collegiate School that nourished him as a poet and writer. He had contributed a poem to the *Century* by the time he was eleven. His favourite author was Francis Bacon, and he was reading everything he could find at hand, from Samuel Johnson's *Rambler* to Captain Marryat and R. M. Ballantyne.

The two leaders of this school of Fredericton poets, Charles G. D. Roberts and Bliss Carman, are associated with the Ottawa poets, Archibald Lampman and Dr. Duncan Campbell Scott, and their work has been lovingly praised by a number of devoted scholars, among whom it will be sufficient to mention Dr. Lorne Pierce, Odell Shepherd, Richard LeGallienne, Muriel Miller, Rufus Hathaway, and the late Professor James Cappon, of Queen's University.

Coming after such critics, it is not necessary to write appreciations of these poets. They have taken their place unchallenged as classics. Instead, it may be useful to suggest the sort of approach that their reputation must now be prepared to withstand: for scholarship and criticism have not yet, except in the brilliant studies by Professor Cappon, submitted the poetry of Charles G. D. Roberts and Bliss Carman to any very rigorous and acid examination. I believe their work is ready for the sort of trial by fire that would burn away the dross and leave the pure gold to shine all the more brightly, unmistakable and permanent. Indeed, literary criticism in Canada is faced with a task not unlike that which Dr. D. C. Harvey, the learned archivist of Nova Scotia, said remained for the historian. "Even on the political and biographical side of history," said Dr. Harvey, "there is still much research to be done; and in doing that research, an effort should be made to overcome the natural vice of eulogy.... Even the Loyalists should be made to stand before the bar of history." Harvey stressed the need "to tone down the harsher criticism of the pre-Loyalists and the undiscriminating eulogies of the Loyalists." Well, in the field of literary history too, we must try to view more sympathetically some of our writers before Confederation and to replace temporarily our impressionistic eulogies of the poets born in the sixties by a scholarly examination of the social and intellectual milieu out of which they have risen. And we must make a more rigorous effort to separate their best work from the larger body of their poetry which is less original, less intense, or less perfect.

When these two undertakings have been successfully accomplished we will be able to assess the true contribution of these men to the broadening stream of Canadian culture.

To relate their poetry to the society out of which it has grown and to disentangle the various threads of intellectual and spiritual influence which made it what it was: there is the task that our literary historians must prepare themselves to undertake. It is not a simple or an easy job, but if successfully accomplished it would be well worthwhile, for we would know our country and our history the better for it.

In these Fredericton poets one observes that a form of expression of varying intensity and varying clarity has been given to such real intangibles as the Tory spirit, the Loyalist tradition, Canadianism, and Imperialism. The student must examine critically the attitude of the poet towards nature, and note also the influences derived not from nature directly but from what other men have felt and thought about nature, from the poetry of Wordsworth, Shelley, Emerson, or Tennyson. And then there is the health-giving strength of the classics absorbed largely through the educational culture of Fredericton in the collegiate and at the university. Lastly, in Carman and in Theodore Goodridge Roberts, and to a somewhat lesser extent in Charles Roberts, there is the spirit of bohemianism, the vagabond spirit, a form of muscular idealism, that prompts the poet to break away—from what? the critic must ask, and why?—and to march off in pursuit of the horizon. The historical critic will try to relate this restlessness to other aspects of the romantic movement, to find parallel instances in German and English literature and above all in American literature and will concentrate on those which actually touched our Canadian poets; and the philosophical critic will examine the motives of our poets and estimate the worth of their revolt.

I myself cannot help feeling that Bliss Carman's "vagabond" poetry shows not so much a desire to get anywhere in particular as the desire simply to get away from the here and now. To Carman the very vagueness of the goal is one of its most attractive features. And this in itself is perhaps not very respectable. Indeed, the presence of this feeling in one of the poets that Carman admired most, Browning, has led the philosopher-critic George Santayana to speak of Browning (and Walt Whitman also) as a poet of barbarism. But perhaps we may discount the vagueness of Carman's goal, not so much because we are charmed by the scenery along the wayside or by the wenches we dally with at the inn door, as because the motive which has prompted the pilgrimage is generous and noble. It is, in the long run, a revolt against accepting the lowest possible view of human nature and of nature. It is an assertion of man's spiritual triumph over time and mortality.

One thing certainly that can be said in praise of all these poets is that they took the responsibilities of their craft seriously and believed passionately in the high calling of the poet. What Theodore Goodridge Roberts wrote in the introduction to a selection of his poems is a credo shared by his older brother and by Bliss Carman. "I believe that poetry is the very essence of mankind's highest efforts to express and interpret life. . . . Poets, as individuals, are as other men and women—brave and timid, false and fair, generous and mean, reckless and cautious, harsh and kind—but when their peculiar gifts of vision and expression are being applied honestly in the cause or quest of any truth . . . theirs is the authority of a sacred office."

I am not sure that we can separate so sharply the inspiration of poetry from the personality and the momentary temper of the individual through whom it is expressed, but I know that the group of poets with whom we are dealing felt that in writing their poetry they were lifted up into a realm of significance that transcended the trivial and shifting accidents of ordinary living. They held, with Tennyson, that

> The poet in a golden clime was born,
>   With golden stars above,
> Dowered with the hate of hate, the scorn of scorn,
>   The love of love.
>
> He saw through life and death, through good and ill;
>   He saw through his own soul
> The marvel of the everlasting will
>   An open scroll.

This "high seriousness"—which was held without any undue solemnity—was partly the inescapable heritage of the Victorian outlook as transmitted through Tennyson, Browning, and Arnold, but it was due in the first instance to the kind of society, in the home, the school, and college, out of which Roberts and Carman sprang and which moulded their personalities in the all-important years of childhood and youth.

The Fredericton of the seventies, as one reads about it in such books as Joseph Whitman Bailey's life of his father, Professor Loring Bailey, or Willison's *Sir George Parkin*, or in reminiscent essays by Sir Charles Roberts, appears like an enchanted city, with its elm-shaded streets, its generously proportioned old homes, its cathedral, and the college on the hill, while the broad river winding through the town and the wooded slopes behind bring the forests and an echo of the sea almost to people's very doorsteps. Charles

Roberts, Bliss Carman and Theodore Roberts have all given ample testimony in their poetry of responding to the special charm of such an environment. It is the charm of a quiet, old-world, gentlemanly society, where the culture is that of the rectory and the classics, perhaps a little provincial, but not raw or uncertain, and saved from any taint of the anemic by the forest and streams and the not-too-distant sea. Indeed, it was these that spoke first and most insistently to Roberts.

> I am a child of the beautiful and storied River St. John, my birthplace being at the mouth of the Keswick stream, ten miles above Fredericton. But a few months after my birth my father was appointed rector of the parish of Westcock and Dorchester, at the head of the Bay of Fundy; and the following fourteen years of my life were spent at the quaint old colonial homestead known as Westcock Parsonage, on the wooded ridge of upland looking out across the green marshes and tumultuous tides of the Tantramar.

Then in 1874 when the future poet was fourteen, his father became rector of Fredericton, and the family moved into the capital. Here he became the inseparable companion of his cousin, Bliss Carman, and though they were not in the same form or year, they attended the Collegiate School and the University of New Brunswick together.

At the collegiate young Roberts and Carman soon came under the close personal influence of the headmaster, George R. Parkin, who had just returned from Oxford. Parkin was a teacher of genius, and he made friends and disciples of his two willing pupils, instructing them in the classics and filling them with an enthusiasm for the great poets of the day, Tennyson and Arnold, and the new exciting writers, Swinburne and Rossetti. Parkin himself had been born on a small New Brunswick farm, and his biographer tells us how in the early days he had learned his Virgil by doing an odd line as the horses were turning around at the end of a furrow. Carman and Roberts have both left direct and eloquent testimony of the way in which Parkin taught them to love and know the classics and to understand the classical foundation of the best English poetry. Carman wrote:

> He was a fascinating teacher ... there was never a dull moment in his classroom or in his society. ... In the classics, which were his chief subjects, his great appreciation of poetry and letters gave unusual scope to the day's work. ... The amount of Greek and Làtin we read before going to college was not so great—two or three books of Virgil, a book or two of Homer, and a book of Horace, in addition to the usual Caesar and Xenophon—but much of it had to be learned by heart, and all of it minutely mastered, with a thorough knowledge of grammar and construction, and

an understanding of all the poetic and mythological references. With him as an instructor, it was impossible not to feel the beauty of Virgil's lovely passages and the greatness of Homer. . . .

This passage, perhaps, will help to refute those who think that a minute and searching analysis of a passage of poetry, whether it be by Virgil or Milton, deadens the feeling for what is truly poetic. . . .

Carman continues his reminiscences, and he tells us of the way in which the teacher's enthusiasm for the Greek and Roman poets spilled over into a passionate exposition of their great English followers. But Charles Roberts has told the same story, and I vary the recital by picking it up now in the words of Roberts:

England just then was thrilling to the new music, the new colour, the new raptures of Swinburne and Rossetti; Parkin was steeped in them; and in his rich voice he would recite to us ecstatically, over and over till we too were intoxicated with them, the great choruses from "Atalanta in Calydon," and passages from "The Triumph of Time",—but above all, "The Blessed Damozel", which he loved so passionately that Bliss suspected him of sometimes saying it instead of his prayers. But Parkin did not confine himself to the Pre-Raphaelites. He would quote Tennyson, Browning, and Arnold to us, and he taught us to know Homer and Horace . . . as supreme poets and masters of verbal music.

From Parkin the two enraptured scholars went on up the hill to the university. The master himself was, to a great extent, a product of the university. In a letter to Professor Bailey, Parkin speaks of the gracious influences that surrounded him in his student days. (He graduated in 1867, and was back again for a master's degree in 1872.) "My wife and I," he wrote almost fifty years later, "often speak of the advantages we gained from living in the Fredericton of our early days. There was an old-fashioned courtesy and dignity—a real interest in things of the mind and spirit which seem to have somewhat disappeared in the rush of life and supposed progress of later times."

Out of all this there comes a picture of the kind of society and the kind of culture that was to find its spiritual expression in the poetry of Roberts and Carman. It was calm, settled, and certain; conservative and no doubt rather narrow; a beautiful flowering of many traditions—the Loyalist, the Anglican, and the classical—all coming to terms with the wilderness after nearly a hundred years of struggle. It is true, of course, that the spirit which finds expression in this poetry is an essence skimmed only from the dominating classes of the New Brunswick social system, and the social historian will find scarcely a hint here of the wide diversity of fortune and standards of living and morality that can be gleaned from the pages of early historians like Peter Fisher or travellers like Patrick Campbell. What we have instead is a society that has established itself firmly through the heroic effort of its ancestors and has now settled down to enjoy and hold the comfortable place it has made for itself. This has its limitations, but it has its advantages too. The lucky artist who is nurtured in such a culture is set free to deal with what is universal, with the fundamental emotions of the human heart, and with the adventures of the soul in its search for an eternal nourishment. He is free, in other words, to write "pure" poetry, a poetry that is almost timeless and changeless, and that deals with the everlasting verities, human love, human loneliness, the sustaining strength of the earth, man's response to the voices, fancied or real, of nature. And in the New Brunswick in which Carman and Roberts grew up this did not mean so complete a withdrawal as might elsewhere have been the case, for the most important industries were farming, lumbering, and fishing—activities that were essentially manly and that brought men into close touch with nature.

Charles G. D. Roberts' finest poetry is undoubtedly the poetry in which he has most faithfully and soberly presented the life of the farmer, the fisherman, and the woodsman going about their eternal tasks under the changing sky of the four seasons. How Virgilian is the spirit of the sonnets he collected in 1893 and published under the title *Songs of the Common Day!* What sobriety and dignity shine in such a passage as this from "The Sower."

> A brown, sad-coloured hillside, where the soil
> Fresh from the frequent harrow, deep and fine,
> Lies bare; no break in the remote sky-line,
> Save where a flock of pigeons streams aloft,
> Startled from feed in some low-lying croft,
> Or far-off spires with yellow of sunset shine;
> And here the Sower, unwittingly divine,
> Exerts the silent forethought of his toil.

And how truly classical, in the richest sense of the word, are these lines from "The Mowing."

> The crying knives glide on; the green swath lies.
> And all noon long the sun, with chemic ray,
> Seals up each cordial essence in its cell,
> That in the dusky stalls, some winter's day,
> The spirit of June, here prisoned by his spell,
> May cheer the herds with pasture memories.

Passage after passage can be found among these sonnets of the common day and in the lyrics from *The Book of the Native* which to my mind represents

Roberts' greatest contribution to the art of Canada. It is a delicate and objective nature poetry, restrained, but all the more significant for that, and I believe that it is here, rather than in his more ambitious mystical poems, that the true worth of Roberts' contribution to our literature lies—in his sonnets of country life, and in such a beautiful piece of recollected emotion as the well-known "Tantramar Revisited" or in such a delicate idyl as "The Solitary Woodsman." These poems are the distant fruit of the country boy, George Parkin, learning his Virgil as the horses paused for a moment turning at the end of the furrow.

When we turn from Charles G. D. Roberts to consider the case of Bliss Carman, the critic finds himself faced with a more difficult task. The problem of the poet's relation to the New Brunswick scene and the culture of Fredericton and the university is not capable of any quick or sure solution. A great deal of research remains to be done and a complete and scholarly biography has yet to be written.[1] A fully documented life of Bliss Carman would throw a most significant light on the intellectual and spiritual life not only of Canada but of the United States also.

A simpler task than the biographical one is the task of evaluating the quality of Carman's poetry and sifting out the clear body of first-rate poetry from the larger mass of his work. Carman's ease and facility of writing was so great he wrote too much, and in many of his poems he has continued on in smooth stanza after smooth stanza long after the laws of concentration and intensity should have cautioned a stop. The first duty of the critic who is anxious to rescue Carman's reputation from the reaction that has followed a too-undiscriminating adulation is to define the special excellence of Carman's best work.

The unique and unforgettable quality that makes itself felt in Carman's finest lines is a magic gleam, intense and troubling, a disturbing mixture of the beautiful and the strange, of the attractive and the frightening. His best poetry is the product of an acute and quivering sensibility, and its successful communication to the reader indicates the presence of great technical accomplishment and the power to create images that are heavily charged with emotion.

At this point, perhaps an example or two are called for. Here are some lines from two poems that show the style and substance of Carman at his best.

---

[1]There is a rather voluminous life of Sir Charles Roberts, but it is not written with the detachment and discernment that the subject demands, and it seems to me to be seriously in error in underestimating the influences of Fredericton and its university upon Roberts in his days prior to graduation from the university.

Outside, a yellow maple tree
Shifting upon the silvery blue
With small, innumerable sounds,
Rustles to let the sunlight through. . . .

And then my heart beat once and broke
To hear the sweeping rain forebode
Some ruin in the April world,
Between the woodside and the road. . . .

The substance, or subject matter, it will be seen, is nothing more than the emotion, the mood, the thrill that the music and the images communicate. A longer extract shows the same control.

Come, for the night is cold,
The ghostly moonlight fills
Hollow and rift and fold
Of the eerie Ardise Hills.

The windows of my room
Are dark with bitter frost,
The stillness aches with doom
Of something loved and lost.

Outside, the great blue star
Burns in the ghostland pale,
Where giant Algebar
Holds on the endless trail.

This is thrilling poetry, but if one stops to examine it closely, one will find that the effect has been gained by a tight perfection of form, a concise sentence, and a richly charged but simple and quite idiomatic language. When with this is considered the metrical subtlety of the lines and the formal stanzaic pattern, I would say that this kind of writing could not have been achieved by one who had not had the kind of classical training that Carman (who had a special aptitude for it, of course) had received from Parkin.

There is much, too, in Carman's descriptive nature poetry which, although not as realistic or severe as that of Roberts, is undeniably native in its origin. As Roberts has written in an article to be found in the Hathaway Collection in the University of New Brunswick library "The savour of Canada permeates" Carman's poetry. "The colour and the scent of Canada which bred him—the Maritime Provinces—cling to him imperishably." The sea that washed the New Brunswick coast and the tides of the Bay of Fundy seem to have entered Carman's blood, and come swinging and surging through some of his finest lyrics:

> Burying, brimming, the building billows
> Fret the long dikes with uneasy foam.

He is restless because in his memory and instinct there is something that responds to a place

> Where the sea with her old secret
> Moves in sleep, and cannot rest.

He is a poet, he tells us,

> Because there lies upon my lips
> A whisper of the wind at morn,
> A murmur of the rolling sea,
> Cradling the land where I was born.

This is a timeless poetry, but it is so because the time and place where Carman spent his youth was so safe and sure that he did not have to think about it. The stability and traditionalism of the society in which he grew to maturity set him free to write a pure and universal poetry in which man and the self and the unknown were isolated from the immediate here and now with its pressing needs and turmoils, its economic and political forces, and its practical methods and social ideals. His poetry was not, like that of an earlier day—the poetry of an Odell or a Howe—social, political, or practical. That is, it did not have to be superficial; it could be universal; and this, at its best, it was; though often, too, it was merely ethereal. Yet it could save its energies for the fundamental problems that touch the heart and spirit, so that its finest flights, if not sustained, at least are high. They enable us to feel some aspect of the mystery and beauty and also the tragedy of life. I do not think anyone who has written about Carman has dwelt adequately upon the underlying sadness of his poetry. "Low Tide on Grand Pré," beautiful as are its finest stanzas, is a poem of disillusionment and frustration. An ecstatic experience, that should have transcended time and become eternal by its very intensity, is only a fleeting and dying memory. Often the expression of joy in Carman's poetry is marred by a kind of jauntiness that rather easily seems forced, but when he gives expression to the Lucretian sense of tears at the heart of things his writing takes on a simplicity and grandeur that is unmistakable.

> ... man walks the world with mourning
> Down to death, and leaves no trace,

With the dust upon his forehead,
And the shadow in his face.

Pillared dust and fleeting shadow
As the roadside wind goes by,
And the fourscore years that vanish
In the twinkling of an eye.

But I do not wish to add another to the long list of impressionistic eulogies of Carman's poetry. Let me turn to something more necessary. Let me conclude by dwelling for a moment on the present and the future. I would like to suggest that those universities in Canada which have benefited by the generosity of bibliophiles and collectors and which have in their libraries valuable accumulations of manuscripts and rare old books have the responsibility of training students to use that material wisely and effectively. These universities should become research centres for the study of Canadian literature and Canadian social history and should make an effort to encourage graduate students to collect and use the material available for the digging....

*from* "Our Poets," *University of Toronto Quarterly*

Turning from these poets as individuals, we must try to make some judgment of their accomplishment as a whole, particularly that of the four leaders, Roberts, Carman, Lampman, and D. C. Scott. Orthodox critical opinion in Canada holds that their poetry represents the most complete and satisfying body of work in the whole range of our literature and is perhaps the most significant artistic and spiritual achievement in our history. These poets are our Parnassians, and the nineties, when their finest work was appearing, is our "golden age." Undeniably, their prolific output was astonishing in a country as careless of culture as Canada was then. And more impressive than the generous bulk of their collected works—or the fact that many of their books bore the imprint of London or Boston—was the unmistakable polish, the genuine literary aura, and the high conception of the responsibilities of their craft which testified to the seriousness of their ambition. Amid the enthusiasm this flowering evoked, it seemed as if the patriotic hopes of Dr. Morgan and Dr. Dewart had been more than fulfilled, and that Canada, within a quarter of a century of Confederation, had produced not one but *four* national poets.

It was harder to realize that the concentration upon personal emotion and upon nature, while it made for an easier success, meant a serious narrowing of range and sometimes a thinning of substance. Delicate sensibility and often accurate feeling went along with a good deal of rather commonplace thinking and conventional moralizing. The highest values were placed on whatever touched the heart and spirit in the beauty of nature.

The claim of this poetry to be truly national, adequately sustained in the field of scenery and climate, must on the whole be denied to a body of work which ignored on principle the coarse bustle of humanity in the hurly-burly business of the developing nation. It was an awareness of a lack of relevancy that led the late Professor James Cappon, the most acute of our older critics, to observe that our best poets "have devoted themselves too much to an almost abstract form of nature poetry."

But this is not the final word on these poets. It defines their limitations, but it does not state their value. This can be done briefly. In one respect their dependence upon literary tradition is not a defect, for it went deeper than any mere surface imitation. It arose out of a belief in the continuity of culture, and in their best work it was a preserving and a civilizing force. Living in the wilderness, they showed it was not necessary to write like barbarians. They have, it is true, except in their second-rate work, no message and no philosophy, but if their theme was narrow, it was important, and they presented it with great variety, charm, and precision. In general terms, it was nothing less than the impingement of nature in Canada upon the human spirit.

*from* Our Living Tradition, *2nd and 3rd series*

I shall not attempt to write in a personal vein about Duncan Campbell Scott. This has already been done well by critics and poets who knew him intimately—Pelham Edgar, Arthur S. Bourinot, and E. K. Brown—and at the memorial service held in St. Martin's-in-the-Field, London, soon after the poet's death, where among the speakers was the Poet Laureate, John Masefield, one of Scott's earliest admirers. The value of warm and intimate personal testimony is incalculable, and we are indebted to those who can offer it. There comes a time, however, as the generations pass and literary conditions change when memories and enthusiasms must give way to calm analysis and objective appraisal. With respect to the poets of the sixties this reorientation has been going on for some time, and Roberts, Carman, and Lampman have all been subjected to close and detached scrutiny. Duncan Campbell Scott, however, who has much to gain from such a re-examination, has not yet, in spite of the memoir of E. K. Brown and an essay by Desmond Pacey, been seen as the remarkably original, if not impeccable, poet he really is. I shall do no more here than present some of the evidence drawn from particular poems and specific passages that have led me to this conclusion and try to indicate, however sketchily, the nature of the sensibility that breathes significance into his poetry. And this may help us, I hope to understand and appreciate his contribution to what has been well named "our living tradition."

If I may anticipate for a moment, I believe we shall discover that Duncan Campbell Scott is a more complex poet than has generally been realized; that his merits have a greater diversity than those of any of his famous contemporaries; and finally that there is a much greater proportion of the work of Scott that can appeal to a modern taste—as there is much also that attains to the universal. Had Lampman lived as long as his friend, disciple, and editor, he might well have broadened his scope, attained more variety, and achieved the philosophic maturity that Scott reached in the two fine volumes of his later years, *Beauty and Life* (1921) and *The Green Cloister* (1936). But, as it is, I believe Duncan Campbell Scott stands first among the poets of his generation. And I say this, fully recognizing that there are some of his poems—mainly the patriotic ones and those in which there is a strong moralistic and didactic impulse inherited from Browning, Tennyson, or Arnold—which seem to wither in the cold climate of a later time. Yet there are fewer such than in the collected writings of Roberts or Lampman, and there is more that contains the preservative of an intensity that rises out of accuracy of vision. The result is that Scott can often speak to us today more directly than the other poets of the sixties.

To illustrate this point of view I shall concentrate on poems that have not often been very closely considered, and in doing so I shall have to pass over some that have been justly admired. I refer particularly to the evocations of Indian life that are unique in our literature. Such poems as "The Half-Breed Girl," "Night Hymns on Lake Nipigon," and "The Onondaga Madonna" seem to be carved out of hard wood and turned and polished to perfection, while the longer pieces such as "The Forsaken" and the two great dramatic narratives of the later years, "At Gull Lake: August, 1810" and "A Scene at Lake Manitou," are the most powerfully realized narratives in Canadian poetry.

Scott's successes in this genre have been dealt with at length by Professor Brown and more recently by Professor Pacey, so that it will be more useful if I turn from them to some of the less well-known poems. I cannot do better, perhaps, than begin with Scott's first book. I shall try to discover there the peculiar nature of the poet's sensibility, and then trace it if possible in later poems of various sorts. We shall note the curious fascination that certain aspects of night and dream exercised upon him, and this will lead us to an examination of what may be called his metaphysic of love and to a discussion of his ambivalent attitude to nature and passion that finds expression in two distinct, if not actually conflicting styles—one tremulous, colourful, and sensuous; the other calmer, more tightly controlled, and possibly more mature.


Duncan Campbell Scott's first poems were published in 1893 in a volume entitled *The Magic House and Other Poems,* and they took their place at once in the mainstream of what was clearly a great new movement in Canadian poetry. In that year appeared also Bliss Carman's first collection, *Low Tide on Grand Pré,* Archibald Lampman's second, *Lyrics of Earth,* Charles G. D. Roberts' third, *Songs of the Common Day,* and Wilfred Campbell's third, *The Dread Voyage and Other Poems.* At a first glance or after a casual reading all these books appear to have much in common. They all have a high literary polish; they show the influence in varying degree of some of the English romantic poets, of Tennyson, of Arnold, or of the Pre-Raphaelites; and all deal with nature, realistically, passionately, or mystically; but there the resemblance ends. Each of these poets, indeed, is remarkably individual, and even when, as all of them more or less consciously did, they submit to literary influences, they choose eclectically and respond to influences each in his own way. Duncan Campbell Scott is closer to his comrade and, in poetic matters, his encourager and inspirer, Lampman, than to any of the others, though, as we shall see, he has at times a passionate intensity and a troubled emotionalism that is matched only by Carman.

What strikes one immediately about *The Magic House* is the sureness with which it takes its place in the tradition of English poetry and at the same time how responsive it is to all the new winds that were blowing in the nineties. Some of the poems, as E. K. Brown has noted, are definitely *fin de siècle*. The two sonnets "In the House of Dreams" cry out for illustration by Aubrey Beardsley and are filled with symbols that modern Jungian critics would recognize as archetypal images and relate perhaps to those of Spenser or Coleridge. The title poem itself catches perfectly the languid note of William Morris and is filled with images and phrases that recall now the Blessed Damozel and now the Lady of Shalott or Mariana in the moated grange. The first two or three lyrics in the book suggest the early Tennyson of Airy Fairy Lillian, but there are other poems that have taken severer models—Matthew Arnold and Robert Bridges—and the result, in such poems as "Off Rivière du Loup" and "In the Country Churchyard," is much more permanently satisfying.

All this sounds a little discouraging I fear. Yet the impression that the book lacks originality, that it shows promise only, or that it makes no positive contribution to Canadian poetry would be a hasty and superficial one. Let us begin to read it more closely. Can we discover from it the nature of the peculiar sensibility—and of the technical accomplishment that enables this sensibility to express and communicate itself; and then beyond that can we trace a line of development running through the whole body of Duncan Campbell Scott's work, and thus define and evaluate his contribution to our literature?

I have spoken of the dreamy lawn Tennysonianism of some of the less successful of the lyrics in *The Magic House*. In the first poem, for instance, where we find such puerilities as "rosy west," "dreamy lawn," and poppies that begin to yawn, we suddenly come upon an intense and accurate image: "A shore-lark fell like a stone." And on the second page in the midst of a flowery and insipid pastoral we are startled to find a hard, clear, sharply etched picture that shows in its most concentrated form the union of intensity and clarity that distinguishes genuine poetry from pretty verses. It is only a moment, but it is a fine one—just the picture of "the little sharp-lipped pools,/ Shrunken with the summer sun." Not even Lampman has excelled that.

As we read further into the book, the vividness and intensity increase. The literary clichés drop away, and more and more poems appear that are almost completely satisfying or that at least can stand as homogeneous and individual works. The nature of their originality, at least, can be discerned in their imagery, and this in turn is a reflection of the poet's individual sensibility. Let me illustrate by quoting some of these images, and before long you will begin to feel for yourselves the quality of the man and the nature of the poetry we are concerned with.

In a lyric called "The Voice and the Dusk" we have this:

> The king-bird *rushes* up and out,
>     He *screams* and *whirls* and *screams* again. . . .
>
> A thrush . . .
>     Throws his *rapid* flexile phrase,
>     A *flash* of *emeralds* in the *gloom.*
>
> The *rapture* from the *amber* height
>     Floats *tremblingly* along the plain. . . .
>
> The *swooning* of the *golden* throat
>     Drops in the *mellow* dusk and dies.

There is a mingling here of sounds and colours; the verbs are intensive and dynamic; the fusion of the senses takes place in a flash, and the resulting disturbance of equilibrium trembles and subsides slowly. The reaction is psychological—a fusion of sense impressions that stimulates an emotional response—here a rapture that slowly dies away. The whole poem is like the striking of a gong that glitters and fades slowly away.

This strangely beautiful poem is full of qualities we meet over and over again in Scott's poetry—its dynamism, the juxtaposition of light and shade, of colours and sounds, of sense impressions and emotional responses, all are characteristic of what is most original in Scott. His is the poetry of a musician and of a man enraptured and enthralled by the song and the sight of birds and by the flash of colours in nature. In another poem, "The Fifteenth of April," appropriately dedicated to A. L., we have an amazing (and accurate) richness of colour discerned in the commonest of places—the muddy soil itself:

> Pallid saffron glows the broken stubble,
>     Brimmed with silver lie the ruts,
>     Purple the ploughed hill. . . .
>
> Down a path of rosy gold
>     Floats the slender moon. . . .

So far, colours; but soon we hear the bird-song, "the vesper sparrow," and

> Ringing from the rounded barrow
> Rolls the robin's tune

and presently, "a hidden shore-lark/Shakes his sparkling song"; and then the night deepens, the dewy sounds dwindle, and in the violet vault of the sky "twinkling tapers touched with steady gold" bring us back again to the "saffron" of the opening earthy lines.

Scott was fascinated by dusk, evening, and night. Of the forty-seven poems in *The Magic House,* sixteen, or more than a third, are nocturnes—evocations of the world after sunset. And nearly all of them illustrate the peculiar power of his sensibility. Darkness is filled with tension and suspense, and the poet chooses those scenes and situations that allow him to deal with nature dramatically and sensuously. In "A Night in June" there is a wonderful evocation of the coming of a nocturnal storm when the oppresive heat of summer seems about to break, and a sudden flash of lightning shows the hidden animal life that suffers also in the darkness.

> There is no stir of air at all,
>     Only at times an inward breeze
>     Turns back a pale leaf in the trees. . . .
>
> A hawk lies panting on the grass,
>     Or plunges upward through the air,
>     The lightning shows him whirling there. . . .

All is movement in the intense warm blackness, and all is hushed and breathless, so that the slightest sounds have an almost unnatural and shattering force: "The beetles *clattered* at the blind"—"The hawks fell *twanging* from the sky." When at last the rain comes, it is with a roar like fire, and after the lightning, thunder *rips* the shattered gloom.

In another poem we have the strangely evocative line, ". . .the bats flew from the black elms like leaves," and in another again the poet notices something as delicate and precise as the reflection in a calm water of "The wan grey underlight of the willow leaves."

In "Night and the Pines," which I think is the finest of all Scott's nocturnes, the darkness is intensified by the darkness of the pine woods. The poem is actually an ode, and it recalls Longfellow's fine "Hymn to the Night" with its magnificent opening chord, "I heard the trailing garments of the Night," but the *décor* is not classic and literary but unmistakably northern. Yet the feeling itself is classical, and after the half-heard thunder of a lonely fall and the eerie cry of the loon—"that cry of light despair,/As if a demon laughed upon the air," the croak of a raven, and the sound of a pine cone dropping in the dark, we come at the end to the invocation of a Sibyl and the reminder that we

> . . . cannot come within this grove
> But all the quiet dusk remembrance brings
> Of ancient sorrow and of hapless love,
>     Fate, and the dream of power, and piercing things,
>         Traces of mystery and might,
>         The passion-sadness of the soul of night.

The association here of love with sorrow, night, dream, mystery, and power may lead us into a consideration of a group of poems even more remarkable than those that deal with the nocturnal aspects of nature—the divided and often ambiguous love poems that bulk large in the body of Scott's collected poetry.

Duncan Campbell Scott's love poems are the product of the clash between a fervid and indeed passionate sensibility and a courtly, gentle, and rather nobly archaic—but very firmly held—conviction about the nature of love as a school of ideals. According to this conviction, love is an act of adoration and the beloved is the object of a truly religious worship, of a service which paradoxically involves an act of desecration, both real and symbolic, as its central mystery and its culminating hope. As a result, many of the love poems express, or betray, an ambivalence that gives them a curious intensity and interest. It is hard to describe, but they seem to have a mercurial and doubtful sensitivity. They are tremulous and a little feverish. They hang in the balance, as it were, and we do not quite know which way they are going to fall. What contributes to this effect is the simultaneous presence of two opposing forces. T. S. Eliot has named them rightly in a famous passage describing the quality of sensibility in one of the lesser known Elizabethan dramatists as *fascination* and *repulsion*.

Let me, however, replace the Elizabethan example with a poem of Duncan Campbell Scott's, and then continue with Eliot's comment. I think you will find it applies perfectly. The poem is a small one, a little serenade or nightpiece from the poet's first volume, hardly more, it seems, than a goodnight kiss. It is called "At the Lattice":

> Good-night, Marie, I kiss thine eyes,
>     A tender touch on either lid;
> They cover, as a cloud, the skies
>     Where like a star your soul lies hid.
>
> My love is like a fire that flows,
>     This touch will leave a tiny scar,

> I'll claim you by it for my rose,
>   My rose, my own, where'er you are.
>
> And when you bind your hair, and when
>   You lie within your silken nest,
> This kiss will visit you again,
>   You will not rest, my love, you will not rest.

It *seems* hardly more than a goodnight kiss, I said. But consider the nature of this kiss. Physically, it is gentle—only a tender touch; but the emotion that prompts it is "like a fire" and like fire it leaves a scar. The kiss is a magic one and its spell is powerful and dangerous. What are we to make of the tone of triumph in the exultant and somehow almost sinister last line—"You will not rest, my love, you will not rest"? Here indeed is love as an act of adoration paradoxically involving as its central sacrificial climax an act of desecration, and at the same time the emotional accompaniment that generates the poem and is generated by it is a fusion of tenderness and cruelty; or, as Eliot has described it, "there is a combination of positive and negative emotions: an intensely strong attraction toward beauty and an equally intense fascination by the ugliness which is contrasted with it and which destroys it." The intensity of the conflict, and therefore of the implied drama, is greater also when, as here, the "ugliness" is in the subconsciousness of the protagonist. To drag it forcibly out from there into the realm of consciousness is the real object of the poem, however deceptively it may pretend to be only a pretty compliment. It is an acknowledgment of what in a poem I shall come to later the poet calls "The little evil thoughts that trouble beauty."

The scar left by the kiss is invisible: what we have is not an image but a symbol. Much later, in *The Green Cloister* of 1936, the symbol appears again. It occurs in a dramatic poem called "By the Seashore" that might have been written by Hardy or Lawrence. At dusk on the sands a man lights a fire of driftwood "as the tide and the sunlight are ebbing away." He is a lover, and he is burning old letters (he promised to burn them)—the image of faith and a sacrificial ritual is clear, and again we have the touch of fire and the symbol of a scar—"The desire of the heart leaves sorrow that lives in a scar." The most powerful moment in this rather subdued and elegiac drama grows out of the restraint with which the poet pictures the ironic destruction by fire of the love-words of the letters:

> The flame flutters and vanishes.
> Here and there the word "love" shines and expires in gold.
> The word "forever" lives a moment in grey on the cinder,
> A shrinking of all the char in a brittle heap—
> It is done, nothing remains but the scar of a sorrow.

This, because of the restraint, the irony, and the controlled passion is a much more mature and satisfying poem than the strange little serenade. It is a song of experience, not of innocence; and if it lacks the tremulous nervous excitement of the divided poems in which there is a clash between pleasure and pain, or between duty and desire, or between the dream and the reality, it has something better—a more universal humanity.

Yet it is the tremulous excitement that provides even some of the less successful of Scott's love poems with a glamour which, if a little fortuitous, is nevertheless significant—for it lights up an important aspect of the poet's metaphysic of love—his chivalric and courtly worship of maidenhood, at the worst destroyed and at the best transfigured by desire and passion. We can examine this theme in two curious and not very well known lyrics, "The Sleeper" from his first volume and "The Water Lily," a later and technically much more accomplished poem. In an article on Scott I wrote for the *Dalhousie Review* I commented:

"The Sleeper" is very fragile indeed. It seems in its opening to be only another echo of Tennyson's earliest style, so the hasty reader may miss the originality and truth of the poem. Actually, a profound perception about the nature and beauty of innocence is expressed and in an imagery that is enticing both for what it reveals and for what it hides. The poem begins by telling how "Touched with some divine repose,/Isabelle has fallen asleep," and the first three stanzas describe the hushed and enraptured loveliness of the sleeping girl, her spirit calmed by a happy dream:

> Then upfloats a planet strange,
>    Not the moon that mortals know,
> With a magic mountain range,
>    Cones and craters white as snow;
>
> Something different yet the same—
>    Rain by rainbows glorified,
> Roses lit with lambent flame—
>    'Tis the maid moon's other side.
>
> When the sleeper floats from sleep,
>    She will smile the vision o'er,
> See the veinéd valleys deep,
>    No one ever saw before.
>
> Yet the moon is not betrayed,
>    (Ah! the subtle Isabelle!)
> She's a maiden, and a maid
>    Maiden secrets will not tell.

This, as I have said, is a very fragile poem. It comes dangerously near to being coy, but it is saved by the essential truth of its perception (which is, I take it, that innocence is a form of arcane knowledge that cannot be revealed to the profane). If the spirit of the youthful Tennyson is here, so is that of Hans Andersen. And that of Sigmund Freud.

"The Water Lily" is placed in Scott's *Selected Poems* next to the allegorical dream poems "The Magic House" and "Avis," and it impresses itself on the mind as a symbolist poem akin to Mallarmé's evocation of the snowy swan or Yeats' of the rose upon the rood of time. There is an exotic, almost oriental luxury about the imagery and atmosphere of the poem that recalls Coleridge and again the early Tennyson. There is a strange and very powerful fusion of whiteness and coldness with passionate, almost tropical, ardours and odours that serves to dramatize what I feel is the hidden theme of the poem—the presentation of an ambivalent attitude towards virginity. "In the granite-margined pool," the poem begins—

> Hot to its shallow deeps,
> The water-lily sleeps
> And wakes in light. . . .

All is rich and luxurious, and everything is tremulous, almost oversensitive, soft, and responsive.

> Like moonstones frail, the waterdrops
> Invade her red-rimmed pads,—
> Tremble mercurial there. . . .

Each of the senses attends and pays court to "the starry-pointed wonder,/ Lolling so languidly by the lotus leaves." The flower is attended by

> Ivory rose petals,
> Fugitive, wind-blown
> Shallops of kindred beauty. . . .

> An odour vibrates upward from the flower,
> An incense faint
> Gathers and floats
> Above the chalice of the breathing lily. . . .

> . . . the distilled and secret odour weaves
> A silver snood,
> Binding the temples of the virgin lily. . . .

Light flock-bells, born of the rains flailing,
Are based on fragile foam and domed with paling
Rainbow flicker;
Thicker the water-beetles ply their oars
Freighting between the phantom shores
The little evil thoughts that trouble beauty;
But heedless the haughty lily
Buoyed in the lymph-clear shallows
Languorously. . . .

But now there is a change. All the virginal and languid lily had been created
for is about to happen:

The intense heaven of her cold white
Is troubled with colour;
The shadow cast by light
On its own substance lies;
The clear etherealities
Are tremoured with fire;
Conscious and still unconscious of the sun,
The petals swoon amorously:
The gold-tipped sceptres of desire
Shine in the warm cradle-cup
Of the luxurious pure lily
Trembling in ecstasy by the lotus leaves.

And then in the beautiful climactic final section we have the creative act
itself, presented as a descent into the dark waters of generation—

Maturity broods in water and air;
The starry-pointed wonder
From the root tangled lair
Feels ripeness lure her under;
She sinks reluctant from sunlight. . . .

Down the dark pool of silence;
The world lost,—
All lost but memory
And the germ of beauty.
O banishment to cloistral water,
The pause in the limpid hush,
There to recreate. . . .

The end of the poem is ecstatic joy, consummation, release, and rest. Nothing in D. H. Lawrence is deeper, more accurate, or more unmistakable.

"The Water Lily" is a symbolist poem and as such it possesses a universality that lifts it above the limitations of the personal. Another of Scott's poems in which the sexual theme is treated with equal frankness is the remarkable "Spring on Mattagami." Here the poem is lifted above the merely personal, not by the use of symbols but by the creation of a mask. The poem, though its rhythms are lyrical, is essentially dramatic, and to identify the protagonist with the poet himself is to underrate the artist and the man alike. Technically, it is something of a *tour de force*. It is written in the complex and striking metrical pattern of "Love in the Valley," and it is intriguing to see the style used by Meredith to present the smiling dales and copses of England employed in the delineation of the Canadian forest. Scott has used the subtle and syncopated metrical pattern to fine effect in conveying the riotous violence of the wilderness. For convenience we can recall E. K. Brown's statement of the theme—the poem is too long to quote in its entirety. "It seems wholly in keeping," wrote Professor Brown, "that he [the poet—or better, the 'hero,' the protagonist, the 'I' of the poem] should pass from stanzas which smoulder with the colours and scents of the landscape to stanzas which flame with his longing for someone in Ottawa, whom he pictures in the midst of wild nature, drawing from it a liberation from her hesitations so that she yields to his passion."

The poem is clearly a dramatic presentation of division, and the two impulses of attraction and repulsion that I have noted in some of the other love poems are here central to the drama. The beautiful and virginal beloved in the scented rose garden and the passionate lover in the rank effulgence of the forest are the opposing poles around which whirl clusters of powerful but uncertain emotions. The drama is presented in two contrasting pictures—the first a garden scene and a gesture of refusal:

> Once I well remember in her twilight garden,
>     She pulled a half-blown rose, I thought it meant for me,
> But poising in the act, and with half a sigh for pardon,
>     She hid it in her bosom where none may dare to see:
> Had she a subtle meaning?—would to God I knew it,
>     Where'er I am I always feel the rose leaves nestling there,
> If I might know her mind and the thought which then flashed
>     through it,
>     My soul might look to heaven not commissioned to despair.

The second picture is of the forest wilderness, and all is enflamed and heightened by desire:

If she could be here where all the world is eager
   For dear love with the primal Eden sway,
Where the blood is fire and no pulse is thin or meagre,
   All the heart of all the world beats one way!
*There* is the land of fraud and fame and fashion,
   Joy is but a gaud and withers in an hour,
*Here* is the land of quintessential passion,
   Where in a wild throb Spring wells up with power.

Everything in nature in this season of northern spring teaches the lesson of surrender and acceptance—the partridge drumming, the laughter of the loons, the "shy moose fawn nestling by its mother," the orient perfume of the marsh flowers, the water-spray weaving iridescent fountains, and at night fireflies and stars tangled in the forest branches.

Then the protagonist—and who can deny that he has an affinity with the hero of "Locksley Hall"?—begins to indulge his fancy and entertain the pleasures of hope:

O, she would love me then with a wild elation,
   Then she must love me and leave her lonely state,
Give me love yet keep her soul's imperial reservation,
   Large as her deep nature and fathomless as fate:

She would let me steal,—not consenting or denying—
   One strong arm beneath her dusky hair,
She would let me bare, not resisting or complying,
   One sweet breast so sweet and firm and fair;
Then with the quick sob of passion's shy endeavour,
   She would gather close and shudder and swoon away,
She would be mine for ever and for ever,
   Mine for all time and beyond the judgment day.

But this is followed by an awakening and a withering into the truth: "Vain is the dream. . . . Fate is stern and hard—fair and false and vain"—and the poem ends with renunciation and submission to a greater law than the law of personal desire:

Vaster than the world or life or death my trust is
   Based in the unseen and towering far above;
Hold me, O Law, that deeper lies than Justice,
   Guide me, O Light, that stronger burns than Love.

This poem is not quite satisfactory, I fear, but not for the reasons hinted at by Professors Brown and Pacey, namely that the bold expression of sexual desire is somehow in questionable taste, but rather that the conclusion is too easily achieved—one does not come to a harmony with the "Love that moves the sun and the other stars" quite so simply—or by a mere act of renunciation. The more natural ending of the symbolic drama unfolded in "The Water Lily" is both aesthetically and humanly more convincing.

From the beginning, of course, there had been present in Duncan Campbell Scott's work another and very different strain from the tremulous and feverish one that pulses through the love poems. From love and from certain aspects of nature, particularly from those associated with night and storm and the hours and seasons of change come the impulses that kindle. But there were also the impulses that restrain. These are derived from the poet's traditions—partly artistic and partly social and religious. An education in the classics, the enthusiastic reading of Wordsworth and Arnold as well as of Keats and Tennyson and Rossetti, and the example perhaps of Archibald Lampman, equipped Scott for the writing of perfectly chiselled lyrics and descriptive pieces that for clarity of expression and delicate precision of observation are worthy of any of his masters. In the first book are "Off Rivière du Loup" with its fine opening lines, "O ship incoming from the sea/With all your cloudy tower of sail—," the haunting lyric, "Memory," the deeply felt elegy written for his father, "In the Country Churchyard," and a number of calm and exact nature poems—the two sonnets called "First Snow," for instance, or the sonnet "September"—which are very close to the spirit of Lampman.

Let us consider for a moment how Lampman and how Scott see nature. As I wrote in *The Book of Canadian Poetry,* "Lampman is an impressionist. Sensation rather than idea is what he derives from landscape. . . . Details of shape and colour, seen in the light of a precise minute and valued for their own sake are what give a sprcial significance to Lampman's portrayal of nature." I think this is true of Scott also; but while it serves to define almost the whole of Lampman's originality, it is only a part of Scott's. And in Scott, nature is usually less exclusively presented as a picture: more often it is a picture *and* an idea.

In Lampman's famous poem "Heat," there is not a single concept until we come to the end of the poem: everything is perception, impression—sounds and sights, colours, shapes, tactile impressions and sensations of movement, and above all a pervasive feeling of heat. There are what might be called *conceits* in the poem, but they are *physical* conceits, not *metaphysical* ones. For example:

> Into the pale depth of noon
> A wandering thrush slides leisurely
> His thin revolving tune

or,

> The grasshoppers spin into my ear
> A small innumerable sound.

At the beginning of Scott's comparable poem, the double sonnet "First Snow," we have this—

> The field-pools gathered into frosted lace;
> An icy glitter lined the iron ruts. . . .

And these lines are pure Lampman; but soon we come upon a touch that is rare indeed in Lampman but frequently met with in Scott—the metaphysical expression of a physical phenomenon:

> Between the dusky alders' woven ranks
> A stream *thought* yet about his summer banks,
> And made an Autumn music in the place.

or,

> The shadow cast by light
> On it own substance.

This is a device that serves a twofold function. It intensifies the expression and gives it an intellectual as well as a sensational significance. Passages like these—and some quoted earlier in this essay—suggest that the characteristic virtue of Duncan Campbell Scott as an interpreter of nature and the real mark of his originality is the glowing fusion in his poetry of keenness of observation with clarity of thought so that the thing and the idea seem to be struck out together.

When we have the happy combination of this kind of sensibility with a classical precision and conciseness of style, we have work of a major excellence. This excellence can be illustrated in all of his books, and in the latest more effectively than in the first. Here are a few examples taken from *The Green Cloister*, the collection of later poems published in 1936.

> . . . a wind-wing on the lake
> Leaves a track upon the water
> Like a quick grey snake. . . .

> The light is like a fluttering bird
> Caught in a cage of blue.

Or, to take a more homely instance, this is how the poet describes a harrow being driven by the farmer up a dry and dusty ploughed slope somewhere on the prairie:

> Where a disc-harrow tears the soil,
> Up the long slope six horses toil....
> ...as they go a cloud of dust
> Comes like a spirit out of earth
> And follows where they go.
> Upward they labour, drifting slow,
> The disc-rims sparkle through the veil;
> Now upon the topmost height
> The dust grows pale,
> The group springs up in vivid light
> And, dipping below the line of sight,
> Is lost to view.
> Yet still the little cloud is there,
> All dusky luminous in air,
> Then thins and settles on the land
> And lets the sunlight through....

Here the poet's eye is sharply focussed on a real object—a homely and unromantic one, a little cloud of dust kicked up by the harrow horses; but we see it as the sun makes it luminous. It comes like a spirit out of earth, and it is felt as a symbol as well as seen as an image.

Again, to cite one more fine passage—still from the volume of 1936—here is the way the poet re-creates a moment of mist and silence in the heart of the mountains. In the intense stillness the attentive ear detects a sound so delicate that we can hardly say whether it speaks to the senses or directly to the heart and mind. It is from the beautiful third lyric in the series called "In the Rocky Mountains":

> For the mist had cloaked the range
> Hiding the vista and the flowing sky-line;
> Almost a silence there, but strange—
> Came a water-sound, a far off crying;
> All the ferns and firs
> Held the mist till they could bear no more,
> Then shed their store
> Of tears with sudden sighing....

It is the intimate interplay of light and shade and the delicate half-states of twilight and mist together with the magnification and slight distortions of sound that seem to appeal most intensely to Scott and set him apart from the other poets of his generation in Canada. He is as sensitive and intense as Carman, and far more accurate; as accurate as Lampman or Roberts, and more truly passionate than either. It is this love of the intermediate stage, the moment of change, when things and qualities are intermingled and partake of one another's characteristics, that contributes much of the movement and drama to Scott's nature poetry. His most vivid and characteristic scenes are pictures of change, flow, and conflict. The times that fascinate him are times of change—sunset, dawn, or spring—and it is movement and change that make even his descriptive pieces dramatic—they are filled with images of storm, of melting, of thawing, of burgeoning or dying; colours are intermingled; sounds, sights and odours are fused with the emotional overtones that generate or accompany them. Sometimes a subtle perception of such a fusing is simply stated—its perceptiveness being its own sufficient recommendation, as in this almost casual sentence from "Compline":

> An odour arises from the earth
> From dead grass cooling in the dew,
> From the fragrance of pine needles
> That smoldered all day in the heat....

or as in the description of what one sees from the window of a train stopping "for no apparent reason" by the edge of a frozen lake in the wilderness:

> The sun is burning in the South; the season
> Is winter *trembling* at a touch of Spring.
> A little hill with birches and a ring
> Of cedars—all so still, so pure with snow—
> It seems a tiny landscape in the moon.
> Long wisps of shadow from the naked birches
> Lie on the white in lines of cobweb-grey;
> From the cedar roots the snow has shrunk away,
> *One almost hears it tinkle as it thaws.*

I do not want to give the impression that these descriptions, sensitive, accurate, and intense as they often are, are placed before us as being self-sufficient—though they might well have been, for they *are* valuable in themselves. But Duncan Campbell Scott is not an imagist poet, and all his observations, impressions, and experiences are put to use. And I do not mean in an obvious or didactic way. The question arises: What use does the poet make of his perceptions and impressions? To answer it, let me continue the description of what the poet saw from the train window. He looks at the foreground now:

Traces there are of wild things in the snow—
Partridge at play, tracks of the foxes' paws
That broke a path to sun them in the trees.
They're going fast where all impressions go
On a frail substance—images like these,
Vagaries the unconscious mind receives
From nowhere, and lets go to nothingness
With the lost flush of last year's autumn leaves.

The theme of the poem, we see, is psychological—the way fleeting impressions fasten on the mind; and it is traditional as well—the great classical commonplace of the impermanence of all things. But the triumph of the poem depends not so much upon the subtlety and precision of the observation as upon the casualness and informality of the occasion. The homeliest and most ordinary experience can be made both unique and universally significant—when it happens to a true poet.

And when we read it and take it in we ourselves become true poets, and our eyes are opened to the possibilities of enrichment in the sensuous world of phenomena. That is why poems like this have a value—I need not hesitate to call it a usefulness—that is incalculable. But quite apart from this, I would cite these lines as characteristic of a new clarity and simplicity that Scott attains to in the poetry of his last years. It is poetry that one might well call modern, if it were not timeless. It owes nothing to Tennyson or Morris or Matthew Arnold, but it can take its place beside the best nature poetry ever written, beside that of Clare, or Edward Thomas, or Robert Frost—and that without being directly indebted to any one of them. It is both traditional and original. This is high praise indeed, but not unjust praise.


I said at the beginning that I was not going to write in a personal vein, and so far I have not. What I have thought it best to offer is literary criticism, which, whether right or wrong, is at least in intention something more significant than a mere chronicle of dates and facts. I cannot end, however, without one brief reminiscence and one word of tribute to the *man*. I only met Duncan Campbell Scott once. It was the same summer that E. K. Brown was so frequent a visitor to the poet's Ottawa home. The classic account left by Professor Brown of an evening "when I talked with him in the huge high-ceilinged room at the back of his rambling house" is such an exact replica of my own experience that I cannot read it without recapturing my vivid impression of the poet's charm and courtliness and of the grace and warmth of his interest in the new poetry that was beginning to be produced in Canada by younger men. He spoke to me also of the poets he had known and admired—

Rupert Brooke, Marjorie Pickthall, and of course Archibald Lampman. As I was leaving, he inscribed for me a copy of that first book of his, *The Magic House and Other Poems,* dating his autograph a day or two earlier—2 August 1942, his eightieth birthday.

He had read me from the book one of the deepest and most beautiful of his classical elegies, the lines to the memory of his father entitled "In the Country Churchyard." In closing, let me repeat them here:

> This is the paradise of common things,
>     The scourged and trampled here find peace to grow,
>     The frost to furrow and the wind to sow,
> The mighty sun to time their blossomings;
>     And now they keep
> A crown reflowering on the tombs of kings,
>     Who earned their triumph and have claimed their sleep.
>
> Yea, each is here a prince in his own right,
>     Who dwelt disguised amid the multitude,
>     And when his time was come, in haughty mood,
> Shook off his motley and reclaimed his might;
>     His sombre throne
> In the vast province of perpetual night,
>     He holds secure, inviolate, alone.
>
> The poor forgets that ever he was poor,
>     The priest has lost his science of the truth,
>     The maid her beauty, and the youth his youth,
> The statesman has forgot his subtle lure,
>     The old his age,
> The sick his suffering, and the leech his cure,
>     The poet his perplexed and vacant page. . . .

Whether we call this Lucretian resignation or Christian humility, its seeming renunciation is actually an affirmation of the high estate of poetry, which is here given no meretricious or gaudy property of outlasting monuments or triumphing over time. Rather its function is that of human life itself—so completely identified with it, that it *is* life—and therefore also death.

*PART FOUR*

*A Choice of Moderns*

## *Some Poems of E. J. Pratt*

### Aspects of Imagery and Theme

*The Second Annual* Pratt Lecture, *Memorial University, St. John's, Newfoundland*

To even the casual reader of Pratt's poems it soon becomes clear that here is a poet of epic proportions, a creator on a large scale, a draughtsman who requires plenty of room, a story teller who spins his yarns at length. This is due in part to the fact that Pratt is fascinated with magnitude, with immense strength and almost incredible power, natural, monstrous, or human, and with geographical if not astronomical distance. It is not due at all to any loquacious inflation of style or structure. Pratt's narratives, even the longest, are not long because they are spun out, pulled thin, or larded with digressions. They are beautifully constructed and are as long as they need be. His imagery, whether expanded like Homeric similes or as concentrated as a fine conceit, is functional rather than decorative and contributes something essential to the progression of the poem.

To look closely at one or two of Pratt's images is perhaps the best way to get into the heart of his poetry and understand the nature of his sensibility. Many of them lead directly to the cluster of closely related convictions about Man, Nature, and God that are implicit in all but the most casual of his poems. "The Submarine," for example, is a narrative of middle length, one of the few poems about war (rather than *the* war) published in the volume of 1943, *Still Life and Other Verse.* It is a remarkably cool and objective piece of what might be thought of as straight reporting were it not for the peculiar, original, and thoroughly characteristic imagery that signs the poem E. J. Pratt. The plot is simple. A (presumably German) submarine stalks and sinks a liner and then escapes into the ocean depths. Heroism and devotion to duty are shown in equal measure by the men below and the men above. Other than this implied comment none is made. The conflict might almost have been a fight between a kraken and a whale. And it is in this objectivity and restraint that the tragic dignity and classic irony of the poem lie.

Consider the imagery. Pratt's dynamism and his inescapable animism, which endow machines and mountain ranges alike with life, are nowhere better seen than here. The launching of the torpedo is shown as animal birth:

> Now like
> The tiger-shark viviparous
> Who with her young grown mutinous
> Before the birth-hour with the smell
> Of blood inside the mother, will expel
> Them from her body to begin
> At once the steerage of the fin,
> The seizure of the jaw, the click
> Of serried teeth fashioned so well
> Pre-natally to turn the trick
> Upon a shoal of mackerel—
> So like the shark, the submarine
> Ejected from her magazine
> The first one of her foetal young. . . .

The target vessel—(probably the *Athenia,* though no ship is named)—is presented as a whale. "The rich-ripe mammal was swimming straight . . . with unconcerned leisure." Her sinking is described like this:

> Three cavernous wounds in the mammal's side—
> Three crumbled dykes through which the tide
> Of a gluttonous Atlantic poured;
> A heavy starboard list with banks
> Of smoke fluted with steam which soared
> From a scramble of pipes within her flanks;
> Twin funnel-nostrils belching red,
> A tilting stern, a plunging head,
> The foundering angle in position,
> And the sea's reach for a thousand souls
> In the last throe of the parturition.

These are very strange lines, and their implications are fascinating: they lead into the heart of Pratt's poetry. The machine in the service of man and as an enemy of man is endowed with life and treated as an animal, ambiguously monstrous or noble. The effect is to create an all-pervading atmosphere of irony that here perhaps just fails of being tragic.

Strangest of all, however, is the closing line of this passage. Death as birth. The last throes of a thousand souls descending into gluttonous ocean are described as a *parturition.* There is nothing in this taut objective fast-moving narrative to suggest that this is to be taken as a hint of faith in the birth into immortality of souls—as there is nothing certain either in the formal, explicit treatment of this theme in "The Iron Door." What comes out of "The Sub-marine" as a whole is Pratt's fascination with silent, stoical struggle that can be equated (as in his well-known poem "Silences") with a primordial, sub-aqueous aggressiveness.

Speaking of the all-pervading themes of conflict and heroism in the narra-tive poems of Pratt, Paul West, the young English poet and critic, noted the poet's "entranced addiction to . . . conflicts in which the primitive defeats the civilized and force defeats ingenuity." In "The Submarine," however, it is ingenuity and civilization, though civilization reduced to mere technical skill, that triumphs over a more primitive machine and a kind of heroic innocence. It is not the primitive that defeats the civilized but the wrong kind of civ-ilization that defeats a better kind, a more innocent kind.

Professor West, thinking of "The Cachalot," "The Great Feud," and "The Titanic," adds that "It is not the heroism that excites him [Pratt], but the pros-pect of destruction."[1] This is hardly true of most of Pratt's poems, certainly not of the greatest and most serious of them, "Brébeuf and his Brethren," or of the purest and most uncomplicated of his celebrations of man, heroic and victorious in his struggle against the sea, "The Roosevelt and the Antinoe."

I still vividly remember reading this poem for the first time, not long after it came out in 1930. Once started, it was impossible to stop until the end. The verse had the lean sinewy swiftness of good prose—(I intend this as a com-pliment)—and I recall not noticing until I had finished it that it was rhymed. The qualities of the writing are speed, tautness, objectivity, and sharpness. A factual exactness has the effect of understatement when what is happening is monstrous or heroic. The total effect depends on two factors: the careful attention to detail (involving the poet in a number of brilliant expository clar-ifications of complex mechanical or scientific processes) and the structural manipulation of events so as to gain the maximum suspense and the dramatic distribution in time and space of the various crises and climaxes of the action.

The poem begins with a sort of prologue in which before sailing from New York the crew of the Roosevelt sign on. They pledge themselves to be

> faithful, true
> And orderly, in honest, sober manner;
> At all times in their duties diligent;
> To the Master's lawful word obedient
> In everything relating to the vessel—
> Safety of passengers, cargo and store,
> Whether on board, in boats, or on the shore.

---

[1]E. J. Pratt's "Four-Ton Gulliver" in *A Choice of Critics,* ed. George Woodcock (Toronto: 1966).

The irony in these lines is not apparent until the middle of the action. Then the reader may recall them as a masterpiece of understatement, a ritual that might have been taken for granted.

With the sailing of the liner what might be considered the first act of the drama begins: "The Gathering Storm." Days and hours are carefully recorded. As the stiff breeze of Wednesday becomes a gale on Thursday and as radio warnings go out from Cape Race and ships at sea, the storm quickens to a hurricane by Saturday.

> South of the Cape within these hours, the *Roosevelt*
> Was driving East by North, with her decks stripped,
> Her lower ventilator cowls unshipped,
> The shafts plugged; battened and wedged the hatches;
> Bell-mouths full-bore discharging from the bilge-pumps
> Under the straining hull. . . .

There follows a description of the storm-swept ocean that more or less runs through the rest of the poem and that need not fear comparison with the storm-pictures in Masefield and Conrad.

The scene shifts now to the wireless room of the British freighter *Antinoe,* battered, waterlogged, listing to starboard, and drifting out of control. The poetry of electronics beautifully informs the account of the radio calls and responses, and we have one of the best of the many imaginative treatments of science and machinery that testify to Pratt's fascination with modern technology:

> Legions
> Unnumbered, moving at the rate of light,
> Pushed out beyond all navigated regions,
> Exploring every cranny of the night,
> Reaching out through dusky corridors
> Above the sea to uninhabited shores,
> Or taking undecoded human cries
> Below the keel to the Atlantic crypts . . .
> To add their wasted sum to a plethora
> Of speed and power in those void spaces where
> Light-years go drifting by Andromeda. . . .

But a few are heard. The *Roosevelt* hears the *Antinoe's* sos. And so does the *Aquitania.* Which shall go to the rescue? The *Roosevelt* is nearer by hours, and Captain Fried turns his ship. The first act of the drama ends.

The second, that might be called "Finding the Ship," is full of suspense and doubt. There is first the wireless probing for the signals now fading, now lost, now found again, of the stricken vessel. Times—hours and days—are meticulously recorded. They are of vital significance. The *Antinoe* radios her condition is precarious. "You say that we sound nearer to you? Cannot/Wait much longer." And the reply: "Coming." There is a vivid description of conditions on board the *Antinoe,* and then:

> Fried knowing that he neared
> The ship's position by the growing power
> Of the signals slowed the *Roosevelt* down to scour
> The closer plotted area, fighting squall
> On top of storm, boring through a pall
> Of snow, till at the heart of the wave-zone,
> With Jack reversed, the freighter like a lone
> Sea-mallard with a broken wing was seen
> Ahead, lee-rail awash, taking it green
> At the bow.

Here is the climax of this part of the story, yet there is one more touch. The master of the *Antinoe* is not yet ready to abandon ship. A flashing lamp signals "Can you spread oil to windward? Please stand-by."

And so the final and most heroic act begins. The liner stands by, but in the blackness and blinding spray contact is lost again—the *Antinoe's* radio has gone dead. The watch on the *Roosevelt* fear she must have foundered. But—

> Dawn and noon and now the afternoon.
> "We picked her up"—so ran the captain's log—
> "One point upon the starboard bow at four
> O'clock, with nineteen hours of delay
> And sixty miles from her last known position."
> Her navigating bridge was swept away;
> Flooded, steam off, lights out, a closing day.

Oil on the water is not enough now, nor is there time enough. They must take the risk and try to send a boat across. Fried calls for volunteers, and a boat is manned by eight seamen under the command of first officer Robert Miller. There is a Homeric roll-call of the eight, their names and their nativity— among them are Germans, Finns, Austrians, Americans, and Danes.

The description of what follows is one of the high points of narrative skill in the poem, and indeed in Pratt's work as a whole. The boat is capsized by the concatenation of a squall and tide-rip close to the liner's side. All but two of the men catch ropes and ladders and are hauled to safety, but two are swept away, one after heroically swimming with a rope to save a comrade.

There is an interlude describing the memorial service held for the two lost seamen in the lounge and the Latin prayer of a Catholic priest on deck.

Meanwhile outside, echoing the ritual—
"Now unto Him who is able to do....
Exceedingly abundantly." ... a wild antiphonal
Of shriek and whistle from the shrouds broke through
Blending with thuds as though some throat had laughed
In thunder down the ventilating shaft;
And the benediction ended with a crack
Of a stanchion on the starboard beam....

And at the end of the priest's prayer and benediction, there is this comment, which just for once and for a moment places this poem in the context of "The Truant" and "Brébeuf and his Brethren."

But no Gennesaret of Galilee
Conjured to its level by the sway
Of a hand or a word's magic was this sea,
Contesting with its iron-alien mood,
Its pagan face, its own primordial way,
The pale heroic suasion of a rood.

Time is running short—news of other ships battered or sinking streams in on the wireless—and efforts are being made to get a rope across to the *Antinoe* by means of the Lyle rocket gun or to drift an empty lifeboat across to the sinking ship, but all fail. The descriptions of these actions are complex, technically accurate, and very vivid, the kind of expository writing that Pratt is able to transform to poetry, almost effortlessly it seems.

Now the speed of the action picks up as the climax of the drama is approached. A second lifeboat, with Miller again in command, is successfully launched and gets into the lee of the *Antinoe*. Twelve of the twenty-five seamen by a feat of almost incredible seamanship are rescued from the tilted deck and safely taken to the liner.

Miller chooses his crew for the third attempt from forty volunteers from deck-hands to passengers. There are four uninjured veterans of the previous boats and five new hands. All, as in Homer, are named. A brief summary can do no justice to the quality of the writing in these climactic passages. A few lines only may perhaps suggest it:

The pitch of the storm, late night and still the snow
Two hundred yards between of yawning space,
And thirteen sailors on the *Antinoe*....
Now one o'clock, and a slight rift revealed
A spatter of light above the running seas—
The freighter's lantern jabbing out in Morse

That the ship's list had reached fifty degrees.
The last hour was on. . .

and the third boat is launched and manages to pull away.

Again courage and superb seamanship defeat the pagan sea. The thirteen
are saved, including Tose, the master of the *Antinoe,* who himself "while
Master of another vessel had, ten years back, rescued a Philadelphia bark" in
a storm only less full of death than this.

Now follows a kind of epilogue or coda: the sinking of the empty hulk of
the *Antinoe,* the siren shout of triumph from the *Roosevelt,* the gradual abat-
ing of the storm, the arrival to a hero's welcome at Plymouth, and then the
characteristic seaman's understatement of the conclusion. The *Roosevelt*
"soon ready for completion of the run/Swung out the Sound, with her day's
work well done,/And in an hour was on the Channel sea."

Although "The *Roosevelt* and the *Antinoe"* is the simplest and most direct
of the major narratives, it is not free of ironic implication and of unsolved or
ambiguous problems in philosophy or religion—problems left unsolved or
ambiguous either to convey an effect of tragic irony or because the poet himself has not made up his mind. Its final effect, however, is more powerful,
because genuinely heroic, than "The Submarine" or "The *Titanic."* Here the
action is aimed at saving life not destroying life, and it is not corrupted by the
merely pathetic *hubris* that enables the passive chance-directed iceberg to
play its role of avenger. Chance, or Fate, does play a part in the drama of
"The *Roosevelt* and the *Antinoe,"* but the master of the *Roosevelt* consciously
accepts its challenge.

> With every tap of the key, the *Roosevelt* knew
> How little would the game depend on skill
> Of hand or resolution of the will,
> How much would all the morrow's gain or loss
> Turn on the unknown chances of a toss.

At this stage of the action this awareness is not a denial of free will or a
betrayal of human courage, strength, and skill. These qualities, which are the
factors of heroism, are the membership cards that give strength and courage
the right to sit in on the life-and-death game with Nature and Fate.

Only in one paradoxical sense can we see here a denial of free will. Unlike
"Brébeuf and his Brethren," this poem is completely secular. Except for the
ritual of the requiem services there is no litany or prayer, and these are more
an act of homage to the courage of the men and the power of the sea than an

act of devotion. No more than in such early poems as "The Toll of the Bells"
or the account of the service that closes "The Ice-Floes" does it express or
lead to faith. Unlike the Jesuit martyrs, the master and seamen of the *Roosevelt* risk death or die not for God—nor because of the contract signed at the
beginning of the voyage—but because they can do no other. Being who and
what they are, they have no choice, and it never occurs to them to ask for one.
In this sense, and in this alone, the poem may be thought of as a denial of free
will. But this is a denial that raises and ennobles man. Why and how? The
poet does not know, but he does know that this act of unquestioning rebellion
against a deadly and mindless Nature makes man godlike. In "The *Roosevelt*
and the *Antinoe*" this affirmation is made by implication only: the naked
deed can be left to speak for itself.

Man's courage, strength, and skill are here shown in a struggle against the
cruel sea, but Pratt is a realist, and he knows that man also is cruel and that
his courage and skill are often put to the service of cruelty—necessarily sometimes, sometimes wantonly. There are passages in "Brébeuf" and in "The Ice-
Floes" that reveal a fascination with blood and cruelty that is only part repulsion but which nevertheless testify to the solidity of Pratt's "world he never
made" and to the honesty with which, like Hardy, he takes a full look at the
worst. Consider in this connection the seal hunt in "The Ice-Floes." As the
poem begins the hunters see from the deck of their ship the mother seals and
their "harps" lying side by side as far as the eye can reach. The hunters have
an easy time and they make short work of it:

> ...off we tore
> In the breathless rush for the day's attack
> With the speed of hounds on a caribou track.
> With the rise of the sun we started to kill,
> A seal for each blow from the iron bill
> Of our gaffs. From the nose to the tail
>     we ripped them,
>         And laid their quivering carcasses flat
> On the ice; then with our knives we stripped
>     them
>         For the sake of the pelt and its lining of fat....
>
> Fast as our arms could swing we slew them,
> Ripped them, "sculped" them, roped and drew them
> To the pans where the seals in pyramids rose
> Around the flags on the central floes,
> Till we reckoned we had nine thousand dead.

There are similar bloody or bloodthirsty passages to be found in "The Cachalot" and "The Great Feud," but in those it is the whale and primeval monsters of the slime who gorge themselves on destruction. And in "Brébeuf" it is the savage Iroquois.

Here one cannot miss the gusto with which the poet has rendered the scene and the act, the knowledgeable technical accuracy that informs the language, and the honesty with which no palliatives are offered—unless two lines almost at the end are to be regarded as justification: "twenty thousand seals were killed/To help lower the price of bread." But they are not intended as such. For the men who risk and lose their lives none is felt to be needed. It is their daily work, the immemorial way of wresting a living from the land and sea that bore them and must support them.

For Pratt, and for these Newfoundland sealers, the essence of the heroic is that there must be no heroics, and when in the tragic climax of the story sixty men are carried away beyond help on a breaking ice-floe, the comment is restrained, and the poem ends with such acceptance as is offered in the secular and sacred rituals of homage and remembrance—a flag half mast, the muffled beat of a drum, a crowded nave. The two sonnets entitled "The Toll of the Bells" form a pendant to the tragedy of "The Ice-Floes." They present in detail the funereal ritual of tribute, but as in "The *Roosevelt* and the *Antinoe,*" its adequacy is denied. Neither the military nor the churchly ritual suffice:

> Today the vaunt is with the grave. Sorrow
> Has raked up faith and burned it like a pile
> Of driftwood, scattering the ashes. . . .

Insistently then the unsolved mystery of death presented itself to the poet, and he kept returning to it, turning it over in his mind and heart. He grappled with it in some of his most characteristic and original poems—"Come Away, Death," "The Truant," "The *Titanic,*" and, most explicitly, in the long visionary ode, written not long after the death of his mother, "The Iron Door."

What makes the problem of death so insistent and so intensely felt for Pratt is his strong sense of life. The poems I have mentioned would not I think have been written were it not for Pratt's eager and jovial relish for the physical side of life. He celebrates energy and good health. He is grateful to the giver of all good things for the blessings of food and drink, and for friendship and convivial fellowship so they can be enjoyed not selfishly in gluttonous solitude but in heart-warming human society. This aspect of the poet's thought is epitomized in the most personal and thoroughly characteristic of all his poems of expansive goodwill, "The Depression Ends." This is a fantasy, more human and more sharply aimed than the delightful "Witches' Brew" in which the poet sets up an apocalyptic banquet table in the skies and invites all the poor, the starved, the misfits and the outcasts of the world to partake of a miraculous feast supplied and served by all the gods of Olympus and the Zodiac. The gift itself is an act of Christian charity and is preceded by a grace offered up by a jolly Chaucerian friar:

> I would select with Christian care,
> To offer up the vesper prayer,
> A padre of high blood—no white
> Self-pinched, self-punished anchorite . . .
> Who thinks he hears a funeral bell
> In dinner gongs on principle. . . .
>         No! rather some
> Sagacious and expansive friar,
> Who beams good-will. . . .

and the prayer he offers as grace is directed to Christ:

> We thank thee for this table spread
> In such a hall, on such a night,
> With such unusual stores of bread,
> O Lord of Love! O Lord of light!
> We magnify thy name in praise
> At what thy messengers have brought,
> For not since Galilean days
> Has such a miracle been wrought.
> The guests whom thou hast bidden come,
> The starved, the maimed, the deaf, and dumb,
> Were misfits in a world of evil,
> And ridden hard by man and devil.

These lines, of course, do not suggest in their imagery or rhythm the quintessential Pratt—only in their substance, the explicit emphasis on hospitality, good cheer, sympathy, and justice, which is one side of Pratt—the soft side, if I may call it that without being invidious. Let me return, however, to the poetry that deals with magnitude and strength, whether mineral, piscine, mammalian, or human, and the struggle for power or survival which is their active property. Aspects of this struggle provide the themes of all Pratt's best and major poems and condition in a peculiar way his figures, tropes, and images, his dynamic diction and aggressive rhythms.

This poet's fascination with the gigantic and the clashing of titanic forces, though it makes for the writing of long poems, does not prevent the utmost concentration in metaphor, simile, or straight description. As I said at the outset, the poems are long not because they are inflated or padded but because there is an almost continuous series of new perceptions and new actions. Pratt's imagination which may well be described as geographical, geological, or cosmological, has the power of transposing the immense and the minute, the macrocosm and the microcosm, and showing us if not "Heaven in a wild flower" the whole geography of the globe in the innards of a whale.

> He was more wonderful within.
> His iron ribs and spinal joists
> Enclosed the sepulchre of a maw.
> The bellows of his lungs might sail
> A herring skiff—such was the gale
> Along the wind-pipe; and so large
> The lymph-flow of his active liver,
> One might believe a fair-sized barge
> Could navigate along the river;
> And the islands of his pancreas
> Were so tremendous that between 'em
> A punt would sink; while a cart might pass
> His bile-duct to the duodenum
> Without a peristaltic quiver.
> And cataracts of red blood stormed
> His heart, while lower down was formed
> That fearful labyrinthine coil
> Filled with musk of ambergris;
> And there were reservoirs of oil
> And spermaceti; and renal juices
> That poured in torrents without cease
> Throughout his grand canals and sluices.
> And hid in his arterial flow
> Were flames and currents....

This is the poetry of wit. The physicians of Lilliput might have examined Gulliver so. It makes me think a little of Andrew Marvell:

> But now the Salmon-Fishers moist
> Their leathern boats begin to hoist;
> And like Antipodes in shoes
> Have shod their heads in their Canoes.

Pratt in his descent into the whale has "world enough and time." The effect is as though he had turned the world inside out and stuffed it into his Leviathan. In "Towards the Last Spike" he pulls it out again and like a cosmic magician turns it into stone and spreads it out over the North American continent to be the Antagonist now not of the New England whaler but of the Canadian railway builders:

> On the North Shore a reptile lay asleep—....
> She lay snug in the folds of a huge boa
> Whose tail had covered Labrador and swished
> Atlantic tides, whose body coiled itself
> Around the Hudson Bay, then curled up north
> Through Manitoba and Saskatchewan
> To Great Slave Lake. In continental reach
> The neck went past the Great Bear Lake until
> Its head was hidden in the Arctic Seas.
> This folded reptile was asleep or dead:....
> Ice-ages had passed by and over her,
> But these, for all their motion, had but sheared
> Her spotty carboniferous hair or made
> Her ridges stand out like the spikes of molochs....

Closely related to these geographical and physiological images, sometimes expanded like a balloon and sometimes shut up like a telescope, are others concerned with alimentation. For Pratt it is not enough to record Gargantuan feasts as in "The Witches' Brew" and "The Depression Ends." He is concerned with the internal flow of the renal juices and the processes of digestion. And with the effects of food. No more than Pope or Swift (to both of whom Pratt here and there shows a curious affinity) does he shrink from a subject or a treatment because it is too homely, too familiar, too common or "unpoetic." It is in the imaginative presentation of the natural that paradoxically enough Pratt's talent for the grotesque is most triumphantly displayed.

One can see this, on a somewhat elementary level, in an image at the beginning of a short poem called "The Stoics" in the volume of 1943, *Still Life and Other Verse:*

> They were the oaks and beeches of our species.
> Their roots struck down through acid loam
> To weathered granite and took hold
> Of flint and silica, or found their home
> With red pyrites—fools' mistake for gold....
> Their *gravitas* had seized a geologic centre
> And triumphed over subcutaneous pain.

Men as trees and roots and rocks, and just a hint of the innards under the flesh. This is a first sketch of the portraits of the Scottish railway builders in the last of the great narratives, "Towards the Last Spike." In the image as it is finally developed we are taken into the very intestinal workings of the men who are made what they are by their food. It is "The Cachalot" all over again—but humanized.

> Oatmeal was in their blood and in their names.
> Thrift was the title of their catechism.
> It governed all things but their mess of porridge
> Which, when it struck the hydrochloric acid
> With treacle and skim-milk, became a mash.
> Entering the duodenum, it broke up
> Into amino acids; then the liver
> Took on its natural job as carpenter:
> Foreheads grew into cliffs, jaws into juts.
> The meal so changed, engaged the follicles:
> Eyebrows came out as gorse, the beards as thistles,
> And the chest-hair the fell of Grampian rams.
> It stretched and vulcanized the human span:
> Nonagenarians worked and thrived upon it.
> Out of such chemistry run through by genes,
> The food released its fearsome racial products:—
> The power to strike a bargain like a foe,
> To win an argument upon a burr,
> Invest the language with a Bannockburn. . . .

The figures here are hyperbole and what might be called the "physical," as distinct from the metaphysical, conceit. "To strike a bargain like a foe" is a pun that goes beyond the ambiguity of a word to the substitution of an action.

As in the description of the inner physiology of the whale, the images here are not mainly pictorial, nor are they intended to be decorative. They are functional, and while they suggest forcefully the characters of the men whose interior workings are thus so vividly laid before us, they are means not ends. The analogies not only *are,* they *act.* What they do is powerfully create a metaphorical identity between these rock-like Scottish financiers and engineers and the hardness and toughness of their antagonist nature.

Here, implicitly suggested by poetic means alone, is one of the recurring and most insistent of Pratt's ideas—an apparently never-questioned conviction of the fatal identity of titanic or heroic antagonists; beast or man against nature, beast against beast, man against beast, or man against man. Dramatically and poetically this identification is right. It gives an all-pervading air of ambiguity, sometimes comic and sometimes tragic, to all Pratt's major poems. Its philosophic or religious validity does not come into question—which is not to say that these struggles are outside a world of good and evil. As I have written elsewhere[2] *"Towards the Last Spike* is a brilliantly original treatment of . . . the theme of power and its analysis into factors of good and evil. The ironic solution to the conflict is that man triumphs over his antagonist, the Laurentian Shield and the Rocky Mountains, by a fusion with it or a merging into it. . . . Pratt's attitude towards Power, whether natural, human, or demonic is complex and ambiguous, and the emotions it arouses in him are ambiguous also—exaltation, terror, and ultimately compassion." It is exaltation and high jinks that prevail in "The Cachalot" and "The Great Feud"; and terror (though controlled) modulating into compassion in "The *Titanic"* and "Brébeuf." In "Towards the Last Spike," while there is plenty of rugged conflict and hard knowledgeable persistent determination, there is hardly the possibility of tragedy. We are among pragmatists, and the struggle between the engineers and the mountains and between Sir John A. and his political opponent, Edward Blake, are in the realm of secular narrative or intellectual comedy.

"The Last Spike" is almost completely free of philosophical implication and in this respect it is something of an exception. Most of his poems, short as well as long, have philosophical and religious overtones. They deal with death and with man's struggle with Nature, and certainly some are complex and difficult. They seem to lead up to an expression of faith and then shy away from it. If this was the whole story, the humanistic and disillusioned view that Vincent Sharman attributed to the poet in his article "E. J. Pratt and Christianity" in the Pratt issue of *Canadian Literature,* might be sustained. I quote Mr. Sharman's summing up because it is partly true and it deserves to be answered.

> For Pratt, what men must understand is that their salvation lies in themselves, not in Nature, God, systems, or in ignorant pride in machines. To maintain life should be the end of men's actions, the accomplishment of which, in times of conflict, is dependent on defiance, determination, and Reason under the control of the heart. But illusions persist: men kill men, die for ideals which embrace death, and delude themselves with hopeful prayers addressed to the "unhearing ears of God." Imperfect men must make direct their feelings for other men for the sake of life. For life is, finally, all that men have, and only men can care at all whether men live or die.

This, to put it bluntly, is to do an injustice to Pratt by misreading or neglecting some of his most important poems, though it does not do the poet so great

---

[2]In the Introduction to *The Oxford Book of Canadian Verse.* See p. 16 above.

a disservice as John Sutherland's opposite error in seeing the Cachalot and *Tyrannosauros Rex* as symbols of Christ! But there are poems that do make an affirmation of faith and without which Mr. Sharman's view might be sustained, and they are among Pratt's finest poems. They mark a stage beyond "The Toll of the Bells," "The Ice-Floes," "The *Titanic,"* and "The Iron Door," and they centre as their climactic point upon the Rood and the sacrifice of Christ's blood. The most impressive of these are of course "Brébeuf and his Brethren" and "The Truant," but these are well known and have been dealt with by other critics, particularly Northrop Frye and Desmond Pacey. I shall look instead at the original and very characteristic lyric "Cycles," printed among the "Later Poems" in the second edition of the *Collected Poems*.

The form is strict and conventional. The poem consists of six six-line stanzas—each a quatrain followed by a couplet—made up of octosyllabic iambic lines. The theme and the imagery are anything but conventional—entirely the poet's own. The theme is the evolution of Man's aggressiveness, or perhaps what science has done to war. Once men knew their foes and fought face to face with fists, then with spears, slings, arrows, and later muskets. But now—

> We need no more that light of day,
> No need of faces to be seen;
> The squadrons in the skies we slay
> Through moving shadows on a screen:
> By nailing echoes under sea
> We kill with like geometry.

Here the first part of the poem ends. The appeal to religion and to God begins, and since man is now engaged in the crucial struggle of the Second World War, Pratt brings his poem home to the men of his own time and culture by developing the controlling image of the prize ring:

> Now since the Lord of Love is late
> In being summoned to the ring
> To keep in bounds the range of hate,
> The Lord of Hosts may be invoked.

Like Kipling, but in a more familiar tone, the poet seems to cry to the stern God of justice: "Lord God of Hosts, be with us yet." But this Eternal Referee is no more a saviour than the Great Panjandrum, and the poem moves to its close by invoking the same symbol that animated the little six-foot rational biped of "The Truant" and the Jesuit martyrs of "Brébeuf and his Brethren"—the Rood.

And then before our voice is dumb,
Before our blood-shot eyes go blind,
The Lord of Love and Life may come
To lead our ebbing veins to find
Enough for their recovery
Of plasma from Gethsemane.

With perfect ease here the poet has translated the Christian dogma of salvation through the blood of the Lamb into the language of modern surgery and blood transfusion, presenting a theological concept in the imagery of modern science and demonstrating purely by poetic means the universality as well as the contemporaneity of religious affirmation.

I have cited enough examples to show you that there is variety and abundance enough in the poetry of Pratt. The *Collected Poems* presents us a world created on the grand scale, surrounded by the eternal sea and spawning monsters, organic and inorganic, that beset the paths of men, whose birth and survival depend on the strength and cunning with which they match and defeat their antagonists. It would seem a meaningless universe were it not for the one inexplicable (or if you prefer, miraculous) intervention symbolized by the Rood.

Pratt is the only Canadian poet who has mastered the long poem or, to put it in a slightly different way, he is the only Canadian poet whose world-view has been large enough to compel forms of a large scale in order to express it. I have called Pratt a Canadian poet, but he is first of all a Newfoundland poet, and while not ceasing to be either of these he is also firmly in the English tradition. The poets one thinks of when reading Pratt are the most English of poets—Hardy, because of the pity and irony that inform his efforts to come to terms with Nature, God, and the riddle of death; Masefield, because of his sea poetry; and, without intending to advance any immodest claim, the father of English poetry and prince of story tellers, Chaucer himself.

I have spoken only of the poems, not of the man who wrote them. I do not wish to end without expressing my own deep gratitude to him for his kindness and encouragement to me and to other younger poets and for the friendly and, indeed, jovial hospitality with which he entertained us. Those who were his students and later his colleagues may have enjoyed the bounty of his wisdom and good humour more frequently than I and others who came to visit him from Montreal but not in any greater measure of abundance.

*F. R. Scott and Some of His Poems*

*from* Canadian Literature, *No. 31*

In Frank Scott we have a figure whom some Carlyle of Canada's second century might write about as The Hero as Canadian Poet or perhaps more soberly as The Poet as Man of Action. Politician, lawyer, teacher, scholar, and public figure, F. R. Scott has been in the forefront of the battle for civil liberties and social justice in Canada. He was one of the doctors presiding over the births of the CCF and the New Democratic Party; he fought and won the Quebec legal battles against the "padlock law" of Premier Maurice Duplessis and against the censorship of *Lady Chatterley's Lover;* he has written studies of Canada's constitution, has been dean of law at McGill, and was a member of the Royal Commission on Bilingualism and Biculturalism. And he has, since his early days as a law student at McGill, been a poet.

The main function of a poet, of course, is to write poems, and Scott has been doing that steadily for more than three and a half decades. But his energy, his generous goodwill, and the natural self-assertiveness that makes him an inevitable and stimulating leader were thrown into the battle for the new poetry in Canada as soon as it was joined in the mid-twenties. The now classic satire "The Canadian Authors Meet" was one of his first shots, while his social and editorial participation in the doings of the *Preview* group and the encouragement he has given to other poets in Montreal have kept up the good work to the present moment. There is hardly a poet in Canada who has not, passing through Montreal, made his pilgrimage to Clarke Avenue, Westmount, and been royally entertained and stimulated with wise and witty talk about poetry and poets; and all of them from the early days of Leo Kennedy, Abe Klein, and myself, through the time of Patrick Anderson, John Sutherland, P. K. Page and the rest, to the overlapping and heterogeneous groups that might include Louis Dudek, Ralph Gustafson, Irving Layton, Doug Jones, and John Glassco, felt the charm, energy and good sense that animate Frank Scott and make him one of the leaders in every group.

Ralph Gustafson has expressed in an appropriate and witty piece of verse

a judgment that I think every one of the poets I have named would agree is
just:

>                         To say
>                         that this man is fantastic
>                         is to be
>                         Frankly wrong.
>                         Real
>                         is the right root
>                         for him.
>                         He bears history,
>                         the lakes
>                         he dives under,
>                         the cold hard sun
>                         he walks in,
>                         Canada perhaps. . . .
>
>                         Praise
>                         he goes into,
>                         padlocks
>                         he gets well out of
>                         and piety. . . .
>
>                         Mortality
>                         moves him,
>                         he goes for wrong-doing,
>                         never lets bad enough
>                         alone. . . .
>
>                         Words
>                         he gets the wear out of . . .
>                         buries with respectable honour
>                         goes
>                         Scott-free.

   "He bears history,/the lakes/he dives under. . . ." These lines will take us
into Scott's "Lakeshore," one of his finest and most characteristic works. It
will serve as a gateway through which to enter into an examination of some of
his most striking themes and interesting techniques. Its theme is Man's history, which extends back into prehistory and before man. Its unifying symbol
is water as the source of life. The poem establishes through a specific concrete
personal experience a contact in awareness with biological history, stretching
back to the primordial beginnings of life and all around to the earthbound
mechanical *now* of "a crowded street."

By the edge of a lake, the poet—or better, the sensuous mind that is the protagonist of so many of Scott's metaphysical lyrics—contemplates water, earth, and sky. There is first "the bevelled edge of land," then "the fretted sands" that the eye follows as they "go slanting down through liquid air." Now the regard is fixed on stones below the surface of the water and held too at the surface where the stones seem to be

> Floating upon their broken sky
> All netted by the prism wave
> And rippled where the currents are.

This is exact, clear, and elegant. There is a seventeenth-century grace about these opening lines. One thinks of Cowley's praise: "His candid style like a clean stream does slide." It is a style that admits, indeed invites, Wit—as we see in the next couple of stanzas. The poet (Man-and-Mind) peers into the water:

> I stare through windows at this cave
> Where fish, like planes, slow-motioned, fly
> Poised in a still of gravity. . . .

The windows are the surface of the water and the surfaces of the eyes. Note also the hushed gravity of the last line and the gentle punning on *still*. But the most striking object that confronts the poet is his own reflection.

> I am a tall frond that waves
> Its head below its rooted feet
> Seeking the light that draws it down
> To forest floors beyond its reach
> Vivid with gloom and eerie dreams.

At the beginning of the fourth stanza the sensuous mind dives down into the depths of the water and into the pre-racial aeons of the past, and for the next four stanzas we become, like the diver, liquid and loosed and silent, "Stroked by the fingertips of love,"

> Too virginal for speech or sound
> And each is personal and laned
> Along his private aqueduct.

But this return to the all-embracing primordial womb can be only a momentary glimpse of a long-lost freedom, a long since forfeited harmony with our environment.

Too soon the tether of the lungs
Is taut and straining, and we rise
Upon our undeveloped wings
Toward the prison of our ground
A secret anguish in our thighs

And mermaids in our memories.

This is our talent, to have grown
Upright in posture, false-erect,
A landed gentry, circumspect,
Tied to a horizontal soil
The floor and ceiling of the soul;
Striving, with cold and fishy care
To make an ocean of the air.

The physical and sensuous exactness of the beginning of the first of these two
stanzas is admirable, as is the emotional and imaginative rightness of the end.
The witty implications in naming our arms "our undeveloped wings" should
not go without notice either. In the next stanza, the aptness of the joke in calling mankind "a landed gentry" adds to the laughter of the mind which it is
one—though only one—of the functions of this poem to provoke.

But it is not with laughter, however philosophical, that the poem ends, but
with wonder.

Sometimes, upon a crowded street,
I feel the sudden rain come down
And in the old, magnetic sound
I hear the opening of a gate
That loosens all the seven seas.
Watching the whole creation drown
I muse, alone, on Ararat.

Here, at the threshold of his book, Scott moves from the poetry of concrete
images through wit and metaphysical imagination to myth and magic. A
long, cool dive into Lake Massawippi and the poet comes up with a rich
hoard of racial memories, dreams and aspirations. All are perfectly fused:
earth, water, air; science and mythology; mermaids, Venus, Noah; the I and
all-mankind; a crowded street and "the water's deepest colonnades."

"Lakeshore" is an excellent starting point for a consideration of Scott's
non-satirical poetry. The themes and the motives of many of his most completely articulated poems are seen here at their clearest and most direct. The
fascination with water, as element and as a symbol; the identification of the
poet's Self with Man and of the sensuous perceptive physical being with

Mind; and the inescapable tendency to identify or interchange the language and imagery of science (especially biology, geology and psychology) with the language and imagery of religion: all of these are here. And they are to be found also, in varying degrees and proportions, in such deeply felt and intellectually stimulating poems as "Paradise Lost," "Eden," "Journey," "My Amoeba is Unaware," and the best of the pieces on India and the Far East— "Bangkok," "Water," "A Grain of Rice," and "On the Death of Gandhi."

"Lakeshore" may also serve as an exemplar both of the "candid" style derived from imagism and of the witty metaphysical style that, without being in the least derivative, recalls Marvell and Waller—or, if you prefer, Auden. Some of the earliest poems dating from the days of the *McGill Fortnightly Review* already have a simplicity of language and an exactness of imagery which are the first fruits of conscious discipline, control, and humility. Little pieces like "North Stream" and "Snowdrift" or the much later haiku "Plane Landing in Tokyo" exhibit these qualities in miniature splendour. A pure and naked perception alone could not, of course, satisfy Scott for more than a moment, and most of his poems that start out as an image soon become images, and perceptions soon become concepts and blossom in metaphor, analogy and conceit. Mind comes flooding in.

Many of the early, very simple verses grouped near the beginning of *Selected Poems* are nevertheless quite delightful, though their importance perhaps is mainly historical (they date from the mid-twenties) and technical (they show Scott's later style beginning to form). "New Names" develops in a personal and indeed almost rapturous way the old thesis that writers as different as Mrs. Traill and Douglas Le Pan have united in expressing—that Canada is a country without a mythology. Scott suggests we must make our own anew. "Old Song" finds and expresses an austere cadence in the almost-silence of the northern wilderness:

> far voices
> and fretting leaves
> this music the
> hillside gives
>
> but in the deep
> Laurentian river
> and elemental song
> for ever
>
> a quiet calling
> of no mind
> out of long aeons....
>
> granite lips
> a stone throat

Here we are back to the purest imagism and a style that is the ultimate in simplicity and suggestiveness. This poem has a theme and a style that are irresistibly appealing to the Canadian poet, as new poets like Bowering and Newlove show as clearly as E. J. Pratt or W. W. E. Ross. Here, as in "Lakeshore," we have the sense of vast distances in space and time and a view of geological prehistory that goes back even farther than the ages of man-as-fish.

Another poem that rises naturally out of such telescopic probings into the geologic and biologic past and therefore has affinities with "Lakeshore" and "Old Song" is the strange meditation called "Mount Royal." This is a Pratt poem with a difference. One thinks of the vivifying dynamism of the description of the Laurentian Shield in "Towards the Last Spike." In Scott's poem time is speeded up: the mountain rises out of the sea; the sea subsides, leaving its deposit of silt and shells; man walks and builds his muddled cities "where crept the shiny mollusc," and the poet or poet-mind observes it all.

> Where flowers march, I dig these tiny shells
> Once deep-down fishes safe, it seemed, on sand....

The joke about the fishes building on sand and thinking themselves safe alerts us to the fact that irony and satire are this poet's chosen weapons. The satire here is directed against man's vanity, pride, and blind self-confidence as in Hardy's lines on the loss of the *Titanic,* where dim moon-eyed fishes stare at the mighty wreck and query "What does this vaingloriousness down here?" The situation is reversed in "Mount Royal." It is the fish who have been stranded and passed by. Now they are cited as an object lesson that suburban and commercial man, who builds his villas on the reclaimed island of the mountain, fails to heed—blindly and foolishly, it is implied, since the forces of cosmic destruction are inexorable. The poem ends in angry scorn.

> Pay taxes now,
> Elect your boys, lay out your pleasant parks,
> You gill-lunged, quarrelsome ephemera!
> The tension tightens yearly, underneath,
> A folding continent shifts silently
> And oceans wait their turn for ice or streets.

There is a curious consequence of this geologic view that we can observe in some of Scott's most characteristic poems. He is a man capable of—indeed unable to refrain from—taking long views, both backwards into the past and forward into the future, an idealist in the popular sense of the word. Both in his political life as a socialist and his literary life as a poet he welcomes the new, the just, and the generous—and always in the broadest and most general terms. Poems that embrace vast cosmic distances, both of space and time, lend themselves to thinking in abstractions. There is "world enough and time" for all the great abstractions to come into being, to evolve and grow, to change, to grow old, and perhaps to die. The good ones we must cultivate, preserve, and nourish; the bad ones we must kill.

There is a very peculiar class of poems in which these consequences of taking large views are quite explicit. Some of its members are "Creed," "Conflict," "Dialogue," "Degeneration," poems concerned with war or with love, and a remarkable series of what for want of a better name I will call "defining" poems—among them "Memory," "Heart," "Was," "Caring," and (with a difference) "Stone."

"Conflict" is a rather Emersonian poem on the tragic paradox of war. It develops the thesis that men on both sides in any conflict fight for the good they know and die with equal courage for the opposite sides of truth:

> When I see the falling bombs
> Then I see defended homes.
> Men above and men below
> Die to save the good they know. . . .
>
> Pro and con have single stem
> Half a truth dividing them. . . .
>
> Persecution's cruel mouth
> Shows a twisted love of truth. . . .

Here speaks the defender of unpopular causes, the idealist who loves the abstract and the universal. It is the wide application of unparticularized truth that such a poetry seeks to secure. Universals and abstractions are employed with the confidence born of an utter faith in their reality and validity. Such words as *good, wrong, bravery, love, truth, prison, ghetto, flag, gun, rack, rope, persecution, sacrifice,* whether abstractions or collective symbols, are made to glow with the vitality of an individual existence—or are used as if they did so glow.

How this is done, the eight quatrains entitled "Dialogue" may demonstrate. In structure and language this poem is as taut and concentrated as "Conflict," but its movement is in the reverse direction—from sensation and particularity (from the concrete, that is) to the universal, a universal which is equated with the spiritual—"spirit takes communion/From every living touch." The progression is straightforward. "Sense is more than mortal." Our bodies are the gateway to a supra-sensual world. Eye, ear, and hand contribute to the synthesis of a new form "to house a new conception."

Desire first, then structure
Complete the balanced picture.
The thought requires the form.

The poem's rhetoric is serpentine, for we have now reached—this is the fifth of eight stanzas—the point where the poem begins:

The hour is ripe for union,
And spirit takes communion
From every living touch.

The end in the last two stanzas is surprising and unheroic. The serpent cannot rear back and strike; instead it sinks down and seems to collapse.

For us, how small the power
To build our dreams a tower
Or cast the molten need.
For us, how small the power.

So few, so worn, the symbols.
No line or word resembles
The vision in its womb.
So few, so worn, the symbols.

Truth, not wishes, hopes, or evasions, is the business of poetry; and this poem would be a lesser one if it ended any other way.

What is needed always is a new language, new images, and a new technique. Scott has been trying all his life—and sometimes with heartening success—to find these. Some of his notable successes are moving love poems that have been placed in this collection immediately after "Dialogue." Their newness and hence their effectiveness lies in nothing more strange than an absolute fidelity to the occasion and the emotion that has brought them into being. One, called "Meeting," begins like this:

If what we say and do is quick and intense,
And if in our minds we see the end before starting,
It is not fear, but understanding that holds us.

Here the conciseness of the syntax contributes potentialities to the meaning. It is not fear that holds us apart but understanding that holds us together.

Other poems that approach or achieve the new style are "Will to Win"—a deceptively light and witty *jeu d'esprit* in which the lightness enables the poet to keep control of the situation and the wit serves to define it; "Vision"—

beautifully rhymed quatrains in which the "newness" or rightness comes from the clarity with which the sharp edge of every idea is defined; and "A l'Ange Avantgardien"—the explicit statement of a romantic view of poetic creation according to which the emphasis must always be on the making never on the made.

One of the most striking paradoxes of Scott's poetic life is that the ceaseless flow of energy which throws up poems of all kinds and in all modes should nevertheless be able to shape them with extreme care, whether the work in hand is a piece of impressionistic and typographical experiment or a closely knit web of thought, like the fine late poem "Vision"—a true metaphysical lyric that begins:

> Vision in long filaments flows
> Through the needles of my eyes.
> I am fastened to the rose . . .
> I am clothed in what eye sees. . . .

and ends:

> Tireless eye, so taut and long,
> Touching flowers and flames with ease,
> All your wires vibrate with song
> When it is the heart that sees.

Here is song that is as well written as prose—a poem that reiterates the validity of the "candid" style of "Lakeshore" and the earlier imagist pieces. This style is seen at its most purely intellectual in what I have called the "defining" poems—lyrics that perhaps have developed out of Scott's training as a lawyer. Lawyers, like poets, are involved with words, with definitions and with subtle quibbles. Some of these pieces, as for example "Memory," are apt and ingenious metaphor:

> Was is an Is that died
>     in our careless hands
> and would not stay
>     in its niche of time.
>
> We crumble all our nows
>     into the dust of Was . . .
>
> forgetting Was
>     cannot be shaken off
>     follows close behind
>     breathes down our neck . . .

> One day we shall look back
> into those staring eyes
> and there will be nothing left but
>                          Was.

Another "defining" poem of the same sort is the one beginning "Caring is loving, motionless," but the lines entitled "Stone" show an interesting difference. In these what is being defined is not an abstraction or a state but an object, a solid item, "a still of gravity." The method is entirely different from that of imagism. The purpose of an imagist poem is to perceive and to present perception, but here we go further in an effort to grasp the idea of the thing and of its place in history. The motion too is just the reverse of that in "Was," where an abstraction was made concrete; here a concretion is seen in the light of thought—the remarkable thing being, however, that the thought is made to seem to radiate from the stone itself:

> A stone is a tomb
> with the door barred.
>
> A still picture
> from a flick of motion.
>
> A stone is a closed eye
> reflecting what it saw. . . .

In these distichs we come back to the sense of time in which Scott is so deeply immersed that it recurs in poem after poem. Here the mind moves from the glacial epochs of prehistory to the bursting stone that falls on Hiroshima.

In closing I should return to the personal. But actually I have not been away from it. The old dictum that the style is the man has never been more clearly illustrated than in the poetry of F. R. Scott. All his poems, from the gayest and lightest expression of delight in life, through his pointed and savage satires, to the profound lyrics I have been mainly considering, are informed and qualified by a sense of responsibility and an inescapable sincerity, which is serious but never solemn and rich without ostentation.

# Earle Birney: A Unified Personality

*from* Canadian Literature, *No. 30*

With the publication of Earle Birney's *Selected Poems,* a generous and representative gathering of a hundred poems, many of them long and ambitious and all of them interesting, we have an opportunity to sum up a long, fruitful, and varied poetic career—a career which this volume indicates has grown steadily in significance. The poems from Birney's two books, *Ice, Cod, Bell or Stone* and *Near False Creek Mouth,* have a power and mastery that was foreshadowed but only occasionally attained in *David* or *Trial of a City,* the works on which Birney's reputation has been founded and established. Though Birney has written two novels, edited an anthology, and published a good many scholarly articles, including an immensely valuable analysis of the poetic reputation of E. J. Pratt, it is as a poet, a teacher of poetry, and a publicist for poetry that he is chiefly and rightly known; and it is his poetry only that I propose to examine here.

I do not remember when I first read a poem by Earle Birney. I know that when Frank Scott and I were preparing the manuscript for *New Provinces* in 1935 we had not heard of him, though we soon began to read the pieces that appeared in the *Canadian Forum,* of which Birney was literary editor from 1936 to 1940. It was not, however, until the publication of *David & Other Poems* in 1942 that it became apparent that a new poet had arrived, a poet who gave promise of being a worthy continuator of the tradition of heroic narrative established by Pratt and perhaps the precursor of a new school of modern poetry in Canada. Now a quarter of a century later we can see that these hopeful anticipations have been amply fulfilled. Birney's career—even more certainly than Frank Scott's—has been analogous to the development of modern Canadian poetry as a whole. Both poets have been leaders in some respects and followers in others. From the beginning both have been adventurous and experimental, and if occasionally they have seemed to be groping or merely wandering, the occasions were remarkably few. Scott, in spite of his liberal and leftist point of view, has been mainly traditional. Birney, who is also politically and socially of the left, takes more naturally to the experimental, though in his case, paradoxically enough, his most successful experiment is the experiment of being traditional. Some of the best of his earlier poems— "Slug in Woods," "Anglo-Saxon Streets," "Mappemounde," and parts of "Damnation of Vancouver" as well—while not mere pastiche or parody, certainly owe their success to the skill with which the poet has utilized his scholarly knowledge of *Beowulf,* Chaucer, *Piers Plowman,* and Hopkins. To the advantages of a western mountain childhood and hard work as a manual labourer and logger in his youth, Birney added those of a thorough academic training in English literature, culminating in a Ph.D. from the University of Toronto in 1936. With the exception of some years spent in study and travel abroad on various fellowships and grants, all his life since the end of the Second World War has been spent as a university teacher of literature and creative writing. The rather touchy remarks about academic critics and anthologists in the preface to *Selected Poems* should not be taken too seriously. They are partly confessional, for Birney has been both. A few of the poems (I shall cite instances later) do suffer because the literary sophistication of the technique calls attention to itself in a way that is distracting rather than expressive. But this does not happen very often, and in any case it is the price that has to be paid for the successes.

There are some things about *Selected Poems* I do not like, and my praise of the poet would be less convincing if I did not say what they are. Some of them, of course, are not the poet's responsibility. The make-up of the book, like so many of McClelland & Stewart's recent volumes of verse, seems to be pretentious and flamboyant, while the illustrations, though good in themselves, seem to be competing with the poems. Poetry ought to be left to speak for itself.

For me the same criticism applies—and here the poet himself must bear the responsibility—to the typographical gimmicks and punctuational nudity imposed on many fine, straightforward, clear poems that when originally published made their point convincingly and movingly without the promptings of visual aids. In his preface Birney is facetiously indignant at the expense of provincial journalists and conservative critics who have registered a similar objection. Actually it is beside the point to cite the practice of E. E. Cummings. Cummings is a unique, highly special, and absolutely consistent poetic individual. If his influence is to be felt in more than a superficial way, it has to be felt in the blood. It will probably be expressed by nothing more showy than the slightly unusual placing of an adverb or the curious elongation of a cadence. To put on another man's hat does not make you that man. Birney is so good a poet when he is himself that he has no need to seek a fashionable "modernism" in typographical eccentricity. Poems like "Appeal to a Lady with a Diaper" and "Mammorial Stunzas for Aimee Simple McFarcin," light and satirical as they are, have been made distractingly difficult to read. The visual aids have become handicaps. The eye has to run an obstacle race.

These are practical and specific objections. I realize perfectly well that there are many typographically expressive passages that are not confusing or difficult at all. Here is a passage from "Letter to a Conceivable Great-grandson":

> Now we've got automation     Our
> letters
>
> are set to de
> liver them
> selves
> fast
> er than
>
> meteors     Soon we'll be
>
> sending wholemanuscriptsprepaidtothe
>
> planets
>
> But what's crazy for real is
>
> we're so damned busy no
>
> body has time to de          what
> cipher
> language it is we're      iting
> r
> w

This is clear enough, though a little inconvenient to read; and its purpose is clear enough—to make the reader experience, physically and mentally, just what the poem is saying at this particular point, that is, that we write and transmit so fast that what we write is inconvenient to read. This, of course, is the modern dogma that Wyndham Lewis and Yvor Winters have attacked— that to express confusion we must write confusedly. My objection to this kind of thing is not that it lacks clarity but that it lacks point: the device is so childishly obvious. However, if, as Birney says in his preface, these devices are spells to appease an intermittent madman within him, let us be grateful and turn to the true poet and the true poems.

*Selected Poems* is divided into six sections. The first, made up mainly of later poems, is entitled after one of the best pieces in it, "The Bear on the

Delhi Road," and is a record of Birney's travels westward from British Columbia to the South Seas, Japan, India, Thailand and back through Greece, Spain, England, and the Arctic, home again. These poems, with one or two not very important exceptions, date from the late fifties and the early sixties, and include half a dozen pieces that are among the best things Birney ever wrote—"A Walk in Kyoto," "Bangkok Boy," "The Bear on the Delhi Road," and best of all, the magnificent "El Greco: *Espolio.*" Here too is one of the not-so-many light, satirical, gently comic poems that is completely successful—successful I think because the satire here directed against the world of tourism and public relations is directed, even if ever so gently, against the poet himself too. This is the delightful "Twenty-Third Flight" that begins:

> Lo as I pause in the alien vale of the airport
> fearing ahead the official ambush
> a voice languorous and strange as these winds
>     of Oahu
> calleth my name and I turn to be quoited in
>     orchids
> and amazed with a kiss perfumed and soft as
>     the *lei*
> Straight from a travel poster thou steppest
> thy arms like mangoes for smoothness
> o implausible shepherdess for this one aging sheep—

and continues to the tragi-comic conclusion of the poet so welcomed being nevertheless soon ruthlessly abandoned: "Nay, but thou stayest not?"—

> O nubile goddess of the Kaiser Training
>     Programme
> is it possible that tonight my cup runneth
>     not over
> and that I shall sit in the still pastures of
>     the lobby
> while thou leadest another old ram in garlands
>     past me . . .
> And that I shall lie by the waters of Waikiki
>     and want?

This is my favourite among the comic poems, but there are many others almost equally seductive, some satirical, some whimsical, and some with a wry seriousness, as in the brilliant series of Mexican poems. I do not know where you will find anything better in modern North American poetry than the combination of wit and sentiment, pertinent observation and auricular, almost ventriloquistic precision than "Sinaloa," "Ajijic," or "Six-sided Square: Actopan."

These last poems are in the second section of the book, which is headed "Trans-Americana." The section begins with a series of satirical pieces on certain unlovely aspects of "civilization" north of the Rio Grande. Most of these, when compared with the charm and sureness of "Twenty-Third Flight," seem weak or forced—a defect which may be partly due to the arbitrary typographical eccentricity that has been imposed upon them since they first appeared in earlier volumes.

When we come, however, to the poems on Mexico, Peru, and the Caribbean islands all such cavilling falls away. These are not only among the finest of Birney's poems; they are just simply and plainly, *man*, the *finest*. The new style that some of our West Coast poets learned from Olson, Creeley, and the Black Mountain writers (and from Birney himself, I suspect) has here been put to uses that transcend the personal and the purely emotional. Poems like "Cartagena de Indias," "Machu Picchu," "Letter to a Cuzco Priest," "Barranquilla Bridge," and others sum up a whole ancient and alien civilization and bring it—and our own—under the scrutiny of a sharp, sensitive, and discursive mind.

When these poems are compared with even the best of the poems of the early forties that make up the next part of the book ("War Winters"), we see how great and how sure has been Birney's development as a craftsman in poetry, a development which depends upon and expresses a development in intellectual and emotional maturity. Perhaps this growth in maturity is the achievement of originality, the setting free of a unique poetic personality that after years of work has at last found itself and its true voice. This is not to be taken to mean that such well-known early poems as "Hands," "Vancouver Lights," and "Dusk on the Bay" are not sincere and accurate expressions of what a Canadian felt in the dark days of 1939 and 1940. But it is easier to see now than it was then that they speak with the voices of Auden, Rex Warner, or Stephen Spender, as we feel they might have recalled Rupert Brooke had they been written in 1915. They are true to their time rather than to a unique person, and they are not, therefore, without their own kind of historical significance. They do certainly present an attractive contrast to the war poems of some of the aged survivors of an older generation. Even today only a few poems written later in the war—Douglas Le Pan's poems of the Italian campaign and Pratt's *Behind the Log*—stand higher than these as interpretations of Canada's war.

In the next section, "Canada: Case History," Birney has grouped those poems, some of them satirical but most of them serious and, indeed, "devout," in which he has come to grips with the problem of what it means to be Canadian and what it is to be a Canadian poet. Viewed as a problem, this theme has become something of a nervous obsession, and Birney, like Scott and some others, is at his best when he approaches it obliquely and allows his hawk's eye and his adder's tongue to do the work for him. Everything that is really important is conveyed in the imagery and the diction. Cadences like

> the moon carved unknown totems
> out of the lakeshore
> owls in the beardusky woods derided him
> moosehorned cedars circled his swamps
> 　　and tossed
> their antlers up to the stars. . . .

> a marten moving like quicksilver
> 　　scouted us. . . .

> the veins of bald glaciers blackened
> white pulses of waterfalls
> beat in the bare rockflesh

—to give but three brief samples, are simple, sensuous, and passionate. Such indigenous music and imagery give to poems like "David," "Bushed," and the poems of transcontinental air travel, "North Star West," and "Way to the West," a richness that Birney and a few other poets rooted in the native tradition seem to have derived from the earth and air of Canada itself. This is a northern style, and an excellent one. Our sense of its validity is increased when we realize that it is not peculiar to Birney but is a common heritage. Here are some examples chosen almost at random from *The Oxford Book of Canadian Verse:*

> No more the slow stream spreading clear in
> 　　sunlight
> Lacing the swamp with intricate shining
> 　　channels . . .
> 　　the mica glint in the sliding water
> The bright winged flies and the muskrat gone
> 　　like a shadow. . . .
> 　　　　　　　　　(Floris McLaren)

> The sachem voices cloven out of the hills
> spat teeth in the sea like nails. . . .
> 　　　　　　　　　(Alfred Bailey)

> On the North Shore a reptile lay asleep. . . .
> 　　　　　　　　　(E. J. Pratt)

> Sinuous, red as copper snakes,
> Sharp-headed serpents, made of light,
> Glided, and hid themselves in night. . . .
>                   (Isabella Crawford)

This last passage, and the poem from which I have taken it, shows better than all the explanations in the preface why Birney is impatient with commas and rhyme.

Of course not every one of the northern poems has the linguistic rightness of "Bushed" or "David." Sometimes his Eng. Lit. sophistication betrays Birney into an overstrained conceit, as for example in these lines from "Page of Gaspé"—

> Between over-generous margins
> between the unprinted river and the
>       rubbed-out peaks
> run the human typelines . . .
> farms split to sentences by editor death
> fattening subtitles of rockfence . . .
>
> In this repetitive prose a sawmill
> sets quotemarks after the stone windmill's
>       period. . . .

or leads him to indulge in a sort of metrical plagiarism. "North of Superior" is filled with more or less erudite allusions to Scyldings, Excalibur, the Green Knight, the Den of Error, Azazel, and Roland, and the metre which recalls Pound's "Seafarer" in the first stanza reminds us of "Evangeline" in the second.

But these are occasional failures. To risk making them is the price every alive and eager artist must pay for his successes. One such success is surely the fine reflective poem "November Walk Near False Creek Mouth," the major work in Birney's last collection of new poems. It is dated "Vancouver 1961—Ametlla, Spain 1963." "November Walk" is a rich, meditative, ode-like poem that gathers up the themes of the long series of descriptive, narrative, and reflective poems set in or near Vancouver from "Dusk on the Bay" and "Hands" to the present, and finally and on a much larger scale achieves what the poet had been groping for from the start of his career—an orientation of himself and his place and his time in terms that are both emotionally and rationally satisfying. This poem stands with the poems on Mexico and Peru as the high water mark of Birney's achievement up to now. Most encouraging of all, it gives promise of fine things still to come, for it shows the poet has found a style commensurate with the theme he has approached in many different ways in many different poems—man's effort as microcosm to come to terms with society, nature, and the macrocosm in the brief moment of allotted time. It is a promise that makes Birney's remark in the preface—"In my next work I am thinking of pasting my poems on mobiles"—seem like the frivolous joke it is intended as.

The fifth section of *Selected Poems*, headed rather journalistically "Letter to a Conceivable Great-grandson," is the least successful part of the book. It is a somewhat haphazard collection of pieces on the threat of atomic extinction and the ironies and confusions inherent in the world of cold-war distrust and science-fiction posturing. The point of view is liberal and humane, and the sentiments are those which all decent men must share. The trouble with this sort of poetry is not something that can be laid at the door of an individual poet. The responsibility is elsewhere. These excellent sentiments are shared (and expressed) by politicians, statesmen, editorial writers, publicists and generals who find them no bar whatsoever to actions and votes that lead in the practical world to the aggravation and perpetuation of the crisis that they (hypocritically) and the liberal poet (ineffectively) lament. The result is a widening of the gap between the poem's practical intention and the possible achievement of that end. Perhaps its most successful accomplishment is to demonstrate the futility of poetry as propaganda and drive home the corollary that action alone is adequate. This built-in demonstration of its own uselessness is what vitiates nearly all poetry that takes a bold stand against sin, and makes the social poetry of Birney, and of Frank Scott too, the weakest part of their work. Two of the finest poems, however, in this part of the book are translations from Mao Tse-tung made with the assistance of Professor Ping-ti Ho. Here the cleverness and strain of some of the poems and the echoes of Spender and Rex Warner in others give way to a simple direct style that is very moving indeed.

There is not much that needs to be said here about "Damnation of Vancouver," which forms the final section of this book. Originally published as *Trial of a City* in 1952, it was recognized as one of the most original and technically accomplished of Birney's poems, a *tour de force* of linguistic virtuosity and a satire as biting as anything in Canadian literature. It marked a distinct advance on the simple and unified narrative "David," mingling as it did the colloquial and the grand styles and the satirical and the affirmative modes. It thus anticipates the South and Central American poems of the sixties and fuses perfectly for the first time in Birney's work the two themes that Northrop Frye has named as central to Canadian poetry, "one a primarily comic theme of satire and exuberance, the other a primarily tragic theme of loneliness and terror."

For *Selected Poems* Birney revised what was originally a poem or masque and turned it into a play, complete with elaborate stage directions, descriptions of actions (business), and statements about the emotional implications and tones of voice to be got into some of the speeches. This is fine for the amateur actor and the inexperienced director, but the reader of poetry, I should think, would prefer to take his poetry neat. The development of the theme—which is the rape of the land of the Indians by the forces of commercial exploitation and "progress"—comes through more vividly in the original version.

What remains to be said in conclusion? Not very much surely. It is quite clear that Earle Birney is one of our major poets, perhaps since the death of E. J. Pratt our leading poet. Certainly he is the only rival of Pratt as the creator of heroic narrative on a bold scale and, unlike Pratt, he has been consistently experimental. He has not always been successful, and he has sometimes aped styles and fashions that are unworthy of his real talents; but without a somewhat boyish spirit of adventure his successes would have been impossible too. The real triumph of *Selected Poems* is that it demonstrates so clearly and forcibly—as does indeed the whole of Birney's career—a unified personality of great charm, wit, strength, and generosity. I recall Louis MacNeice's description of the modern poet: "I would have a poet able-bodied, fond of talking, a reader of the newspapers, capable of pity and laughter, informed in economics, appreciative of women, involved in personal relationships, actively interested in politics, susceptible to physical impressions. . . ." This is the man I know, and the poet who rises out of this book.

*A Reading of Anne Wilkinson*

### *Introduction,* The Collected Poems of Anne Wilkinson

When I heard of the death of Anne Wilkinson I read once again, and at a single sitting, all the poems she had written—her first small collection *Counterpoint to Sleep*, published in 1951, the volume of 1955, *The Hangman Ties the Holly*, her three lyric sequences in the *Tamarack Review* No. 5 and No. 18, and later the notebooks and manuscripts containing the poems which are here published for the first time, pieces written mostly in the last year of her life.

I read with a newly sharpened awareness—an awareness of small, immensely significant details of imagery, music, language, and emotion. There is a stanza of Emily Dickinson which describes the strange clarification brought about by death, and it kept running in my head as a sort of counterpoint to what I was reading:

> We noticed smallest things,
> Things overlooked before,
> By this great light upon our minds
> Italicized, as 'twere.

I could not help thinking how well these lines applied not only to my own state of mind but to one of the special qualities and peculiar virtues of Anne Wilkinson's poems—their being saturated, as it were, with light, a radiance of the mind, cast often on small, familiar things, or things overlooked before, and reflected back into the mind and heart.

"The poet's eye is crystal," she noted in "Lens," one of the few poems that state an explicit *aesthetique,* and her "long duty" and "daily chore" is to keep and cherish her good lens. The crystal eye, the craftsman's lens, the light that animates them, and the green world on which it falls: these are the instruments and materials, and the colours and lights that flash through her verse. She never knew the tragedy of not living in a sensual world. It is a sensuousness of the eye that most vividly brings her world to life, but the æther through which this light vibrates is a tremor of the mind and the vision of her green world is made fruitful by love.

In the first lines of the first poem in *The Hangman Ties the Holly* she announces one of the two main themes of her book:

> Who has the cunning to apprehend
> Even everyday easy things
> Like air and wind and a fool
> Or the structure and colour of a simple soul?
>
> New laid lovers sometimes see,
> In a passion of light. . . .

Light is everywhere here a symbol of truth, reality, and, above all, life. Green signifies Nature, sensation, happiness, grace, and again life. If these aspects of her sensibility make one think of Vaughan or Traherne in the one case and of Andrew Marvell in the other, the newness, freshness, and uniqueness of her vision are not diminished but enhanced.

A traditional background is a help, not a hindrance, when it is entered into with all one's wits about one and purified by the senses. Earth, air, fire, and water have an immediate sensational significance in the poetry of Anne Wilkinson—as well as a medieval and metaphysical one. In a poem that develops out of an aphorism by Empedocles—"I was born a boy, and a maiden, a plant and a bird, and a darting fish in the sea"—she enters, through the twin gates of sensation and wit, into the phenomenal world and becomes a part of its life:

> Yet always I huff out the flame with breath
>     as live
> And green as Irish grass, recalling the gills
> Of my youth when I was a miner
> Deep in the hills of the sea.

The union of the four elements and her own identification with them is everywhere assumed, but occasionally it is explicitly, concretely, and dynamically *stated*, as in the *fiat* of the last stanza of "Poem in Three Parts":

> The stone in my hand
> IS my hand
> And stamped with tracings of
> A once greenblooded frond,
> Is here, is gone, will come,
> Was fire, and green, and water,
> Will be wind.

This is as close perhaps as this poet has come to a religious statement—or at least to a religious statement untouched by irony—but hers is the classic religion of Empedocles, Heraclitus, and Lucretius. What it celebrates is a metamorphosis. Over and over again she descends into the earth like Flora or Eurydice or merges white flesh, red blood, into the leafy green of a tree like Daphne:

> Let the world go limp, put it to rest,
> Give it a soft wet day and while it sleeps
> Touch a drenched leaf; . . .
>
> Before you turn
> Uncurl prehensile fingers from the tree,
> Cut your name on bark, search
> The letters for your lost identity.

The twenty or so stanzas which form the "postscript" to "Letter to My Children" and which, regrettably, I think, were dropped from the *Hangman* volume, afford many other illustrations of this sensuous imagery. The greatest gift she can bequeath her children is:

> Five full and fathomed senses,
> Precision instruments
> To chart the wayward course
> Through rock and moss and riddles. . . .

There is a flowing together and intermingling of the senses in some of her most characteristic expressions as, for example, in the magical stanza beginning:

> You'll shiver but you'll hear
> The sharp white nails of the moon
> Scratch the slate of midnight water. . .

or in the image of the eye, the hungry eye, as tiger:

> Uncage the tiger in your eye
> And tawny, night and day,
> Stalk the landscape for the contour
> Of a fern or arm. . . .

The poem is long and somewhat discursive, perhaps, but it both epitomizes and illustrates the poet's sensibility and wit and has its own delightful ingenuity. Images derived from an urban sophistication are used for the expression of a universal and quite classical hedonism. Praise of the senses as the

source of joy and wisdom is recorded in many of the poems—usually in the
language of romantic convention. "The ear . . . will mark the drop in pitch of
towns adrift in fog." The "luminous dial" of the eye will read the "gold
numerals of dawn/Thin on the face of the midnight watch," and nose must

> Smell the vigour
> Packed in snow at noon and metal
> In the air
> When stars show up for duty
> On the dim lit wards of winter. . . .

For Anne Wilkinson the body and its senses were the instruments through
which nature and reality entered the mind and became a part of being. "I put
on my body and go forth/To seek my blood," she writes in the lovely poem
"The Red and the Green":

> I walk the hollow subway
> Of the ear. . . .
>
> Skin is minstrel, sings
> Tall tales and shady
> Of the kings of Nemi Wood. . . .
>
> My new green arteries
>
> Fly streamers from the maypole of my arms,
> From head to toe
> My blood sings green. . . .

"My blood sings green": this is one aspect of her poetry—its intimate sensuous identification with life as a growth out of the earth; and it implies a
Pan-ic or Lawrencian forgetfulness of the non-living, dry, and essentially
irrelevant intellection of much of our routine living. But knowledge, intellect,
and the motions of thought are by no means absent from this poetry. They
are seen in the buried literary allusions and the puns. The former are perhaps
not essential, but they are not merely ornamental or snobbish either—they
italicize and connect rather than make an initial or final assertion—and it is
good to find confirmation of one's feelings in Sir James Frazer, Mother
Goose, Shakespeare, and the author of "Greensleeves." The puns, as elsewhere in these poems,[1] not only give an impression of liveliness, sharpness,

---

[1] Some examples: "new laid lovers"; "the warm gulf stream of love"; "happily lived ever water-
ward,"; "the curd and why of memory,"—to cite only a few.

and wit, but convey with greater precision and intensity, and immensely greater compactness, a relationship that might take clauses and sentences instead of a single word to get across. "The curd and why of memory," for instance, presents the mental gropings after something forgotten with an almost physiological suggestion of the tremblings of the membrane of nerves and brain.

This poetry of "green thought in a green shade" is connected also with the red of the earth and of blood. The identification of the poet with nature is sensuous and emotional. It is achieved in love, and it is achieved in death. These two themes—and a union of them both in a sort of love-hate relationship with death—are found in some of the earliest of the poems as well as in some truly terror-inspiring poems which give a sombre intensity to *The Hangman Ties the Holly*. They are found too, as might have been expected, in the last, uncollected, poems.

Love in the poetry of Anne Wilkinson is sometimes, as in "Strangers," a game of wit, but it is always also a sensuous involvement, not a twining of bodies and minds only but a mingling with the green sap of Nature in a wholly holy communion. This is the significance of the delightful and lovely poem beginning "In June and gentle oven. . . ."

> In June and gentle oven
> Summer kingdoms simmer
> As they come
> And flower and leaf and love
> Release
> Their sweetest juice. . . .

The music is impeccable. Presently there is one faintly sinister image, which soon we realize is intended to hint at the necessary serpent in every Eden:

> An adder of a stream
> Parts the daisies. . . .

But lovers are protected by Nature, instinct, and joy, and are "saved":

> And where, in curve of meadow,
> Lovers, touching, lie,
> A church of grass stands up
> And walls them, holy, in.

The closing stanza of this poem is one of the most beautiful expressions in modern poetry of the divinity of love achieved in the sensuous community of the green world:

> Then two in one the lovers lie
> And peel the skin of summer
> With their teeth
> And suck its marrow from a kiss
> So charged with grace
> The tongue, all knowing
> Holds the sap of June
> Aloof from seasons, flowing

Something of this fertile richness is found in a later love poem—the sequence of five lyrics entitled "Variations on a Theme." Here, however, the pure and innocent religion of love and nature has been clouded by an intense awareness, amounting almost to a foreknowledge, of death, and there is an air of faint desperation in the spells and magic rituals that are tried as exorcisms.

The poem is a series of variations on a sentence of Thoreau: "A man needs only to be turned around once with his eyes shut to be lost in this world." The key words are "turned" and "lost." Each of the five lyrics explores one of the ways of being lost. Thoreau thought of losing the world in the Christian sense of a spiritual achievement, but there are many ways of being lost—some are a kind of ecstasy and all are bewildering. In the first of the variations it is childhood's "first flinging of the blood about in circles," a recollection of games in the green meadow when the child spins round and round in dizzying circles until the world and his own identity are lost. The second and fourth lyrics are visions of horror—the second of death, the fourth of madness.

> From arteries in graves, columns
> Rose to soil the sky; and down
> Their fluted sides the overflow
> Slid to earth, unrolled and spread
> On stalk and stone its plushy red

The elegance of the writing enhances the horror of this second section, but the intensity increases still more in the nightmare-like fourth:

> ... where above me one black crow
> Had cawed my spring, two dirty doves
> Sang daintily. I stoned the birds
> But no stone hit, for of white gloves

My hands were made; I stole a stick
To break the sky; it did not crack;
I could not curse—though I was lost,
Had trespassed on some stranger's dream. . . .

The third section, like the first, is a happy one. It deals with the magical trans-
formation of being "lost" in love. Significantly, it is the only poem in the
sequence in which the protagonist is "we" not "I." It is a very beautiful poem,
and short enough to quote in full:

We shut our eyes and turned once round
And were up borne by our down fall.
Such life was in us on the ground
That while we moved, earth ceased to roll,
And oceans lagged, and all the flames
Except our fire, and we were lost
In province that no settler names.

The fifth poem rises almost directly out of this one and develops the theme of
death more simply and traditionally than it had been treated in the second
and fourth:

Death turned me first, will twirl me last
And throw me down beneath the grass
And strip me of this stuff, this dress
I am, although its form be lost.

If the green, light-riddled poetry in which Anne Wilkinson celebrated life
and the love of life makes one think of Marvell and Vaughan, she is also, like
Webster (and not in her last poems only), much possessed by death. I mentioned earlier the love-hate relationship with death that seems almost inherent in her sensibility and that animates in a truly terror-inspiring way a few of
her most powerful poems, "The Pressure of Night," "Strangers," "Topsoil to
the Wind," as well as the recent deceptively light and witty "Notes on Robert
Burton's *The Anatomy of Melancholy*" and the brilliant "A Cautionary Tale."
To these we must now add some of the poems written in her last year when
she knew her illness mortal—"Summer Storm," with its terrible evocation of
pain pressing "on nerve ends in the brain"—

Skull's skin is paper thin
Migraine is seeping in—

and "Waking," "A Room for Sleep," and the fearful poem beginning "Accustom the grey coils/Locked in the skull/To the silence" and ending

> the swelling
> Predicts at its pressing point
> Hoarded night bursting, the
> Black sky unloading
> Its stars till the skull is alight.

The sequence "A Sorrow of Stones," and particularly its culminating poem "When a Body Breaks," represent the most original and terrible of the later poems:

> It is other than I had imagined. I thought
> To travel behind two plumed white horses,
> I thought to lie like cream in a long black hearse
> I had not calculated on this
> Fall without end.

Yet even in these final poems Anne Wilkinson was able to integrate the witness of all the senses into an affirming testimony of the beauty and richness of life. They consolidate her position among the small group of women poets who have written of love and death with a peculiarly feminine intuition, an accuracy and an elegance that do not hide but enhance the intensity of the emotion—Emily Dickinson, Christina Rossetti, Elinor Wylie, and Leonie Adams. Her work as a whole puts her, certainly, in the forefront of contemporary Canadian poets. She has helped us to be a little more aware and hence a little more civilized. Her poems are a legacy whose value can never be diminished.

# Critical Improvisations on Margaret Avison's Winter Sun

*from* The Tamarack Review, *No. 18*

In the beginning was the Word.

Let us begin then with the word. Start with discrete particles. Look at the bricks.

"My house," she says, "is made of old newspapers."

But newspapers, like poems, are made of words. Let us look at the words.

Epithets are significant in poetry. Here are some of her favourites: *odd, curious, brave, bleak, deft, forlorn, fair, desolate, precious, Muscovite, wry.* A strange, courtly, almost Spenserian flavour. Remark a few other words: *fabrique, old Mutabilitie, remarked, iwis,* and the exclamation *but soft!* and we would be well into the Wood of Error. Better stop, turn round, look again, and pick another batch—words and phrases these: *patch of altitude, ultimate Recipient, administrative wing, winnowed navigators, quilted tumulus, bullshop, moustache-cut, micro-astronomical amaze.* Time wobbles, we appreciate, and space is telescoped. The diction is as modern as it is archaic.

Predicates and copulas give us concepts. She stars an unlikely young verb in a difficult part: *Daydreams . . . disk woodenly; Clenches the green-blue Bow; He stood, and gnarled silently.* She arranges unexpectedly happy marriages between impossible substantives and unrecommended adjectives: *Horning farness, These packaged us-es; This rabbinical gloss*—a working pun.

Wrenched out of context these fall harshly on the understanding. Epithets, of course, make phrases; predicates sentences. They create a harmony, or cry out for one. Put these words and phrases into their place in the jigsaw of the poems and they take on a radiance, or impart one. They lead to image, conceit, and apothegm.

Imagery is physical; conceit is intellectual. Here they often fuse. But let us isolate the sensory perceptions first. All the senses are pressed into service. Light and sight are so sharp they hurt, hence such painful felicities as *pinpoint multiple sunrise*. Colours are minutely distinguished, and we have *purple-blue, green-blue, old snapshot-blue, slick-paper blues and greens*. This last describes the *flanks* of mountains. In one short poem "Banff" the eye discriminates between *pencil-blue, Chalk blue, green-blue, milk-green, white, blazing white, blazing keen,* and *Anthracite. Shellack orange* in one poem is separated in another from the colour of a horse seen as *thin-coloured as oranges ripened in freight cars....* The tactile senses and the sense of smell are almost as accurate as sight. *Things I can't know I smell.* She speaks of "a mushroom and root-cellar coolness" and notes the impingement of an urban culture on the country by observing that "The toasted evening spells/City to hayrick."

The metaphysical conceit arises when nice distinctions in the realm of sensation are made to imply value judgments on things seen or felt, as they do when these are man-made things, not "Nature." Here, for example, is how the coming of darkness at twilight over the shanties on a city's waterfront is recorded:

> Lost, like the committing of sins
> crag-shapes are sediment,
> chopped down, minced, poured to pave
>     the shelving
> parade ground for pinioned grotesques
> in the pink shadow-lengthening
> barracks of evening.

Here the way things are seen and communicated is criticism (examination, interrogation, evaluation) as well as perception. The result is to transform perception into vision.

The success with which this is sometimes achieved is seen in such astonishing and difficult though not obscure poems as "Dispersed Titles," "Civility a Bogey," "Intra-Political," or "The Fallen, Fallen World." In these, it seems she uses experience to illustrate and clarify philosphical ideas, rather than *vice versa.* And to announce a faith—a faith all the more sure because held with irony. In "The Fallen, Fallen World" she casts an approving eye on Revolutionaries, Idealists, and the Learned who are "in snow and sleep's despite/ Straitly sustained." Each in his way impatient, each nobly wrong, and each exonerated with a tender or gently mocking irony—the Learned perhaps especially:

> They, stubborn, on the frozen mountain cling
> Dreaming of some alternative to spring.

Again: the boldness, originality, and all-inclusiveness of Avison's imagery can be seen in many places, but nowhere more dazzlingly than in the gently punning, critically ironic "Intra-Political," a poem subtitled "An Exercise in Political Astronomy." In the opening lines, World is seen as Supermarket and we, the people, are in turn and all at once the packaged and regimented comestibles, grocer, shopper, warehouse trucker, and child—"lion-hearted four-foot haggler with a hot dime."

She uses the pun charged with irony as if with TNT like a critical battering ram. What was it boxed us in to the geometrical prison of our rational and mechanical culture? The answer is brief, quick, and accurate:

> Strait thinking set us down in rows.

But there is hope in energy, humour, light. Fallen man can still dream of emerging from this pre-creation density into the light and space of a new Genesis. Like the phoenix we carry the seed of a new birth within ourselves—humour is a sign of it ("Glee dogs our glumness so"). And energy—"even our own energy will out." We are invited to "Look at the platinum moon," and by an act of the will to partake of the Pentecostal feast:

> If, with dainty stepping, we unbox ourselves
> while still Explosion slumbers,
> putting aside mudcakes,
> and buying, selling, trucking, packaging
> of mudcakes,
> sunstormed, daring to gambol,
> might there not be an immense answering
> of human skies?
> a new expectant largeness?

The peculiar virtue of this poetry arises from the intimacy with which the poet invites us to share her improvisational insights and home-made constructs. She writes to herself—as well as for the reader. She has to discover things and the ubiquitous unexpected connections of things for herself. Only after that can she point them out to the rest of us.

This method (and the necessity for it) can be seen in the rather small poem

"Chronic" near the beginning of the book. The title is the fraction of a pun, for the theme of the poem is the difficulty (impossibility?) of writing a chronicle that will be a meaningful or comprehensible record of the chronic, habitual, inescapable, peculiar reality that each of us lives in. The poet here can only speak for herself. "My house," she says—I repeat the quotation—"My house is made of old newspapers." *House* bears a richness of implication, armorial, ancestral, and astrological, that comes down to us from at least Chaucer. But even if we recognize or invent these associations, she addresses us rather sharply and with a directness that is obviously no respecter of persons:

> And don't pretend you recognize it.
> You don't. Because it doesn't look like a house,
> ... and *I* wouldn't know
> Except it's where I live.

The house on the street, the street in the sky, the sky in the head—and at the tip of the senses. This is the "house" she has set out to blueprint. Will her forms and figures be "accepted"? She isn't sure. This poem, like all of Avison's poems—even (or especially) the most fanciful—makes a fetish of sincerity. It includes the admission:

> ... I become accustomed
> To failing more and more
> In credence of reality as others
> Must know it...

and ends in private allusions, the relevance of which we have to assume. Here on page 8 we are a little doubtful, but by the time we have reached page 89 (the last), we will have become so convinced of the poet's integrity and keenness of scent that we accept with delight the relevance of whatever she is prepared to vouch for.

Even the unexplained references in the most obscure of her poems—"Our Working Day be Menaced" or the ambitious "Agnes Cleves Papers"—serve the purpose of affirming a dignity and revealing a method:

> The shaft of vision falling on obscurity
> Illumines nothing, yet discovers
> The ways of the obscure. . . .

To sum it all up very briefly: rarely has a poet so compactly and richly identified sensation and thought. If there really *has* been a dissociation of sensibility, here we return magnificently to the old unity, and join with her among the guests at Bemerton who "Did sit and eat."

*from* Canadian Literature, *No. 50*

Of the Canadian poets who led the second wave of modernism in the forties and fifties, P. K. Page holds a curious and somewhat anomalous position; she has certainly not received the critical attention that the remarkable fusion of psychological insight and poetic imagination which characterizes and individualizes her poems would lead one to expect. Perhaps the effort to discriminate between the subjective and objective elements in her work, or between image and symbol or memory and desire, has been thought by the critics too unprofitable or found too fatiguing. There is no doubt that she is a difficult poet—at least I have found her so—and the difficulty is not intellectual. Her moons are not reason's, so that what the reader who is to get the maximum enjoyment needs—or the critic who is to get the maximum comprehension—is a sensibility and an intuition that have to be nourished and educated by the poems themselves as he reads and re-reads them. Though I feel a certain presumption in approaching this subject, I can say that I have found the experience of trying to come to terms with it an absorbing one. Her gardens may be imaginary, but more than the toads in them are real; and are not her angels also?

Of course the fact that P. K. Page has not received the attention that has been given to some other poets of her generation can be partly accounted for more charitably and more prosaically. Her output has not been large. She published only three volumes of verse at rather long intervals—*As Ten, As Twenty* (1946), *The Metal and the Flower* (1954)—which won the Governor-General's Award—and a retrospective selection, *Cry Ararat!* (1967), which contained seventeen new poems. For some ten years of the fifties and the early sixties she was out of Canada with her husband, who was in the Canadian diplomatic service in Australia, Brazil and Mexico, and for much of this time she gave up writing (or publishing) poetry for painting. "Gave up," of course, is not really true; her painting and her poetry complemented one another; each, I think, made the other better, or made it more deeply what it was, which is much the same thing. And then the immersion in the language, landscape and mythology of the strange, intense, and perhaps intensely un-Canadian places had a stimulating and enriching influence on all her latest poems. One does not have to rely on the evidence of the poems alone to cor-roborate these remarks—though that would be ample. In the tenth anniver-sary issue of *Canadian Literature,* she wrote her own account of her experi-ences during the years of fruitful "exile," and in another article, "Traveller, Conjuror, Journeyman" in *Canadian Literature* 46, she gave an account of her philosophy of composition and of the part played by memory, dream, sensation and technique in both her poetry and her painting. These essays and her recent poems will mark, I believe, the beginning of a new, far juster and far higher estimate of her standing among our poets.

The comparative lack of attention given to P. K. Page's early work, pub-lished in the little magazines of the thirties and early forties when she was an active member of the *Preview* group in Montreal, is due partly no doubt to the fact that they were overshadowed by the flashy political poems of Patrick Anderson and the simpler satirical or amatory verses of Frank Scott. Even when she was most herself she was associated in the mind of a critic as alert as Milton Wilson with Anderson as a writer of "decadent pastorals . . . whose glass-tight but vulnerable aquarium leaves me gasping for air."[1] This did not prevent Professor Wilson from giving us some just, discerning, and generous analyses of one or two of the most striking of the early poems.

No critic or literary historian, however, has made any serious attempt to deal at length with Miss Page's poetry or to define, illustrate, and evaluate her psychological symbolism and her strongly personal treatment of the univer-sal themes of isolation and frustration—much less point to their trans-figuration in certain epiphanies at the close of some of her most remarkable poems. This, for want of a better workman, I shall try to do.

I begin with a few generalizations and then shall turn immediately to a close reading of some of her finest and most characteristic poems. This will perhaps enable us to isolate the special quality of her excellence and help place her in the developing pattern of modern poetry in Canada.

There are certain themes that occur over and over again in her poetry and a number of archetypal images and symbols that leave their impress on most of the best poems in each of her three books, and on her work as a whole.

Her subjects are:

Childhood, its innocent eye, its clarity of vision, and its imaginative rich-

---

[1] *"Other Canadians* and After," in *Masks of Poetry,* ed. A. J. M. Smith (Toronto: McClelland & Stewart, 1962), p. 126.

ness of invention, all leading to the discovery of a new and other reality than that of adulthood and reason;

Love, either faithful, happy and unifying, or faithless, disillusioned and lonely—the end-point of self-regarding love—that must be mastered by a conscious effort of the will;

and lastly, Dream, where child, poet, artist and wit live and have their being in what in some poems is a garden of innocence, Eden before the Fall, and in others a briary wilderness or a sinister painted arras.

Her images and symbols are white and green, images of snow, winter, ice and glass; or of flowers, gardens, leaves and trees; or else glass again, and salt, the transparent green suffocating crystal sea. Her symbolic world seems mostly mineral or vegetable, but there are symbols also of birds—the swan and the peacock especially—and fish. And there are breathing human creatures also: girls, adolescents, lovers, and some selfish, isolated, lonely men. But what most vividly lives and breathes here is the eye, the lung, the heart, and the feeling and perceiving mind.

What is most strange and most revealing in this world is that the workings of the mind are almost unconscious, often as in dreams, and that even the wit is controlled from elsewhere. Hers is in its final effect a poetry of vision, and it demands a quality of sympathy in the reader that its poetic richness helps to create. Indeed, to speak for myself, it casts a spell that has made it possible to value it not as vision only but as revelation.

I would like then, from the point of view of theme and imagery to discuss, analyse, or perhaps just talk about some of the poems that have impressed me most deeply. A rough classification might go something like this:

Poems in which images of winter predominate, where white is the colour, and ice, snow, glass, and a breathless cold make the mind and senses tingle—among these are "Stories of Snow," "Photos of a Salt Mine," "The Snowman," "Now This Cold Man," and many lines or stanzas of other poems, such as the last few disillusioned or awakening lines of "Images of Angels."

Poems of flowers and gardens, where vegetable dominates mineral, and green is the primal symbol; many of these are dream gardens, and there are two opposed or contrasting gardens, gardens of innocence and grace, and gardens of imprisonment or exile, or perhaps they are one garden, before and after the fall. Until its close "Images of Angels" is of this group; so in part is "Stories of Snow." In this group also are many of the poems that deal with childhood and some of the newer poems such as "After the Rain," "Giovanni and the Indians," and "The Apple," which is followed by its sad and desolate retrospective sequel, "To a Portrait in a Gallery." The garden songs of innocence give way to songs of experience, and here are the most intense and powerful of all the poems. Close to these in theme is "The Metal and the Flower," though perhaps the antidote for the poison it contains is found in the much later "This Frieze of Birds."

Along with the poems centred on snow and ice, or green gardens of pleasure or terror—not too strong a word for "Arras" or "Nightmare"—are those where image and symbol are derived from the sea—the sea of poet and psychologist, where sleep is a drowning and the submarine world is the world of the unconscious. Among the most striking of these are "Element," "Portrait of Marina," "Boy with a Sea Dream," and "In a Ship Recently Raised from the Sea."

Other classifications might list poems under such heads as childhood, love, self-love and dream; but in all of them the same dichotomy of innocence and experience, happiness and despair, or good and evil could be discovered. Classification carried too far defeats its own end; it is time for a close reading of some of the poems I have named.

"Stories of Snow" grows out of memories, reveries, and dreams of childhood—"some never-nether land"—where snowstorms are held "circular, complete" in the crystal globes kept in a high tall teakwood cabinet. Encapsulated here are evocations of innocence and perfection opening "behind the sprouting eyes" caught in the "vegetable rain." The conciseness and allusive richness of the language and imagery of the brief opening stanza set the tone at once and imply as a leading theme the contrast between childhood's innocence (or ignorance?) and the safe and changeless purity of the sterile snowflakes imprisoned or preserved in the small glass globe where the child (or poet) may shake up a storm. The major contrast in the poem, however, is that between the white world of innocence and art and the lush tropical landscape of "countries where the leaves are large as hands/where flowers protrude their fleshy chins/and call their colours," which stands for the natural world of instinct and appearance, of uncontrollable organic growth, that strangles and betrays but which child and poet, or poet as child, can escape from into what the couplet that ends the poem names "the area behind the eyes/where silent, unrefractive whiteness lies."

This somewhat esoteric ending is led up to through a series of anecdotal pictures that seem like a multiplication of the famous ice-locked swan of Mallarmé—but with a richness and dramatic variety that needs more room than the sonnet can offer.

The illustrative central part of the poem begins with the lines "And in the early morning one will waken/to think the glowing linen of his pillow/a northern drift, will find himself mistaken/and lie back weeping." The dreams of this wakened sleeper in a land of fleshy flowers proliferate out of the opening stanza, become the whole poem, and lead to its climax. In Holland, in winter—we realize now that the "never-nether land" of the opening was the embryo of a pun—hunters, their breath in plumes, "part the flakes" and sail in their white winged iceboats over the frozen lakes to hunt the swan. All the images here are of whiteness and no-colour, of snowflakes and ice, and we see that the innocent world of the child's glass globe has taken on a new, beautiful but sinister significance.

> And of the swan in death these dreamers tell
> of its last flight and how it falls, a plummet,
> pierced by the freezing bullet
> and how three feathers, loosened by the shot,
> descend like snow upon it.
> While hunters plunge their fingers in its down
> deep as a drift, and dive their hands
> up to the neck of the wrist
> in that warm metamorphosis of snow
> as gentle as the sort that woodsmen know
> who, lost in the white circle, fall at last
> and dream their way to death.

"Stories of Snow" is the outstanding success of P. K. Page's first volume, comparable in magnificence and complexity to "Images of Angels" in her second. These are perhaps the finest of the many very individual poems that seem to grow like beautiful flowers out of childhood memories, recurring dreams, and a crystal clairvoyance. Innocence and experience, illusion and disillusionment, find expression in an overflowing of powerful emotion, remembered not in tranquillity but with a craftsmanly excitement and an exquisite shiver that sets the rhythmical pattern of all her most moving poems.

"Images of Angels," like "Stories of Snow," "Photos of a Salt Mine," and some of the newer poems, "After Rain" and the finest of all, "Cry Ararat!," is a kind of sentimental education—*sentimental* not in any pejorative or ironic Flaubertian sense—that, recognizing worlds without love, seeks to explore ways of transforming them or coming to terms with them. Here images of ice and snow give way at the beginning to the daisy fields of childhood. This is the sharpening contrast to the close of "The Snowman," the poem immediately preceding "Images of Angels" in the inclusive volume of 1967. Here are the concluding lines of "The Snowman":

> And as far as I could see the snow was scarred
> only with angels' wing marks or the feet of birds
> like twigs broken upon the snow or shards
>
> discarded. And I could hear no sound
> as far as I could hear except a round
> kind of an echo without end

rung like a hoop below them and above
jarring the air they had no need of
in a landscape without love.

And here is the beginning of "Images of Angels":

Imagine them as they were first conceived:
part musical instrument and part daisy
in a white manshape.
Imagine a crowd on the Elysian grass
playing ring-around-a-rosy,
mute except for their singing,
their gold smiles
gold sickle moons in the white sky of their faces.
Sex, neither male nor female,
name and race, in each case, simply angel.

This gives us the traditional, almost Sunday school picture of the angel, innocent, whimsical, happy, but it is done with the wit and knowledge of the mature and *critical* grown-up poet. The angels are white, and gold, and holy; but they are to be pitied—they were made (by whom?) "never to be loved or petted, never to be friended." Almost at once a sinister note intrudes. Somehow the angels are realized now to be "mixed with the father, fearful and fully/ . . . when the vanishing bed/floats in the darkness. . . ."

In the body of the poem we have three witty and dramatic characterizations—representative figures who might be thought of as imagining angels: the "little notary," the financier or businessman, and "the anthropologist, with his tidy science."

For each the angel is a special symbol. For the little notary—the scene is surely Quebec—"given one as a pet," it is his private guilt, and might, if discovered, be his private shame, and he keeps it "behind the lethal lock/used for his legal documents," guiltily shut up. Reading this today one thinks of the legal and political repression of the Duplessis days before the Quiet Revolution, an allusion impossible to have been in the author's mind when the poem was written in the early fifties. This is an illustration, I think, of the growth into an even wider significance that some poems undergo with time.[2]

The eleven-line stanza devoted to the businessman is lighter in tone than the rest and more frankly witty; could this be the reason it has been omitted from the reprinted version?[3] "Angels are dropping, angels going up."

---

[2]Poems by Shelley, Auden, Anne Hébert and Frank Scott might be cited in further illustration.
[3]The stanza on the businessman has been deleted from the poem as it appears in *Cry Ararat!* (1967). I enjoyed the passage and cannot feel that it is out of keeping with the rest of the poem.

What business man would buy as he buys stock
as many as could cluster on a pin?

But the stanza ends by humanizing the businessman by filling his heart with uneasiness and shame as he remembers childhood tying a tinsel angel to his children's Christmas tree, and the poem returns for a moment to the world of such innocent poems as "Christmas Tree—Market Square."

For the anthropologist, the angel is the miraculous transcendence and perhaps the condemnation to futility of all his classifiable observations. Where in the writings of philosphers or poets has the triumph of imagination over reason been more brilliantly and wittily put than here?

The anthropologist with his tidy science
had he stumbled on one unawares,
found as he finds an arrowhead, an angel—
a what-of-a-thing
as primitive as a daisy,
might with his cold eye have assessed it coolly.
But how, despite his detailed observations,
could he face his learned society and explain?
"Gentlemen, it is thought that they are born
with harps and haloes,
as the unicorn with its horn.
Study discloses them white and gold as daisies . . .

as they were described, indeed, at the beginning of the poem. This is the tone and language of light verse and intellectual prose, but the poetry rises out of the thought as naturally and inevitably as in Marvell. The union of the homely and the profound is so quietly accomplished that hasty readers may never notice it. Somewhat in this vein the poem ventures other perceptions: "Perhaps only a dog could accept them wholly/be happy to follow at their heels . . ." and again, "Or, take the nudes of Lawrence and impose/a-sexuality upon them; those/could meet with ease these gilded albinos."

The next and penultimate stanza returns to the child's world and the child's faith of the beginning, where the sphere of consciousness and imagination is reduced to something as small and self-contained as the glass globe of "Stories of Snow." This prepares us for the close of the poem—unexpected and very strange: the summer imagery of daisies, sun-dazzle, and lamb-white gives way to the white of cold and snow. The child, "*this* innocent," (the poet herself) "with his almost unicorn" (his imaginary angel, the poem up to this point) "would let it go . . ."

and feeling implicated in a lie,
his flesh would grow
cold
and snow
would cover the warm and sunny avenue.

Does this ending repudiate imagination, faith and the fairytale world of childhood so convincingly recreated not only in this poem but in many others such as the beautiful "Christmas Eve—Market Square" and the pieces gathered in the last book under the title of one of them, "The Bands and the Beautiful Children"? I do not think so. These closing lines are an affirmation of sincerity and of an integrity that is moral as well as aesthetic—a look at the worst as the images in so many poems of flowers and sun and summer are an attempt to find the best.

Before attempting an analysis of "Arras," which I think is the finest, if among the most difficult of the poems, let me jot down a few notes on others in which imagery and symbol are drawn from the sea and from salt or metal. In some the sea is clearly, like sleep, a symbol of the unconscious and, indeed, for the sensitive and perhaps easily hurt spirit of the poet, a dark place of refuge. This is the theme of one of the shortest but most explicit, the beautiful and touching "Element": "caught and swung on a line under the sun/I am frightened held in the light that people make/and sink in darkness freed and whole again/as fish returned by dream into the stream." Although the key statement is the line "I am not wishful in this dream of immersion," the poem ends with the agonizing image of "gull on fire or fish/silently hurt—its mouth alive with metal."

Much more objective and therefore free to be more witty, but inevitably less intense is "Boy with a Sea Dream." Here are images of masts of ships, ancient hulls, and keels rusting in the iodine air—a dream of immersion again "where like a sleep/strange men drown drowsily/spiralling down the sea's steep underlip. . . ." Once again the sea is a symbol of dream as the cinema of the unconscious, but without any of the jargon of the clinical psychologist. For the critic, who like the poet ought to have a poetry-crammed head, the associations are with the music and imagery of "Lycidas," "Full Fathom Five," and the "Voyages" of Hart Crane.

The end is strange and subtle, a sort of inside-outside reversal recalling, distantly, of course, some passages in Jay Macpherson and Robert Graves.

. . . like the perfect schooner which is pushed
through the slim neck to fill a bottle's shape

> his dream has filled the cavern of his head
> and he, a brimful seascape,
> a blue brine,
> with undertows and sudden swells
> which toll his bells
> and watery laws to be obeyed
> and strange salt death to die. . . .

Images of sterile salt and metallic cold are found in a number of poems that analyse self-love with what can only be described as a kind of cold fury. Among these are "Isolationist," "Only Child," "Foreigner," "Man with One Small Hand," "Mineral" and "This Cold Man." The last three are particularly impressive for the concentrated angry wit that turns experience into a new universal and instant myth.

A striking quality of many of these poems is the sudden immediacy of perception and emotion.

> Look, look, he took me straight
> to the snake's eye . . .

begins "The Apple"—a magnificent opening, equalled only perhaps by Anne Hébert's awakening in "La Chambre fermée":

> Qui donc m'a conduite ici?
> Il y a certainement quelqu'un
> Qui a soufflé sur mes pas. . . .

It is these quick exclamations of bewilderment, horror or agony that give so much of its intensity to the haunted dream garden of "Arras." Here the perfection and purity of the classical Eden has been violated by a strange and somehow sinister intruder:

> . . . a peacock rattling its rattan tail
>             and screaming
> has found a point of entry. Through whose eye
> did it insinuate in furled disguise . . .?

The agonizing questions come thick and fast: "Who am I or who am I become that walking here/I am observer, other. . .?" "What did they deal me in this pack?" Alice's looking-glass garden has grown menacing and lonely. "I want a hand to clutch, a heart to crack . . . the stillness is/infinite. If I should make a break. . . ." Then the truly terrifying line:

> The stillness points a bone at me.

And now the prisoned dreamer breaks under the reiteration of the self-imposed questioning:

> I confess:
> It was my eye.
> Voluptuous it came.
> Its head the ferrule and its lovely tail
> folded so sweetly: it was strangely slim
> to fit the retina. . . .

This fearful magnificence gives way to a simple homely cry, which in its context has a grandeur beyond the reach of rhetoric—"Does no one care?"

This poem alone would be sufficient to place P. K. Page among the fine poets of this century, and it is good to know that while it is perhaps the high point of her achievement it is also the high point of a school of symbolist Canadian poets among whom I would name Anne Wilkinson, Anne Hébert, Jay Macpherson, Daryl Hine and Gwen MacEwen. These are the poets in Canada who write not for the immediate moment alone. They are the poets who will live when the urbanized hitch-hiking social realists or the lung-born egoists of instant experience have been long forgotten.

After Confederation

*from* Canadian Literature, *No. 38*

When we turn from the poetry of the generations just before and just after Confederation to that of the present or the near-present, we find that there is the same distinction to be drawn between the explicit and somewhat journalistic *verse* that states or discusses in explicit terms the problems which face the people living north of the United States border, and the *poetry,* which expresses, indirectly and implicitly, the *spiritual reality* which makes a nation.

To speak first of what I call the explicit verse, a very sharp difference will be observed at once. The poets of the earlier time wrote, as Lighthall pointed out, cheerfully, hopefully, eagerly. They were expressing a faith—not necessarily a very informed one, but natural and very tenaciously held, something akin to what passes for conviction and opinion in the mind of the mythical man-in-the-street and is the basis upon which democratic elections are lost or won—a faith in the common interests and common heritage of all Canadians or, at least (and this cannot be left unremarked today), of all English-speaking Canadians. Sangster, Mair, Roberts all testified to this in their patriotic and political verse. The verse of the modern poet, on the other hand, tends to be critical and satiric. It is the flaws, shortcomings, and failures that the poet now sees looming large, while the ideal and the hope somehow fails to move him deeply enough for him to make poetry out of it.

One of the most explicit of the attempts made by a modern poet to come to terms with the problem of what it means to be Canadian was made—ironically enough, perhaps—by a young English writer, Patrick Anderson, who lived in Montreal in the late thirties and the early forties, became a Canadian citizen, and edited an influential little poetry magazine called *Preview,* along with F. R. Scott, P. K. Page, and others. Anderson was a fellow-traveller, if not actually a Communist, and his view of Canadian history and the future of Canada was an orthodox Marxist one: "And the land was. And the people did not take it." But in a section of the poem called "Cold Colloquy," Anderson presented us with one of the first and one of the wittiest expressions in contemporary verse of our self-conscious and confused hestitation to enter into what the poet (in this case, at least) seems to believe is a great and manifest destiny.

In the poem the spirit of Canada speaks. It is in reply to "their" question—not "my" question or "our" question I must not fail to notice:

> What are you . . .? they ask, their
>     mouths full of gum,
> their eyes full of the worst silence of the
>     worst winter in a hundred years.
> And she replies: I am the wind that wants a flag.

[That want at least has been supplied.]

> I am the mirror of your picture
> until you make me the marvel of your life.
> Yes, I am one and none, pin and pine
>     snow and slow,
> America's attic, an empty room,
> a something possible, a chance, a dance
> that is not danced. A cold kingdom.

> Are you a dominion of them? they ask, scurrying . . .

> Most loyal and empirical, she says, in ice ironic. . . .

And so the poem goes on, purring in puns and definitions. After "What are you?" the question is, "What is the matter then?" And the answer is, "The matter is the promise that was never taken." Inevitably there comes another question:

> What shall we do then . . .? they ask, English
>     and French, Ukrainians, Poles, Finns . . .

and the poet answers—and now at the end the writer ceases to be a satirist, a writer of clever verse, and becomes a patriot and an idealist—like Sangster or Roberts. Though with this difference. They thought the Fathers of Confederation were God. They uttered their *Fiat,* and lo! Canada was; the modern poet—if a poet writing in 1945 is modern—places the creation of a true Dominion still in the future. But he answers the question in spiritual and idealistic terms, not in terms of economics or sociology or the close-reasoned reports of royal commissions, but in poetic terms:

> Suffer no more the vowels of Canada
> to speak of miraculous things with a cleft palate. . . .

How apt, how true, and how contemporary this is, after more than twenty years. What a perfect illustration of Ezra Pound's definition of literature as "news that stays news!"

Two other distinguished contemporary Canadian poets have dealt with this theme, Earle Birney and Irving Layton, but in their treatment of it neither deviates very deeply into poetry. They have kept carefully on the surface of things, hewed to the line of satire, and steered religiously away from faith, hope, and patriotic enthusiasm. Birney is the wittier of the two and his destructive but very impressive analysis of our national weaknesses is salutary. It is found at its clearest in the poem called "Canada: Case History," written in 1945. The definitions are witty and deadly, and their truth will be recognized immediately by men of all parties.

> This is the case of a high-school land,
> deadset in adolescence,
> loud treble laughs and sudden fists,
> bright cheeks, the gangling presence.
> This boy is wonderful at sports
> and physically quite healthy;
> he's taken to church on Sunday still
> and keeps his prurience stealthy.
> He doesn't like books except about bears,
> collects new coins and model planes
> and never refuses a dare.
> His Uncle spoils him with candy, of course,
> yet shouts him down when he talks at table.
> You will note that he has got some of his French
>     mother's looks,
> though he's not so witty and no more stable.
> He's really much more like his father and yet
> if you say so he'll pull a great face.
> He wants to be different from everyone else
> and daydreams of winning the global race.
> Parents unmarried and living abroad,
> relatives keen to bag the estate,
> schizophrenia not excluded,
> will he learn to grow up before it's too late?

It's a good question, and we should thank the poet for asking it. I don't think we should expect him to answer it. It's for us to answer.

Let us consider now the Confederation ode in Irving Layton's collection, *Periods of the Moon*. This ode is not of course a patriotic encomium like the cheerful exhortations of Mair or Roberts. It is an angry and effectively coarse satire. And it is not really about Confederation; it is about something more important than Confederation; it is about the way Canadians today think and feel (or *don't* think and feel) about Canada and Confederation and the centennial—about what, in fact, is going to make Confederation a reality or a sham. It is a satire on the artificially inseminated enthusiasm that government agencies, civic agencies, business organizations, and ad-men are feverishly drumming-up and which the poet feels—not without a certain grim satisfaction—will be in vain.

It is easier, no doubt, to point out weaknesses and errors, and cry "stinking fish" than to suggest remedies, corrections, and reformations. That is the job for the historian, the political scientist, the economist, the statistician, the member of a royal commission. Perhaps the poet may cheer when the good work has been accomplished, but if in the meantime he makes use of "satire, invective and direspectful verse"—to steal a phrase from the title page of *The Blasted Pine*—to prick the bubble of our complacency and jolt us awake to a proper realization of our true position in relation to one another, to the United States, Great Britain, and the world at large, he will have performed an essential service.

What the poet as satirist and critic has been saying in verse, which when well written has the advantage of being concise and memorable, has been stated over and over again by our academic historians and political philosophers. Compare, for example, with the passage from Patrick Anderson's "Poem on Canada" I was quoting above, these sentences by Professor John Conway, writing in the *Atlantic Monthly* for November 1964:

> We Canadians have so far failed to enter fully into our legacy, and this is our one great, overreaching problem as our centennial approaches. On its solution everything else depends. We have failed to vest sovereignty where it properly belongs—in the Canadian people. Instead, we have allowed it to remain in the British monarchy, and in doing so we have divided our country and inhibited our emotional and creative development as a people.

It is significant perhaps that here too, in the essay of a professor of history writing exactly a hundred years later we have the same conviction as that which the Reverend Hartley Dewart expressed in his introduction to our first anthology—that creative maturity in poetry and the arts is the result of true nationhood. Professor Conway continues:

> When we take the long overdue step and transfer sovereignty to where it properly belongs, it will become clear that Canadians—British, French, and European alike—have been and are engaged in a common enterprise which is of far greater concern than the separate concerns of each group; and just as the United States has given classic expression in literature, philosophy, and political theory to its interpretation of the New World, so will we begin to give classic expression to ours.

One might pursue this subject farther and give illustrations of the instructive and often amusing parallels between the writings of historians or social critics and those of the poets, or at least of the satirists among them, and place beside the verses by Frank Scott entitled "W. L. M. K."—

> —He never let his on the one hand
> Know what his on the other hand was doing.

and

> Do nothing by halves
> Which can be done by quarters—

some sentences by Professor Underhill:

> His statesmanship has been a more subtly accurate, a more flexibly adjustable Gallup poll of Canadian public opinion than statisticians will ever be able to devise. He has been the representative Canadian, the essential Canadian, the ideal Canadian, the Canadian as he exists in the mind of God.

Here you will see the arts of verse and prose coming close together—prose as concise and pointed as verse, and verse as sensible as prose. But I must leave this tempting field to the graduate student of Canadian literature who wishes to find a subject for a dissertation that may prove both useful and entertaining. Instead, I will offer some general observations about the state of poetry and the status of poets here and now.

The situation today is immensely different, not only from a hundred years ago but from the time in the middle twenties when I, along with F. R. Scott,

Earle Birney, A. M. Klein, Eustace Ross, and Raymond Knister, began to write, I say "along with," but that's not quite accurate. I knew Scott and Klein, of course, but Ross and Knister and Birney were unknown to us. I followed avidly the European and American literary journals and little magazines—particularly the *Dial* in New York and *transition* and *This Quarter* in Paris. (In Canada there was only the *Canadian Forum*—and it had one fine feather in its cap: it had printed E. J. Pratt's "The Cachalot.") We were astonished and delighted to find in the pages of the avant-garde magazines writing by Canadians—Morley Callaghan's first stories and poems by Raymond Knister—and when some of my poems appeared in the *Dial* I found also those of another Canadian, W. W. E. Ross—hailed recently by Raymond Souster as "the first modern Canadian poet."

These were the first stirrings of the new poetry movement in Canada. But for the most part as the twenties came to a close the picture was still pretty dismal. The Maple Leaf school of patriotic nature poetry under the aegis of the Canadian Authors' Association and a group of genteel traditionalists among editors and publishers forced most of the new young poets to look outside Canada, knowing that acceptance by the *Dial* or *Poetry* (Chicago) or one of the Parisian experimental magazines meant that we had attained a higher standard of excellence than was demanded by any Canadian journal—always excepting the *Forum.*

The atmosphere indeed, when I began to write, is very well summed up and expressed in Frank Scott's now famous poem "The Canadian Authors Meet." It was not until 1936 that we were able to persuade a Toronto publisher to bring out a little group anthology called *New Provinces* containing work by the Montreal poets Scott, Klein, Kennedy, and myself and the Toronto poets Finch and Pratt—the latter only being well known. The book made no impact at all—except perhaps on other still younger poets—only eighty-six copies were sold, and the new poetry movement, which in Canada seemed to be limited to the books of E. J. Pratt, had to wait until the early forties to get under way. Then, with the criticism of W. E. Collin and E. K. Brown and the first books of Birney, Klein, Scott, myself, and a little later P. K. Page, Patrick Anderson, Raymond Souster, Dorothy Livesay, Louis Dudek, and . . . but the list grows too long, and has never ceased to grow.

Today, after the amazing acceleration, starting in the forties and continuing through the fifties and sixties with an ever-increasing ferment, Canadian poetry presents at first sight a bewildering spectacle of schools and individuals busily writing, gesticulating, reading, declaiming, quarrelling, praising, lecturing, teaching, applying for grants, appearing on television, grinding out little mags on mimeograph machines, and frequently producing new and genuine poetry.

At one time it seemed to me that Canadian poets could be roughly divided into two schools, the native and the cosmopolitan, and I think it was Northrop Frye who added the necessary corrective—that this dichotomy is not a matter of division between poets or groups of poets but a division within the mind of every poet. The division that exists today, however, between poets and groups of poets is between the traditional or academic, the cultivated poets, you might say, and the new primitives, whose tradition goes back no farther than to William Carlos Williams, Charles Olson, or his disciple Robert Creeley, and, in some cases, to Allen Ginsberg. This is an American school of (if I may be allowed a paradox) sophisticated primitives. They hail from San Francisco and Black Mountain College—Cid Corman's little magazine *Origins* was published at Black Mountain and rather surprisingly, among the Canadian writers it published were Morley Callaghan, Irving Layton and Margaret Avison. The chief influence of these western American experimentalists has been felt in Vancouver, in the little poetry magazine *Tish,* and in the verse of such poets as John Newlove, George Bowering, Lionel Kearns, and the younger writers featured in Raymond Souster's recent anthology *New Wave: Canada.*

In Canada, however, it is not groups or broad general divisions that stand out most clearly, but individuals—men of vigorous personality, who go striding up and down the land (aided and abetted by the Canada Council, the CBC, and the universities) speaking their poetry and standing up for the poetic way of life, as opposed to the life of unimaginative acceptance in the mechanized world of ad-men, mass communications, and pollster politics, It is their immersion in this world they never made and do not like that makes so many of our poets—Earl Birney, Frank Scott, Irving Layton, Leonard Cohen—satirists and ironic comedians in a surprisingly large proportion of their work and forces some of the younger poets into abstract expressionism, black humour, and the cultivation of pop art as a revolt against the conformist art of the establishment.

Of recent years also some of our poets have realized that to be Canadian is not enough, just as to be British or American is not enough. In the thirty years that include what happened at Guernica, Belsen, Dresden, and Hiroshima, events of such stupefying horror occurred—and are still occurring in Vietnam—that the poet is forced to realize that his responsibility rests with all mankind and that he shares the guilt of all mankind. Something of this is felt in the poems of India and the Far East of Scott and Birney, of South America and Mexico by Birney and Louis Dudek, and in the poems of Germany and Spain by Irving Layton.

In the prefaces to several of his latest books, Layton has presented the conception of the universal moral responsibility of the poet with vigour and clarity; and while the presentation is sometimes marred by an accretion of personal "soundings-off," these do not invalidate the truth and passion of the poet's main message. "Today, poets must teach themselves to imagine the worst. . . . If the poet is to win back the praise he once enjoyed as the supreme 'interpreter of the age' he must learn again to address himself to the moral and psychological dilemmas of his time. Though satisfying verbally and technically mere blabbermouthing is out. . . ."

If this should mean discarding about sixty percent of Layton's own poetry, the rest would be the stronger for it. And I take it as a sign of continuous development that this element of responsibility, strength and sincerity has been increasing in proportion with every volume he has written in this decade.

As I close, I would like to set beside the prefaces of Irving Layton the preface written in 1941 by a young Canadian named Bertram Warr[1] to a small pamphlet of his poems published by Robert Graves. Warr was a pacifist, who had tried to enlist in the Red Cross but was drafted into the Royal Air Force and killed in action over Germany 3 April 1943.

> Ours is an age of renunciation. It is an age of probing and reflection, of scrutiny of tradition and dogma in the hard light of reason. And with each abandonment of the outworn things that for so long had meant security to us, we grow just a little more tight-lipped. We feel the new hardness of scepticism, and as tie after tie is cut, in manners, religion, science, the whole field of contact between man and man, there comes over us the lassitude of disillusionment. . . . We are not yet ready for this new world that has grown up from the second decade of the century. Successive shocks have proved too much for us and we have been driven into retreat, still clinging to the shreds of old things, and too untried to step forward and gaze upon the new in their true light. We have gone backward to lick our wounds and debate, somewhat morbidly, whether to carry on the fight, or to renounce with all the rest, those other bases of our being, Beauty and Love and the Search for Truth.

Many of the most serious of our younger poets have, perhaps, gone backward to lick their wounds, but one thing is clear, even in the most far-out of the beat poets, that the search is still, if sometimes in the most unexpected places, for beauty, love, and truth. The contemporaries and compatriots of the Canadian poet today may not be any longer Yeats or Eliot but rather Lorca and Brecht, Pablo Neruda, René Char, William Carlos Williams, and Mayakovsky, and the art that he must aim at is neither native nor cosmopolitan but universal.

---

[1]Some poems by Bertram Warr will be found in *The Book of Canadian Poetry* (1957) and *The Oxford Book of Canadian Verse* (1960).

# PART FIVE

## Some Polemics: Early and Late

*Wanted — Canadian Criticism*

*from* The Canadian Forum

One looks in vain through Canadian books and journals for that critical enquiry into first principles which directs a new literature as tradition guides an old one. Hasty adulation mingles with unintelligent condemnation to make our book reviewing an amusing art: but of criticism as it might be useful there is nothing. That this should be so at a time when we are becoming increasingly "Canada-conscious" may seem strange, but the strangeness disappears when we examine the nature of the consciousness in question. This, judging from its most characteristic forms of expression, is a mixture of blind optimism and materialistic patriotism, a kind of my-mother-drunk-or-sober complex that operates most efficiently in the world of affairs and finds its ideal action summarized in the slogan "Buy Made in Canada Goods." There is, perhaps, something to be said for this state of mind if cultivated within certain very definite limits, if it be regarded solely as a business proposition and with due regard for economic laws; but when duty and morality are brought in and the above mercantile maxim is held to apply to things of the mind and spirit: that is an altogether different matter.

The confusion is one between commerce and art, an error which a society such as ours has some difficulty in escaping. A small population engaged in subduing its environment and in exploiting the resources of a large new country may very easily develop an exaggerated opinion of the value of material things, and has some quite understandable doubts as to the necessity of artists. Indeed, most of our people are so actively engaged in tilling the soil or scrambling to the top of the tree in the industrial and commercial world that they have neither the time nor the inclination for reading poetry on the back porch—unless it be inspiration stuff or he-man Canadiana. The result is good for business but bad for poetry, and if you happen to think that poetry is the more important you are tempted to ask what is to be done about it.

To the serious Canadian writer this is a vital question, for to him the confusion between commerce and art presents itself in the light of a temptation to effect a compromise. If he chooses to work out his own salvation along lines which cannot be in keeping with the prevailing spirit of pep and optimism he finds himself without an audience, or at least without an audience that will support him. The one Canadian magazine, it must be noted, for which such an artist would care to write is at present unable to pay contributors, while poor imitations of the *Saturday Evening Post* are ready to pay him handsomely if he will cease to be an artist and become a merchant. This is the temptation with which the devil has assailed the Canadian Authors' Association, and the whole communion has succumbed in a body. There would be little harm in this if everyone knew the nature of the compromise that has been made, if, for instance, the Canadian Authors had the honesty to change the name of their society to the Journalists' Branch of the Canadian Manufacturers' Association and to quit kidding the public every Christmas that it (the public) has a moral obligation to buy poor Canadian, rather than good foreign books.

So far, it is true, literature as an art has fought a losing battle with commerce, but the campaign as a whole has barely begun. Reinforcements are on the way. Young writers like Morley Callaghan and Raymond Knister have contributed realistic stories of Canadian life to foreign radical journals. Mazo de la Roche, having won an important literary prize in the United States, has a firmly established reputation in her native land. E. J. Pratt and Edward Sapir are demonstrating that Canadian themes are improved by modern treatment. All these examples are definite, if modest, successes, but reverses are encountered too. A good poet such as Wilson Macdonald is praised for the wrong things, and seems likely to succumb to the blandishments of an unfortunate popularity, the sort of popularity that appears to be at the command of any poet who hammers a vigorous rhythm out of an abundant assortment of French and Indian place-names. If you write, apparently, of the far north and the wild west and the picturesque east, seasoning well with allusions to the Canada goose, fir trees, maple leaves, snowshoes, northern lights, etc., the public grasp the fact that you are a Canadian poet, whose works are to be bought from the same patriotic motive that prompts the purchaser of Eddy's matches or a Massey-Harris farm implement and read along with Ralph Connor and Eaton's catalogue.

The picture, on the whole, is one of extreme confusion. There are little skirmishes, heroic single stands, but no concerted action. Without a body of critical opinion to hearten and direct them, Canadian writers are like a leaderless army. They find themselves in an atmosphere of materialism that is only too ready to seduce them from their allegiance to art and with an audience that only wishes to be flattered. It looks as though they will have to give up the attempt to create until they have formulated a critical system and secured its universal acceptance.

What are the tasks that await such a criticism?

First and foremost, as a sort of preliminary spadework, the Canadian writer must put up a fight for freedom in the choice and treatment of his subject. Nowhere is puritanism more disastrously prohibitive than among us, and it seems, indeed, that desperate methods and dangerous remedies must be resorted to, that our condition will not improve until we have been thoroughly shocked by the appearance in our midst of a work of art that is at once successful and obscene. Of realism we are afraid—apparently because there is an impression that it wishes to discredit the picture of our great dominion as a country where all the women are chaste and the men too pure to touch them if they weren't. Irony is not understood. Cynicism is felt to be disrespectful, unmanly. The idea that any subject whatever is susceptible of artistic treatment and that praise or blame is to be conferred after a consideration, not of its moral, but of its aesthetic harmony is a proposition that will take years to knock into the heads of our people. But the work must be done. The critic-militant is required for this, not a very engaging fellow, perhaps, but a hard worker, a crusader, and useful withal.

It is the critic-contemplative, however, the philosophical critic, who will have the really interesting work. It will be the object of such an enquirer to examine the fundamental position of the artist in a new community. He will have to answer questions that in older countries have obvious answers, or do not arise. He will follow the lead of French and English critics in seeking to define the relation of criticism and poetry to the psychological and mathematical sciences and will be expected to have something of value to say as to the influence upon the Canadian writer of his position in space and time. That this influence, which might even become mutual, be positive and definite seems desirable and obvious: that it should not be self-conscious seems to me desirable, but not to many people obvious. Canadian poetry, to take a typical example, is altogether too self-conscious of its environment, of its position in space, and scarcely conscious at all of its position in time. This is an evident defect, but it has been the occasion of almost no critical comment. Yet to be aware of our temporal setting as well as of our environment, and in no obvious and shallow way, is the nearest we can come to being traditional. To be unconscious or overconscious—that is to be merely conventional, and it is in one of these two ways that our literature today fails as an adequate and artistic expression of our national life. The heart is willing, but the head is weak. Modernity and tradition alike demand that the contemporary artist who survives adolescence shall be an intellectual. Sensibility is no longer enough, intelligence is also required. Even in Canada.

*A Rejected Preface to* New Provinces, *1936*[1]

*from* Canadian Literature, *No. 24*

The bulk of Canadian verse is romantic in conception and conventional in form. Its two great themes are nature and love—nature humanized, endowed with feeling, and made sentimental; love idealized, sanctified, and inflated. Its characteristic type is the lyric. Its rythms are definite, mechanically correct, and obvious; its rhymes are commonplace.

The exigencies of rhyme and rhythm are allowed to determine the choice of a word so often that a sensible reader is compelled to conclude that the plain sense of the matter is of only minor importance. It is the arbitrarily chosen verse pattern that counts. One has the uncomfortable feeling in reading such an anthology as W. W. Campbell's *The Oxford Book of Canadian Verse* or J. W. Garvin's *Canadian Poets* that the writers included are not interested in saying anything in particular; they merely wish to show that they are capable of turning out a number of regular stanzas in which statements are made about the writer's emotions, say "In Winter," or "At Montmorenci Falls," or "In A Birch Bark Canoe." Other exercises are concerned with pine trees, the open road, God, snowshoes or Pan. The most popular experience is to be pained, hurt, stabbed or seared by beauty—preferably by the yellow flame of a crocus in the spring or the red flame of a maple leaf in autumn.

There would be less objection to these poems if the observation were accurate and its expression vivid, or if we could feel that the emotion was a genuine and intense one. We could then go on to ask if it were a valuable one. But, with a negligible number of exceptions, the observation is general in these poems and the descriptions are vague. The poet's emotions are

---

[1] *In 1936 appeared the historic anthology,* New Provinces, *which has always been regarded as one of the most important events in the history of English-Canadian poetry. A. J. M. Smith was one of the six contributors, together with Finch, Klein, Kennedy, Pratt and Scott. Smith wrote the original preface to* New Provinces. *E. J. Pratt objected to its contents and it was withdrawn in favour of a preface written by F. R. Scott. Now, almost thirty years later, we print that original preface for the first time.*—G. Woodcock.

unbounded, and are consequently lacking in the intensity which results from discipline and compression; his thinking is of a transcendental or theosophical sort that has to be taken on faith. The fundamental criticism that must be brought against Canadian poetry as a whole is that it ignores the intelligence. And as a result it is dead.

Our grievance, however, against the great dead body of poetry laid out in the mortuary of the *Oxford Book* or interred under Garvin's florid epitaphs is not so much that it is dead but that its sponsors in Canada pretend that it is alive. Yet it should be obvious to any person of taste that this poetry cannot now, and in most cases never could, give the impression of being vitally concerned with real experience. The Canadian poet, if this kind of thing truly represents his feelings and his thoughts, is a half-baked, hyper-sensitive, poorly adjusted, and frequently neurotic individual that no one in his senses would trust to drive a car or light a furnace. He is the victim of his feelings and fancies, or of what he fancies his feelings ought to be, and his emotional aberrations are out of all proportion to the experience that brings them into being. He has a soft heart and a soft soul; and a soft head. No wonder nobody respects him, and few show even the most casual interest in his poetry. A few patriotic professors, one or two hack journalist critics, and a handful of earnest anthologists—these have tried to put the idea across that there exists a healthy national Canadian poetry which expresses the vigorous hope of this young Dominion in a characteristically Canadian style, but the idea is so demonstrably false that no one but the interested parties has been taken in.

We do not pretend that this volume contains any verse that might not have been written in the United States or in Great Britain. There is certainly nothing specially Canadian about more than one or two poems. Why should there be? Poetry today is written for the most part by people whose emotional and intellectual heritage is not a national one; it is either cosmopolitan or provincial, and for good or evil, the forces of civilization are rapidly making the latter scarce.

A large number of the verses in this book were written at a time when the contributors were inclined to dwell too exclusively on the fact that the chief thing wrong with Canadian poetry was its conventional and insensitive technique. Consequently, we sometimes thought we had produced a good poem when all we had done in reality was not produce a conventional one. In Canada this is a deed of some merit.

In attempting to get rid of the facile word, the stereotyped phrase and the mechanical rhythm, and in seeking, as the poet today must, to combine colloquialism and rhetoric, we were of course only following in the path of the more significant poets in England and the United States. And it led, for a time, to the creation of what, for the sake of brevity, I will call "pure poetry."

A theory of pure poetry might be constructed on the assumption that a poem exists as a thing in itself. It is not a copy of anything or an expression of anything, but is an individuality as unique as a flower, an elephant or a man on a flying trapeze. Archibald MacLeish expressed the idea in *Ars Poetica* when he wrote,

> A poem should not mean, but be.

Such poetry is objective, impersonal, and in a sense timeless and absolute. It stands by itself, unconcerned with anything save its own existence.

Not unconnected with the disinterested motives that produce pure poetry are those which give rise to imagist poetry. The imagist seeks with perfect objectivity and impersonality to re-create a thing or arrest an experience as precisely and vividly and simply as possible. Kennedy's "Shore," Scott's "trees in ice," my own "Creek" are examples of the simpler kind of imagist verse; Finch's "Teacher," tiny as it is, of the more complex. In "Shore" and "Creek" the reader may notice that the development of the poem depends upon metrical devices as much as on images; the music is harsh and the rhythm difficult.

Most of the verses in this book are not, however, so unconcerned with thought as those mentioned. In poems like "Epithalamium," "the Five Kine," "Words for a Resurrection" and "Like An Old Proud King" an attempt has been made to fuse thought and feeling. Such a fusion is characteristic of the kind of poetry usually called metaphysical. Good metaphysical verse is not, it must be understood, concerned with the communication of ideas. It is far removed from didactic poetry. What it is concerned with is the emotional effect of ideas that have entered so deeply into the blood as never to be questioned. Such poetry is primarily lyrical; it should seem spontaneous. Something of the quality I am suggesting is to be found in such lines as

> The wall was there, oh perilous blade of glass

or

> This Man of April walks again.

In the poems just mentioned thought is the root, but it flowers in the feeling. They are essentially poems of the sensibility, a little bit melancholy, perhaps a little too musical. A healthier robustness is found in satirical verse, such as Scott's much needed counterblast against the Canadian Authors' Association, or in the anti-romanticism of Klein's

> And my true love,
> She combs and combs,
> The lice from off
> My children's domes.

The appearance of satire, and also of didactic poetry that does not depend upon wit, would be a healthy sign in Canadian poetry. For it would indicate that our poets are realizing, even if in an elementary way, that poetry is more concerned with expressing exact ideas than wishy-washy "dreams." It would indicate, too, that the poet's lofty isolation from events that are of vital significance to everybody was coming to an end.

Detachment, indeed, or self-absorption is (for a time only, I hope) becoming impossible. The era of individual liberty is in eclipse. Capitalism can hardly be expected to survive the cataclysm its most interested adherents are blindly steering towards, and the artist who is concerned with the most intense of experiences must be concerned with the world situation in which, whether he likes it or not, he finds himself. For the moment at least he has something more important to do than to record his private emotions. He must try to perfect a technique that will combine power with simplicity and sympathy with intelligence so that he may play his part in developing mental and emotional attitudes that will facilitate the creation of a more practical social system.

Of poetry such as this, there is here only the faintest foreshadowing—a fact that is not unconnected with the backwardness politically and economically of Canada—but that Canadian poetry in the future must become increasingly aware of its duty to take cognizance of what is going on in the world of affairs we are sure.

That the poet is not a dreamer, but a man of sense; that poetry is a discipline because it is an art; and that it is further a useful art: these are propositions which it is intended this volume shall suggest. We are not deceiving ourselves that it has proved them.

*Canadian Poetry — A Minority Report*

*from* University of Toronto Quarterly

Professor E. J. Pratt's article on the present status of English-Canadian poetry[1] has sent me to a number of other attempts by Canadian poets or critics to evaluate the contemporary native product in terms of the achievement of the past, and I have been struck by the fact that the only thing all the articles have in common is a more or less all-pervading, but usually ill-defined, sense of uneasiness or dissatisfaction. Occasionally this is given direct and even truculent expression; sometimes the reader absorbs it rather furtively, reading between the lines; and sometimes it is rationalized out of existence or sublimated into patriotic boasting. Yet whether the critic denounces, excuses, points with pride, or merely throws out a smoke screen, he betrays, it has seemed to me, a feeling of insecurity that sometimes amounts almost to bewilderment. Canadian poetry is lost, or it has not found itself; new vistas are opening ahead of it, or it has come to a dead end. It is either up a tree or it has slipped from its high estate, and it needs somebody to give it a fresh direction. It should mirror the aspirations of the struggling masses; or it should return to the grand manner and high morals of our fathers. The older poets are too sentimental, and the young are too brainy. The denizens of the Canadian pantheon have not much to say, but they feel deeply and they love God and nature; the modern poets are obscure. . . .

One may be pardoned if he succumb to a feeling of mild bewilderment too. Everyone seems to be giving directions at once. Some hopeful souls are urging the use of whip and spur; others, more cautious, advise check-rein and curb. But where, after all, as Roy Campbell boldly demanded in a somewhat similar connection in South Africa, where's the bloody horse?

Now I am not one of those people, gently castigated by Professor Pratt, who love every literature but their own and who hear the muses singing in the

---

[1]"Canadian Poetry—Past and Present," University of Toronto Quarterly, VIII (Oct., 1938), 1-10.

isles of Greece but never stop to listen for them on the old Ontario strand; nor am I one of those lovers of the new who have no patience with whatsoever our fathers have found of good repute. I certainly do not wish to blow frost on the idea that Canada has produced a considerable body of respectable and interesting poetry. The belief, however, which most of the standard anthologists and pontifical critics assume, suggest, and sometimes even state, namely that our "great poets" have given us a national poetic literature comparable in power and fidelity to that of England or the United States—this belief is so fantastic that no one outside Canada can be made to believe anybody really holds it.

Here, by way of illustration, is an example, and not a particularly flagrant one, of the undiscriminating praise bestowed on our standard poets by our most influential critics. Professor Pratt rightly maintained that the true goodness of Archibald Lampman's poetry lies in its direct and sincere realization of the Canadian landscape and the Canadian atmosphere, that Lampman is essentially a nature poet, and that this is enough. But it is not enough for the representative critic whose judgment I wish to examine. I quote from William Arthur Deacon's *Poteen:*

> There is a fineness about Archibald Lampman that, coupled with an instinctive artistry, spells immortality.... Too much stress has always been laid upon him as a Nature poet: the phrase is so unnecessarily limiting. A quiet, serene poet, he did describe and interpret Nature more beautifully and adequately than any other has yet done, but to him man was as much a part of Nature as the autumn maples and he was seer enough to perceive the same life quickening all things:
>
> > Not to be conquered by these headlong days,
> >    But to stand free; to keep the mind at brood
> >    On life's deep meaning, nature's altitude
> > Of loveliness, and time's mysterious ways.
>
> A liking for Lampman is sure proof of taste in poetry.

Now, however much we may admire the sentiments of the lines quoted, it is surely impossible to find in them much more than a rather sluggish movement and a succession of trite and pseudopoetic phrases—the verse, indeed, is far below the level of Lampman's best; and that such a passage should have been selected by our critic as a touchstone of taste effectively invalidates the assertion with which he concludes. Furthermore, when he declares that Lampman has described and interpreted nature more beautifully and adequately "than any other has yet done," I, at least, can only assume he means "than any other *Canadian poet* has yet done." Reading the passage in its context does not, however, lend any support to my assumption, and I am left wondering whether, after all, Deacon really does fancy Archibald Lampman is the greatest of all nature poets. The difficulty of deciding is increased by the fact that it is not quite certain such an opinion would be rejected by all our critics, some of whom, apparently, have not read Wordsworth, Crabbe, John Clare, Robert Frost, or Edward Thomas. Lampman is inferior to any of these poets. But they have set high standards, and to be excelled by them is in itself no disgrace. Canadian critics should realize this.

I have said that most of the articles on Canadian poetry published in the last few years have seemed to express in one way or another a sense of uneasiness or even alarm. What seems to be troubling the well-wishers to our literature most is the fact that Canadian poets—the quick and the dead alike—are not read, indeed, are hardly even known, in England and the United States. A number of explanations and excuses have been advanced. I shall leave out of consideration the theory that the underlying cause is national jealousy, that it is attributable to the Englishman's contempt for the colonial or to the hard-headed Yankee's rejection of all spiritual values, and concentrate instead on two factors that without doubt do contribute to the isolation of our poets.

The first is the fact that our anthologies do not represent our poetry as effectively as they might. This is due partly to copyright difficulties, but more to the artificial (non-poetic) standards set up by the estimable persons who compiled them. The result is that collections like *The Oxford Book of Canadian Verse* (1912) and Garvin's *Canadian Poets* contain, in addition to a rather small minority of living poems, a "great majority" made up of the worst poems of the best poets and the best poems of the worst poets, in such abundance that the stranger is distracted and dismayed. The one test that the anthologists never fail to make is the test for "Canadianism." If a poem does not exhibit some obvious and often superficial manifestation of being Canadian, it must treat the grand, serious themes with solemnity and unction. But if it is unmistakably Canadian, it may be as trivial as it likes.

There are exceptions, of course. All the anthologies contain some good poems, though these are hopelessly outnumbered. A revision, a weeding out, a new discovery—this is the task that is waiting for an anthologist with taste and courage. There is an immediate and vital need for a revaluation of our standard poets, based upon a careful examination of every poem, line by line and stanza by stanza. What it is useful to know is not the historical significance of a poem in the development of Canadian literature but its absolute poetic vitality. We want to know whether the poem is alive or dead. Can it speak to us in a language we recognize as that of a man, not of a bird or a book? Can we accept it without putting half of our personality—the mind—to sleep? Has it ever been, or can it become again, a part of life? Very few of the pieces in *The Oxford Book of Canadian Verse* could survive such a scrutiny, but those that could would gain immeasurably in effect if set free from the cloying atmosphere in which they exist there.

Let us consider for a moment the treatment of Bliss Carman in the anthologies. This poet, because his appeal is the easiest and his lyric note the purest, is the most widely known of all Canadian poets. At his best, his technique is sure and his line firm. No other Canadian has ever quite achieved the strange union of rapture and awe that makes his best poems so magical. . . .

But Carman's work is extremely uneven. The good is very good, and the bad is very bad, and in the earlier books the proportion of good poems is high, while in the later it is low. That a man capable of the majestic music of

> The sun goes down, and over all
> These barren reaches by the tide
> Such unelusive glories fall. . . .

should also be capable of echoing "The May Queen" in a long jingle beginning,

> Make me over, Mother April,
> When the sap begins to stir!

and ending,

> Make me anything but neuter
> When the sap begins to stir!

is, perhaps, not without precedent in literary history, but that the two poems last quoted should be placed side by side in *The Oxford Book of Canadian Verse* emphasizes a point that is close to my present thesis. And that point is this. When English and American anthologists, like Sir Arthur Quiller-Couch in *The Oxford Book of Victorian Verse,* E. V. Lucas in *The Open Road,* and Louis Untermeyer in *Modern American Poetry,* have represented Carman— the only Canadian, by the way, that any of them includes, and that, too, I suspect, under the assumption that he is an American—they have represented him, it seems to me, by poems of uniformly high quality. But the Canadian anthologists, such as Campbell and Garvin, seeking apparently for the bulk commensurate with a major national poet, have mingled the good, bad and indifferent all together. Yet it is not, one soon discovers, so much that they wish to represent the poet completely, at all levels of achievement, as that they cannot distinguish between different levels of achievement. Discrimination has never been an essential part of a Canadian anthologist's equipment. Enthusiasm, industry, sympathy, yes; but taste, no.

But the inadequacy of our anthologies cannot be held responsible for the failure of living poets to win recognition outside the Dominion. Some Canadian bards, of course, are content with the more modest rewards and the greater glory that is comparatively easily attained at home, and find in the plaudits of the Authors' Association an adequate compensation for the neglect of New York and London. But if our literature is to make good its claim to be a living voice of national significance, our poets will have to realize that they cannot live to themselves alone; they will have to recognize that, whether they like it or not, they are in open competition with the whole English-writing world. If they shrink from imposing on themselves standards as high as those of the literary world of England and the United States, they will have to expect neglect and resign themselves to bask forever in the tempered airs of the native nursery.

Instead of this, let our younger writers at least send their poems to the best literary magazines in London and New York, and their books to the great publishing houses. They will stand every bit as good a chance of being judged on their merits and, if talented, of being encouraged as any other writer. And this is what our most vigorous poets have always done. Bliss Carman's work was first published in Boston, E. J. Pratt's in London. Morley Callaghan, our finest novelist, won his first success in Parisian "little magazines" and in New York. After he had been acclaimed by American and English critics, whether or not the Canadians followed suit mattered very little. Yet, notwithstanding such exceptions as these, it is mainly true that Canadian writers—and particularly Canadian poets—have failed to win recognition abroad. The going, to put it bluntly, has been too tough. Our poetry is, for the most part, a provincial poetry—good enough for home consumption, but not strong enough for export.

A few critics are beginning to face this fact, and our publishers must always have had to. But most Canadians, instead of being willing to pull in their horns, admit their limitations, and seek in our very narrowness a source of strength (as, for instance, by opposing the claims of regionalism to those of nationalism), are raucous and busily practical. Canadian Book Weeks are inaugurated to supply artificial stimulation to the home market, and the producer is pepped up by being herded into the sheepfold of an authors' association, where, from the very first, commercial, social, and patriotic ideals have taken precedence over all others.

In the meantime, explanations have been probed for, and some scapegoats have been found. One of these is the Canadian public, which, if any public should, ought to support Canadian poets. It is accused of neglecting this high responsibility, of being indifferent to poetry, and, indeed, of practically entering into a tacit conspiracy to starve all poets to death. Yet this is hardly fair. Taken by and large, the Canadian public is no more boorish and no less boorish than the British public or the American public. Poetry does not pay (in the sense that stockbroking does) in any country today.

But the Canadian public is, in one respect at least, an unusual one. It is, and inevitably still must be for a considerable time to come, a colonial public. While self-reliant and self-assertive in the field of material conquest, in the realm of culture and intellect it is timid, eager to please, and stupid. It is half conscious of its weakness, and terribly anxious, therefore, to be assured of its strength.

One of the characteristics of colonialism is ambition. Energy, pride, self-assertiveness, the sense of property, these the North American colonist always possessed. It was not long, therefore, before the claims of nationalism made themselves heard. Most of the American colonists made good the claim in a political sense and by force of arms in 1776. Those who remained loyal to England, held Quebec and Lower Canada, and finally spread westward through the Prairie provinces to the Pacific, carried with them the germs of the nationalistic ideal—an ideal which in Canada has been as significant and influential as if it were real. While the Canadians were not and could not be an independent and homogenous race, and while politically they do not, even today, think of themselves as a wholly independent nation, they have with an ever-increasing intensity been dreaming of themselves as a people that ought to have (and hence by an easy transition as a people that does have) a national literature.

Critics arose, mostly college professors or journalists, who made it their main business to look for, and find, some special quality, tone, or *thing* in the verse written in Canada which was uniquely expressive of the Canadian soil or of the Canadian landscape or of Canadian human nature. The worst of these critics wrote the fattest books, and since the field was a new one and everyone was glad to be praised, their work was accepted as a just and sensible evaluation of the highways and headwaters of Canadian literature.

And yet it is not only the extremists among the patriotic critics who have been led astray by the search for a national spirit. An objective and uncompromising study of Canadian poetry *as poetry* remains to be written. Poetic excellence is taken for granted, or brushed aside as of only secondary importance, provided a piece of verse is an obvious manifestation of "the Canadian spirit." As a matter of fact, a sort of double standard has unconsciously been set up. Canadian poetry is treated as if it were produced in a vacuum. It is written by, for, and about Canadians, and it is evaluated solely in terms calculated not to wound Canadian susceptibilities. Our academic critics have been so bookishly revelling in the joys of Canadian lyricism with the "Group of '61," or noting their raptures anent the trills of such indigenous throstles as Wilson MacDonald or Audrey Brown, that they have no idea where in the world today significant poetry can be found. I wonder whether any Canadian critic over forty has ever heard of—much less read—such significant modern poets as Wallace Stevens, Marianne Moore, Louis MacNeice, Laura Riding, John Crowe Ransom, or—one might almost dare to add—Gerard Manley Hopkins and Ezra Pound. How many of them have read the *Faber Book of Modern Verse*, or studied the criticism of Ogden and Richards, T. E. Hulme, Wyndham Lewis, William Empson, Herbert Read, Kenneth Burke, or Christopher Caudwell? Would it ever occur to a Canadian critic to apply the standards of such men as these to the analysis and appraisal of Canadian poetry?[2]

Form is always important, and if I seem to diverge for a few moments from my main theme to examine certain peculiarities of style which our critics praise or indulge in, I do so because in reality it is only to return to my thesis from a new point of departure.

Most writers on Canadian poetry, one soon discovers, have felt it necessary to assume a somewhat heightened style, to indulge in a rather spectacular display of metaphor, and, instead of saying anything fresh about the poetry, have given us their own impression of it in a sort of appreciative prose substitute. It is the critic's sensibility, not the poet's, we really learn about. For instance, Deacon quotes, apparently with approval, Wilson MacDonald's characteristic assertion that Charles Heavysege's little poem, "Self-Examination," was "the breaking of the golden flagon of song in Canada." This means that the poem marks the appearance in Canadian literature of a pure and intense lyrical quality, and the style of the statement is intended to suggest in itself that lyric quality. The first stanza of the poem is as follows:

> Open, my heart, thy ruddy valves;
>   It is thy master calls;
> Let me go down, and curious trace
>   Thy labyrinthine halls.

Now, about this, two things are obvious: that it looks like a piece of diluted Poe, and that the lack of feeling for the sounds and connotations of language, revealed by "thy ruddy valves" in the all-important opening line, effectively prevents the thought and mood from being communicated today with adequate intensity. And when in the second stanza one finds the awkward noun "ken" pressed into service for the sake of the rhyme, and in the third stanza the writer's heart apostrophized as "thou covered nest/Of passions," one realizes that the golden flagon of song is, indeed, a broken one, and that the wine spilled is of a rather poor vintage year. Deacon, however, reaches no

[2]This was written in 1939. These strictures would not apply today so much has the situation changed for the better.

such conclusion, for he complacently indicates that the poem is one which usually represents Heavysege in the anthologies, and after quoting MacDonald's trite metaphor, exposes its absurdity by quoting the mediocre poem.

One more example of florid writing and confused criticism must be cited. It will lead us quickly back to the heart of our present inquiry. I quote from Dr. J. D. Logan's *Highways of Canadian Literature.* The subject is Charles Mair's unassuming lyric called "The Fireflies." Dr. Logan writes as follows:

> They who, with master artistry, write delineative poetry, shall hardly achieve, in short and single phrase, so apt and clear and vivid a picture of the Canadian firefly as Mair's incisively realistic and genuinely poetical line:—
>> Thou fairy hunter of the moonless night.
> That is masterly....

This bit of verbiage was held up to ridicule by A. M. Stephen in a brilliant and well-informed attack on the critics, read—apparently in vain—to the Canadian Authors' Association two or three years ago in Vancouver. It is a sample of jargon that would have delighted Fowler. What, for instance, is "delineative poetry"? And why should Dr. Logan forbid those who "with master artistry" write it from achieving, if they can, a picture of the Canadian firefly?

A more important point, however, is this. The line quoted may well be what the critic considers genuinely poetical, but the one thing it is not is realistic, incisively or otherwise. It presents no detail, no picture, no concrete image. *Fairy, hunter, moonless,* and *night* are all perfectly general words, and the line, therefore, is abstract and vague. Its connotations are mildly romantic, and this is what Dr. Logan means by "genuinely poetical." Lastly, and most important of all, how the line applies to the Canadian firefly and not to the New England firefly or to the English glow-worm is a mystery that only a Canadian critic would dream of concocting.

This, indeed, is but another instance, small but significant, of the rabid determination to find an elusive Canadianism in every bit of verse published in the Dominion. It is a determination that has distracted our critics for too long from the real problem of evaluation and has led them to judge the worth of a poem not in terms of the whole range of English poetic experience but in terms only of Canadian things. They view the poem in its northern isolation, through the mists of which it looms larger than it is. What the critic who would be useful in Canada today would do with Mair's verses I am not prepared to say, but of one thing I am sure. Before making any assertions about their aptness, vividness, concision, delineative excellence, or genuine poetic quality, he would compare them carefully with certain poems on a similar theme by Herrick, Marvell, and Lovelace.

We find ourselves again, then, concerned with what I think is at the centre of our present discontent. Let me state this as directly as possible. The most pernicious influence upon Canadian poetry is, and for a long time has been, the optimistic spirit engendered by our adoption of special standards. We have stealthily acquired an enervating habit of making allowances, which in turn has cajoled us into accepting the mediocre as the first rate—*for us*. And it has meant in the long run (and, of course, with some exceptions) the condemnation of our poetry to a lonely exile within our borders.

And now after so much petulant jingling of the harness, the time has come to remember the bloody horse. What of the poetry being written in Canada today—what is it like? What is its value judged by other than native standards? Who is writing it, and under what conditions? To answer such questions fully is not possible here. I can do no more than present a few rather general observations and suggestions.

In the first place, I do not think the best poetry is to be found in the books of the best known and most highly praised names. Wilson MacDonald has written a few poems of power and dignity, but an examination of his best book, *Out of the Wilderness*, reveals the general havoc wrought by the self-deceiving desire to be a Canadian bard, to be popular, to be bold, to say everything as loudly as possible, and to be sure that nothing will be beyond the comprehension of even the dullest son of the Dominion. As a result, he produces poems that are almost as good as Alfred Noyes and others that are worse than Robert W. Service. And Deacon writes that ". . . at times he is invested with an originality of conception savoring of seership. For versatility we have had nothing to equal him, varying as he does from the sweetest of light lyrics to the profoundest meditations. . . ."

Audrey Brown is another poet who has won academic praise and popular applause. This time it is for writing longish mythological narratives, nature poems, and romantic lyrics in a lush redundancy of secondhand Keatsian vocables. The plain sense of her work, such as it is, is easy to grasp; the language is recognizably "poetic"; the imagery is richly coloured but not startling, and the emotions are those a poet is expected to have. But that the whole thing has been incomparably better done by Keats and the Pre-Raphaelites and that this, after all, is a real world, not a dream world—these considerations weigh little with the critics and the public.

No, for the most part, our best poetry will not be featured on the shelves of the fashionable booksellers. It will be found in a couple of volumes by Dorothy Livesay and Leo Kennedy, in E. J. Pratt's *Newfoundland Poems, Titans,* and *The Witches' Brew*, in two volumes, *Laconics* (1930) and *Sonnets* (1932) by W. W. E. Ross, of Toronto, and scattered through the pages of the *Canadian Forum.*

Among the most important of the contributions which the *Forum* has made to the intellectual life of the Dominion has been the encouragement it has given two very significant types of poetry, the metaphysical lyric and the political satire. It has been especially distinguished by the satirical verse of L. A. MacKay, which for polish, wit, and epigrammatic force deserves to rank with the best work of this kind that any English poet has produced in the last score of years. I may cite among examples of MacKay's weight and brilliance, the lines on General Franco's Moors in Spain, the dialogue between the shades of Cromwell and Walpole on Chamberlain's foreign policy, and the excellent ballad of Ontario's shabby-genteel liquor laws called "Frankie Went Down to the Corner." Other contemporary Canadian poets, also, are doing a good deal to make up for their predecessors' neglect of satire, some of A. M. Klein's most richly living poetry being of this sort. The comic vitality of Pratt's *The Witches' Brew*, while not satiric, is nevertheless a welcome relief from the traditional solemnity of the Canadian bard. F. R. Scott's best verse is entirely in the field of satire.

There is little need to say much here about the work of Dorothy Livesay and Leo Kennedy. Both of these young writers have rigidly disciplined themselves in their craft, and they have succeeded in lopping away from their style all extraneous ornament and all extravagance or clumsiness of diction. And at the same time they have found what is for them a significant subject matter in the Marxian class struggle. It is no exaggeration to say that they are making a contribution to proletarian poetry that is also a contribution to poetry.

To me, however, the most interesting of all the Canadian poets of today are two men who are not nearly so well known as anyone I have yet mentioned— Robert Finch and W. W. E. Ross. Finch is an intellectual poet. Of the six contributors to *New Provinces*, he is the most elegant and the least sensuous. His verse is not without feeling, but the feeling is so carefully husbanded and so fastidiously winnowed that one is impressed with its delicacy and precision rather than with its abundance and strength. At its most intense, it expresses an aesthetic emotion: an emotion which rises out of the effort to compel an order from a given experience. Finch's poems are interesting for more than their subject matter. They illustrate excellently a quality that has not previously appeared in Canadian literature, a quality that may be named *dandyism*.

Ross, though almost completely unknown in Canada, has been welcomed by such a distinguished literary journal as the *Dial* and has been printed and discriminatingly praised by *Poetry: A Magazine of Verse*. The fact that those of us concerned in the preparation of *New Provinces* failed to include some of his poems was a mistake that left the book poorer than it might have been.

Ross's verse differs fundamentally from that of Finch. Where the latter is complex, subtle, and sophisticated, Ross is astonishingly simple, fresh, naive. He responds to experience with a naked simplicity and directness that makes us see things set free from the scale of habit. It is as though the poet and hence his reader were looking at a train or a fish or a meadow for the first time, and with a childlike eagerness that instinctively rejects whatever is non-essential or derivative. Let me quote one poem in illustration.

THE DIVER

I would like to dive
Down
Into this still pool
Where the rocks at the bottom are safely
    deep,

Into the green
Of the water seen from within,
A strange light
Streaming past my eyes—

Things hostile,
You cannot stay here, they seem to say;
The rocks, slime-covered, the undulating
Fronds of weeds—

And drift slowly
Among the cooler zones;
Then, upward turning,
Break from the green glimmer

Into the light,
White and ordinary of the day,
And the mild air,
With the breeze and the comfortable shore.

It is such a return as this, to the light of the ordinary day and the mild air of the comfortable shore, to simplicity, directness, and humility, that our poetry and criticism most urgently need to make.

Allow me to address a word directly to the young man who has talent and sincerity, who lives in Canada, and who wishes to be a poet. Talking over the heads of the petty versifiers that Professor Pratt, as editor of the *Canadian Poetry Magazine*, is so acutely aware of, I would say to such a writer something like this:

Do not be anxious for fortune or fame. You will probably get neither. Do not think of writing as a game or a racket. Do not try to get in the literary swim. Do not flatter reviewers or butter the critics.

Set higher standards for yourself than the organized mediocrity of the authors' associations dares to impose. Be traditional, catholic, and alive. Study the great masters of clarity and intensity—Dante, Chaucer, Villon, Shakespeare, Dryden. Study the poets of today whose language is living and whose line is sure—Eliot, Pound, the later Yeats, and Auden. Read the French and German poets whose sensibility is most intensely that of the modern world—Baudelaire, Rimbaud, and Rainer Maria Rilke. Read, if you can, the Roman satirists.

Send your verse to the best English and American literary magazines. Until you are sure that your work is acceptable there, leave the Canadian magazines alone.

And remember, lastly, that poetry does not permit the rejection of every aspect of the personality except intuition and sensibility. It must be written by the whole man. It is an intelligent activity, and it ought to compel the respect of the generality of intelligent men. If it is a good, it is a good in itself.

## *from* Writing in Canada

"The one staggering generalization," Professor Daniells has written—"The one staggering generalization that may safely be made of Canadian poetry, past, present, and far into the future, is that its excellence has sprung from the vision, the self-nurtured impulse, the self-taught craftsmanship of a handful of individuals in the face of an immense public indifference, deadly though unspoken, and none the less menacing because it is polite." This is something that all of us are acutely aware of. But we must not deceive ourselves by thinking that this is a local or national state of affairs, or even a peculiarly contemporary one, though it is certainly different and probably more acute than it was in the seventeenth or eighteenth centuries. Today anyway it exists in England and the United States quite as acutely as here.

Michael Roberts in his introduction to the now classic *Faber Book of Modern Verse* wrote: "More often than prose or mathematics, poetry is received in a hostile spirit, as if its publication were an affront to the reader. . . ." Again, A. M. Klein in his "Portrait of the Poet as a Landscape"—at first entitled "Portrait of the Poet as Nobody"—dealt with the problem in his characteristically vivid and ironic way. At the beginning of the piece, the poet seems to be dead—at least as far as recognition, honour, or influence in our society can be seen. He is unmourned, indeed unmissed: "Nobody, it appears, missed him enough to report." "It is possible that he is dead, and not discovered"—"like the corpse in a detective story." "We are sure only that from our real society he has disappeared; he simply does not count. . . ." The poem only hints at the cause of this isolation; it is concerned mainly with its effects—and not upon society but upon the poet. Thus it leaves something to be desired, but it serves as a beautifully made springboard from which to plunge into our subject. But let us stay for a moment with the poem, and with the poet.

> He is alone; yet not completely alone. . . .
> Each city has one, sometimes more than one;

> here caretakers of art, in colleges;
> in offices, there, with arm bands, and green-shaded;
> and there, pounding their catalogued beats in libraries,—
> everywhere menial, a shadow's shadow. . . .

It is a discouraging picture. But the results are worse. Or worse for the poet in the character I am a little surprised to find Klein depicting him in—a proud, romantic, egocentric, frustrated, and inward-turned intellectual, who, rejected by the world of normalcy, cultivates his private madness. This, of course, is not the picture of a real poet—not even the picture of what the poet must be and has inevitably become in our society. It is a picture of what the world of business and journalism likes to think the poet is. And I think it is a weakness of Klein's poem that this distinction has not been made unmistakably clear. Only in the climactic last two stanzas does Klein suggest something of the real value of the poet's work—and its true reward.

> To find a new function for the déclassé craft
> archaic like the fletcher's; to make a new thing;
> to say the word that will become sixth sense;
> perhaps by necessity and indirection bring
> new forms to life, anonymously, new creeds—
> O, somehow pay back the daily larcenies of the lung!
>
> These are not mean ambitions. It is already something
> merely to entertain them. Meanwhile, he
> makes of his status as zero a rich garland,
> a halo of his anonymity,
> and lives alone, and in his secret shines
> like phosphorus.

And then this poet—in his bitterness and anger—cannot help adding one final touch of savage irony. "And in his secret shines," he says, "like phosphorus. At the bottom of the sea."

Well, there is the picture. The poet as exile, as the rejected man, as nobody. How do we explain it? How can we account for it?

The commonest explanation offered today concerns itself with the alleged obscurity of modern poetry. Those who level this charge forget that it is not only modern poetry which they ought to find obscure, but Shakespeare, Donne, Milton, Blake, and other poets of the past to whom they pay lip service, or take for granted, or do not read. Even the most accomplished and richly experienced readers have testified to the obscurity of these poets and have found their richest rewards in making the effort to penetrate and lighten it. In dealing with the question of obscurity in poetry, we must ask by whose standard we are to judge and condemn. Certainly not that of the lowest common denominator. Whenever complexity of subject and subtlety of treatment are to be found, poetry will be obscure to the commonplace mind; and it is most often the commonplace mind which ignores, derides, or condemns the poet as being obscure. After that he is called "intellectual," or "over-intellectual." And then "out of touch with life" or "ignorant or contemptuous of humanity."

To believe this is to take too mean a view of the human mind and, indeed, of human nature itself. It is a view which would deny not only all art and poetry but also the analogous disciplines of mathematics, science, and technology. For there is another kind of obscurity—a genuine and often necessary one. Poetry—and especially modern poetry—is sometimes a useful form of technical language—even sometimes a jargon, if you will—that is uniquely adapted for the presentation and examination of psychological and emotional problems, and of philosophical and theological problems. "Problems" is perhaps a dangerous word to use, because it suggests a dry, calm, objective, intellectual activity. But I would remind you that I am talking about poetry; and that poetry is the application of emotion to ideas. And furthermore, that ideas themselves are not dry and unemotional in their results. They kindle emotion, and are generated out of emotion.

No. Poetry is not unpopular because it is obscure, any more than mathematics or science or theology are unpopular because they are obscure. The real reason for the unpopularity of the poet lies elsewhere. Not in the fact—which is not a fact at all—that the poet has isolated himself from either the world of men and affairs or the world of nature; but that, on the contrary, he has identified himself too closely and in too critical a spirit with those worlds. Like the modern painter he looks at things more closely and more accurately than it is usually convenient for the self-satisfied, active, "practical" man to do. And he penetrates beneath the surface. His feelings are more accurate and more intense, and they are laid bare for evaluation and critical analysis in a way that cannot help but seem subversive of the busy uncritical complacent activity of the unexamined life. As Louis MacNeice has put it: "I consider that the poet is a blend of the entertainer and the critic or informer. . . . As informer, he is not a photographic or scientific informer, but more like the 'informer' in the derogatory sense." He is the one, in other words, who tells on us, the teller of unpleasant truths, the secret conscience of society, the revealer of unconscious guilt. No wonder he is derided, exiled, driven into the wilderness, and made a scapegoat.

If he is to fulfil this role—his historic role—he must do so without self-consciousness and without vanity: not by standing apart from society or humanity (even if this were possible for a Poe or a Mallarmé), but by being true to the reality of nature and of human nature—above all in his language and in his imagery. He must cultivate in himself accuracy and clarity; he must identify himself with things and men's feelings about things. Rilke has said it in his *Letters to a Young Poet:*

> There is only one single way. Go into yourself. Investigate the reason that bids you write; find out whether it is spreading out its roots in the deepest places of your heart. . . . Then draw near to Nature. Then try, as a first human being, to say what you see and experience. . . . If your daily life seems poor, do not blame it; blame yourself that you are not poet enough to call forth its riches; for to the creator there is no poverty and no poor indifferent place. . . .

This is what Irving Layton means when he writes:

> And me happiest when I compose poems,
>     Love, power, the huzza of battle
>     are something, are much;
> yet a poem includes them like a pool
>     water and reflection.
> In me, nature's divided things—
>     tree, mould *on* tree—
>     have their fruition;
> I am their core. Let them swap,
>     bandy, like a flame swerve.
> I am their mouth; as a mouth I serve.

As a mouth, *I serve.* We return, through the self, to a sense of responsibility—nothing so limited as a merely personal responsibility, or even a social responsibility, but a responsibility to the nature of reality—in truth itself. It is to return—as a mouth—through language, rhythm, and the sound of verse—to humanity. The rhythms of verse have a natural, physical basis. Its occasions, whether public or private, are always human occasions. It has both a personal and social *use.* It draws mankind together by extending the powers of feeling, while at the same time it sharpens and intensifies them. Thus poetry performs not merely a useful function, but an essential one.

Poetry is an instrument of self-awareness.

It is the art especially, which as R. G. Collingwood said of art in general, "is the community's medicine for the worst disease of mind, the corruption of consciousness."

It is an art of concentration. Complacency, urbanity, sentimentality, whimsicality—all those qualities that make a pleasant folksy radio talk, a good-humoured popular magazine article, or an effective advertisement—these are foreign to the hard, sharp, concentrated intensity of poetry.

Poetry is language and feeling purified of the superficial.

All the smooth, polite, gentle compromises that make for easiness and good humour in everyday life in a suburban society poetry brushes aside or ignores or penetrates beneath. Either directly or by implication, it is *subversive* of this spirit.

It is serious but not solemn; witty or humorous, but not good-humoured; sharp, not vague; imaginative rather than fanciful; condensed, concentrated, and savage rather than diffuse and genial. It is language that refuses to make compromises. That is why it is so difficult—difficult to write, I mean—and why it arouses opposition and anger, why it is bound to be unpopular. It convicts the reader of all sorts of humiliating things—dullness, blindness, superficiality, complacency, sentimentality: and he responds in nine cases out of ten by calling poetry obscure, or perverse, or mad. I am afraid the muse in our age is named Cassandra. She is a stranger at the party; and no amount of nationally advertised deodorants, perfumes, and prophylactics will transform her into a popular hostess or a welcome guest. As a result the poet *as a poet* is left to starve; that is unless he is willing to compromise—to play the game—to enter into the general conspiracy of *not* seeing beneath the surface of things. But to do that is to cease to be a poet.

Real poets know it is naive to expect that society should reward them for what they write as poetry. One speaks of the professional writer; but is there a professional poet? Even among the most successful and influential of the best, Hopkins was a priest, Bridges had private means, Eliot is a publisher, Robert Frost, a farmer, William Carlos Williams, a doctor, Wallace Stevens, an executive of an insurance company, Marianne Moore was a librarian and editor, Auden is a lecturer and journalist. Most of the younger poets in England, the United States, and Canada teach in the universities. Hardly any one depends for his livelihood on poetry. It does not have to be a mercantile commodity. As Eric Bentley has written:

> We today cannot take the arts for granted. We have destroyed the old aristocratic culture, which, for all its faults, had a place for the arts, and have created a culture of commodities, which, to be sure, has a place for everything—upon one condition; that everything become a commodity. Thus there is one sort of literature that flourishes today as never before: commodity literature, as promoted by the book clubs and publishers' salesmen.

If we as poets are willing to forego our role as tellers of unpleasant truths, as examiners of hidden guilt, as guardians and innovators of language, there are easy rewards awaiting us—as least at home: popularity, even a modest fame, acceptance, at first in academic circles, then by the middlebrow public catered to by *Maclean's* magazine, *Saturday Night*, the Canadian Authors' Association, and the CBC. Simplify (that is superficialize) your language and conventionalize your imagery; deal with large generalized themes, as often as possible with some heroic episode of Canadian history or some grand stark aspect of nature in the north; deal in bold outlines; paint with broad strokes; be dramatic, or better, melodramatic; and you will achieve a successful and popular journalistic poetry that will be able to compete with soap operas and popular fiction.

This is a real temptation that a few, but not many, of our poets have shown signs of succumbing to. Most have gone quietly about their work of presenting experience as intensely and accurately as they can, handling the tools of their craft, which is language, with care and inventive intelligence, each one concerning himself, inevitably and almost unconsciously, with the life in which he finds himself immersed.

And who shall say that the rewards are negligible, even if intangible. For the poet, after all, they are nothing more nor less than to fulfil a need of his nature. He is a lover of language, of life, and of art. In the best sense of the word, he is an *amateur*. He is a lover, an enthusiast, the master of a special craft, the guardian of a cult. And the audience he writes for primarily is made up of specialists, enthusiasts, craftsmen and experimenters—in other words, *other poets*. Only in this way can there be development, advancement, genuine accomplishment. It is the criticism and approval by knowledgeable practitioners that is meaningful and helful. This is true of the research chemist, the advanced mathematician, the original philosopher as well as of the poet. Their papers are published first in the learned journals and are judged by an academic society before their influence is felt in the larger world.

I said that the audience a poet writes for is *primarily* other poets. This primary audience keeps the creative artist on his toes. It makes for care, subtlety, and precision. It demands that one strive for perfection and be dissatisfied with any easy solutions or cheap effects. But there is also and must ever be a pull from the other direction: the language really used by men and women in everyday occasions is there for the poet to select from; the feelings common to all and therefore accepted by all are his also and must not be violated.

When the poet is working he is not (and must not be) thinking of payment—at least in terms of money or material advantage; of reputation, perhaps—fame, after all, is the spur, and the honourable esteem of one's peers, and betters, is not an unworthy incentive. A poem is a work of art—a thing made; and the first responsibility of the poet is to see that it is well made—made as well as he can make it. This responsibility is primarily to himself. And it is for this reason that self-discipline, self-control, and the humility that comes from submission to the laws of craftsmanship are so essential. These are virtues that must be cultivated, exercised, and indeed *trained for.*

Everyone has a prejudice in favour of his own work, just as everyone else has a prejudice against it; and it is necessary that the first of these prejudices should not tempt us into overestimation, vanity and misplaced pride. The second prejudice is not so dangerous. It is salutary. It puts the poem on its mettle. It *has* to be good, or a little bit better than good, if it is to win its fight for survival and force its way into the approval of the world.

But one may very well ask how one's own judgment of a new poem is to be tested, confirmed, or modified. First, as I have suggested, by the cultivation of skill and technical accomplishment in one's craft as a poet; and by the difficult and conscious acquirement of objectivity and humility. Then by submitting the work to the best technical journals in the field of poetry criticism and literature in the United States and England as well as in Canada.

We are particularly fortunate in Canada in writing for a small knowledgeable, intensely interested audience of poets and critics who are concerned with the good name of poetry and anxious to show that our work is not unworthy to be placed beside that of poets in the United States or England. And we are fortunate too in the quality of reviewing in the University of Toronto annual survey of "Letters in Canada," in the *Queen's Quarterly*, particularly under the editorship of Malcolm Ross, in the *Canadian Forum*, and in such more specialized magazines as *Northern Review* and *Fiddlehead*. This more than makes up for the inanity, ignorance and prejudice found (with some occasional exceptions) in the daily press and popular periodicals.

The audience, it is true, is always important. We must never forget for whom we write. But there has been altogether too much consideration of the audience in terms of quantity, magnitude, volume—and what it can or ought to pay—and not enough in terms of quality. I am prepared to maintain that a restricted, knowledgeable, exacting audience is more valuable to the poet than a large and undiscriminating one.

The position of the poet in Canada today is much more fortunate than it was fifteen years ago. A fairly large group—or a number of groups, if you like—of poets and critics has arisen. And this has its readers, who provide—if you will judge qualitatively and not persist in counting noses—a sufficient stimulant for our vanity and enough hard-boiled well-informed you've-got-to-show-me sort of criticism to keep us on our toes. There are plenty of opportunities for mutual discussion, for good shop-talk, and friendly, though pretty tough, competition. A number of good anthologies (and a couple of bad ones) have helped to bring our poetry before a wider audience, particularly in the universities, and at the same time have helped to teach discrimination. The work of the university quarterlies and especially of the "little magazines" has been of incalculable value.

But it is the poets themselves whose response to the challenge of the international world of art and letters has created an art movement in Canada that challenges comparison with that of our painters and which, without producing a master or a "great" poet, has raised the level of poetic awareness and expression so that we need not be ashamed of it in London or New York or (if we write in French) in Paris. Perhaps best of all: modern poetry in Canada has become one of the lively arts. It has demonstrated that it can be serious and significant without being in the least solemn. Its high spirits are shown in the richness, vividness, exuberance, and colloquial freshness of its language and its imagery. Language is seen as high-spirited play—rarely as pedantic euphuism.

Your tall French legs, my V for Victory . . .

one of our poets[1] begins a triumphant love poem. And another,[2] writing of childhood memories of playing in the secret cave of the catalpa tree, weaves syllables and sense-impressions in a way that is the essential act of the poet:

Catalpa, in you a song, a cache
A secret story hidden,
A cat, an alp to climb, an ahhh—
Winedrinker's joy and almost the apache
Of violent lunges, whisperings backstage.
And still the greenery, the lacings of the leaves
With quiet, wind outside
And inside cool, cool as caves
Of water, cool as waves
And welcome as water is
On salted skin and ankle.

I could cite dozens of illustrations of this union of sensuous richness with verbal exuberance: James Reaney's "The Chough," A. M. Klein's poem in praise of Montreal written in a bilingual Canadian, Patrick Anderson's "Cold Colloquy," F. R. Scott's "Bonne Entente," or the many bitter, inward-turned flowerings of perhaps frustration that one finds in the poems of P. K. Page or Anne Hébert, and which serve to show that these high spirits and this metaphorical exuberance have nothing to do with an absence of genuine seriousness. They are generated often out of the bitterest and most disillusioned response to experience. . . .[3]

[1]F. R. Scott.
[2]Miriam Waddington.
[3]The concluding paragraph which dealt with eclectic detachment is omitted. The subject is discussed at length on pages 22 to 29.

# A Survey of English-Canadian Letters — A Review

*from* University of Toronto Quarterly

The need for a complete and comprehensive literary history of Canada—one that should also be something of a cultural history—has been felt for a long time. A number of handbooks and outlines were published in the twenties, but the studies of "headwaters" and "highways" produced by the academic critics of that time were lacking in discrimination and were vitiated by a sort of schoolmarmish primness and coyness. Somewhat better was the less pretentious "outline" by Lorne Pierce, and some good fragmentary work was done by R. P. Baker in his *English-Canadian Literature to the Confederation* (1920) and Lionel Stevenson in *Appraisals of Canadian Literature* (1926), but it was not until the literary revival of the forties that a modern approach to "the problem of Canadian literature" was begun by E. K. Brown and continued by the university writers who collaborated in the annual survey of "Letters in Canada" published in UTQ. Apart from some studies of poetry and of the western novel very little was attempted in the way of historical criticism, and the field was left, as far as any synoptic survey was concerned, to Professor Desmond Pacey. Until now, Pacey's *Creative Writing in Canada: A Short History of English-Canadian Literature* has been the most complete and up-to-date handbook available to the student and the general reader. The book is not written with any particular distinction of style, and a few of its judgments are of doubtful validity; nevertheless its general consistency and singleness of purpose give it a certain value which is not greatly diminished by the appearance of this new large, ambitious volume,[1] which aims at virtues of another kind.

These are the virtues of catholicity, variety, and fullness. There is to be a new look at the whole of Canadian literature in English and the society and culture that produced it; and the new look will be based upon fresh, original

---

[1] Carl F. Klinck and Others, *Literary History of Canada: Canadian Literature in English* (Toronto: University of Toronto Press, 1965.)

research, a good deal of digging into sources, and a good deal of reading of the unreadable. The task, I fear, could not always have been congenial. In any case, it was felt at once to be beyond the scope of a single scholar. "The programme," as the introduction states, "for basic research . . . which led to this book has taken six years to complete and has been carried out by many hands. . . . The book now being published has in fact been written by the editors [Carl F. Klinck, general editor, Alfred G. Bailey, Claude T. Bissell, Roy Daniells, Northrop Frye] and twenty-nine other scholars. . . ." These collaborators are drawn from every one of the leading Canadian universities, except those in the three Prairie provinces, with Toronto, Western Ontario, and New Brunswick predominating.

"The divisions and periods of this history," to quote again from the introduction, "have not been arbitrarily imposed, but have rather been discovered in the light of the evidence." The contributors were given the freedom and responsibility "to dictate the approaches, methods of classification, critical concepts, and descriptive styles most appropriate to the truth as the respective authors saw it. . . . Flexibility, freshness, and authenticity were placed in the balance against strict orderliness, but an order emerged. . . ."

This has a fine scientific ring, but if such a method and so much freedom are to be ultimately successful in an undertaking as ambitious, comprehensive, and new as this one, certain conditions are demanded, only some of which obtain here. First, there must be a powerful, dominating, and unifying mind at the editorial helm; and secondly there ought to be an equality of distinction among the contributors—all require alike the virtues of both scholar and critic: industry, patience, discrimination, taste, intelligence, and a sense of style—powers difficult enough to find in a single author and next to impossible in an editorial committee. There also should be, I think, a general agreement among the writers on aims, principles, and values. Diversity is not always a sign of tolerance and humility; it may be a sign of confusion and its effect may be confusing.

The above remarks are not intended as condemnation of the present book but rather to point out the difficulties inherent in the task the editors have set themselves—difficulties which will explain, and go far to excuse, any weakness or partial failure.

As far as the order is concerned, certainly, what evolved from the interplay of various minds seems eminently reasonable and not particularly new—except perhaps that 1880 rather than Confederation is taken as the most significant date of division in our literary history. A glance at the table of contents will reveal the structure. The book is divided into four main parts.

The first, an excellent one on the early voyagers and explorers, was written by David Galloway and Victor G. Hopwood. Here are chapters that one wishes were longer. Speaking for myself, I would like to have read a fuller appreciation of Hearne's Boswellian personality and of his narrative art as shown in his dramatic account of the slaughter of the Eskimos at the mouth of the Coppermine River. Greater note might have been taken also of the education, training, and early reading of men like Hearne and David Thompson. The fine account here of the genius of David Thompson, however, more than makes up for any such omission. It should help us to realize that Thompson was not only one of the greatest explorers and surveyors this continent has known but, incorrect and unliterary as he may be, one of Canada's greatest writers.

The second section, called "The Transplanting of Traditions" deals mainly with the "literary activity" of the Maritimes and the Canadas to 1880. This is the work, in great part, of Professor Fred Cogswell and the general editor, though with some good chapters on peripheral subjects by other scholars. Especially useful is Dr. Edith Fowke's account of folk tales and folk songs from Newfoundland to the Pacific coast. Relevant to almost every article in the early part of the book is H. Pearson Gundy's survey of "Literary Publishing." This is an excellent and, indeed, an essential chapter—as far as it goes, which is only to about 1900. Why was it not continued in a later section to bring the story of the relations between publisher, author, and the public up to the present? The as yet unexplained breakthrough at the beginning of the forties, when several leading Canadian commercial publishers suddenly became receptive to modern poetry deserves analysis and discussion. So perhaps does the struggle of small private presses, of which the most influential has been Raymond Souster's Contact Press, to advance the cause of experimental verse and secure an audience for the new young poet. Paralleling this development has been the somewhat more successful exploitation, through showmanship and the use of modern advertising techniques, of the more sensational aspects in the work and personality of poets and novelists, who might have been better, if less popular, writers had they been left alone. This is a controversial subject, but had it been aired in a later chapter like Gundy's, the book would have been just that much more useful and interesting.

The third part, "The Emergence of a Tradition," deals with the literature from 1880 to 1920, chiefly popular fiction and poetry, though again other forms and other modes are taken up in separate chapters. Here the finest work is that of Professor Daniells, whose treatment of the Confederation poets fully deserves the editor's commendation for flexibility, freshness, and authenticity. So too do the chapters on historical writing, on Canadian English, and on the literature of protest, by Kenneth N. Windsor, M. H. Scargill, and Frank W. Watt respectively.

The fourth section is headed "The Realization of a Tradition" and deals with fiction from 1920 to 1940 and from 1940 to 1960 in chapters by Desmond Pacey on the earlier period and Hugo McPherson on the later; Poetry from 1920 to 1960 in four chapters—there is a separate one on Pratt and breaks at 1935 and 1950—all by Munroe Beattie; and lastly with miscellaneous genres in a series of short chapters on history, the social sciences, literary scholarship, religious and theological writing, philosophical writing, travel books on Canada, essays and autobiography, children's books, and drama and the theatre. This, as can be seen, is rather a mixed bag. Some of the chapters are scarcely more than a cursory summary while others are thoughtful and stimulating essays, particularly those on historical writing, on literary scholarship, and on the theatre.

The book is brought to a close in a characteristically brilliant coda by Northrop Frye, which I shall discuss at the end of this article.

The book, as I have said, begins well, for after the fine chapters on the voyagers, explorers, and fur-traders we come to Alfred Bailey's immensely useful "Overture to Nationhood," which serves as a general introduction to the second part. This is a brief but concentrated survey of the principles that can be applied to the study of all forms of literary activity in the period before Confederation. The really significant writers—all of them, I think, and none who is not—are placed in perspective, and the social and political conditions that made them and which they in turn illuminate are sketched deftly and clearly. The special usefulness of this chapter is due to Professor Bailey's firm understanding of what a true literary history of Canada ought to be and what it ought and ought not to include. He knows, for instance, what in Newfoundland before admission to the Dominion or in New England before the revolution must be considered a legitimate part of our literature. "It is an illusion," he writes, "that literary and other cultural phenomena can be fitted to a procrustean bed of territorial nationalism." This is very far from any chauvinistic desire to claim anything and everything "Canadian," including things written by visitors or late-comers. Professor Bailey, indeed, utters a warning that all of us, and, indeed, some of his colleagues, would do well to ponder:

> Twentieth-century scholars, in looking back upon the early history of Canada, may find it difficult to draw an inference of inevitability from what they see. The Dominion as we now know it could not have been predicted by the generation of men, both French and English, who began the task of laying its foundations in the seventeenth century. That it might have turned out to be quite a different thing, with ethnic and territorial components at variance with those of the present, may serve to warn us against the habit of reading back the modern mystique of Canadianism into earlier epochs in which it must of necessity be quite alien. The reader will therefore not be asked to join in pursuit of the *ignis fatuus* of the "distinctively Canadian."

This is excellent. So too is Bailey's intriguing analysis of the consequences of the annihilation of the Huron language and culture in the seventeenth century by the French in Canada and the British Loyalists from New York. This material is properly relegated to a footnote, but it is a mark of competence that a writer on Canadian literary history should be able to take into consideration the *might-have-been* as well as the *was*. "There is a sense in which the Huron catastrophe is the most crucial event in Canadian history," Professor Bailey tells us. Had it not taken place, "Canada might well be a largely Indian state as is Mexico."

As an historian and anthropologist Bailey has a breadth of vision that is lacking in some of the critics whose training has been focussed mainly on English belles-lettres. One is struck, indeed, by the fact that many of the chapters on non-literary, or rather non-bellelettristic, subjects seem to be more cogent, brighter, and better written (with some significant exceptions, of course) than those on fiction and poetry. This is due in large part to the greater simplicity and greater general attractiveness of much of the less self-consciously literary material, so that the critic who has to do with it has both an easier and a more congenial task. The explorers, fur-traders, some of the early settlers, and the writers on political, biographical, or historical subjects are less pretentious and generally more competent than the practitioners of poetry and the concocters of romance. The practical authors can be dealt with in a simple straightforward way and their virtues, which were often moral or heroic rather than "literary," presented without apology. But not so the hordes of minor poets and popular novelists. Confessions and lamentations appear everywhere in this book. If the mediocrity and inferiority of our literature is affirmed once, it is affirmed a dozen times, and often at length. The effect is unfortunate both for readers and for the critics themselves. The former will wonder, if things are as bad as all this, Why such a big book? Why so meticulous an examination? Why such a public display of dirty linen? Some of the latter have fallen back on the theory that it is not their business to evaluate; it is more scientific to describe, to list, and to classify; to enumerate and compile statistics; and finally to draw sociological conclusions about the milieu revealed by, for example, the production of 1,400 volumes of fiction written by 400 Canadians between 1880 and 1920.

Professor Roper and his two collaborators, whose chapters on the novel between these years suffer most seriously from this view, put it this way:

> Our knowledge of the fiction of those years has become fragmentary, partly because with the passing of time almost all of it has disappeared from library shelves, and partly because historians of Canadian literature, judging by literary standards current in mid-twentieth century university departments of English, have dismissed all but one or two books as less than first rate. Reading them in the spirit in which they were

written, their contemporary readers judged differently. This chapter and the following two do not quarrel with either judgement: their primary aim is descriptive not judicial.

This amounts to saying that the chief purpose of these chapters is to recover the names of books and authors better forgotten. "Less than first rate" is something of an understatement, if the judgments which (despite the disclaimer in the last sentence) are scattered throughout the chapters in question are anything to go by. What is regrettable, however, is the frank abandonment of literary standards—even those "current in mid-twentieth-century university departments of English," from which, as a matter of fact, most of the contributors to this literary history come.

As a result of this attitude a good part of the book—and not in these three chapters alone—is cluttered up with brief note-like statements about hundreds of ephemeral minor writers, most of whom were merchants guided by a sickly public taste for sensationalism and sentimentality, while the few serious and genuinely significant writers are given less than the space needed for a full and penetrating account of their work. Collectively a great many more pages are devoted to authors better relegated to bibliographies, catalogues, and check lists than to a writer of real living interest like Sara Jeannette Duncan Cotes. The value of Mrs. Cotes is recognized, of course, but the two-and-a-third pages devoted to her work are hardly commensurate with her superiority.

Much labour has gone into the making of these chapters, and I would be the last to suggest that it has been wasted. The information here recorded about the numbers and kinds of novels published and the circumstances attending their success or failure throws a great deal of light on the social and economic motivations of authors and publishers as well as on the public taste. But this light does not illuminate very much beyond, though it helps us to form an opinion as to the cause of the mediocrity of so much of our fiction and offers a necessary supplement to the quite valid but ultimately unsatisfying explanation: "Our builders were with want of genius cursed."

When we read at the beginning of the three chapters on the novel a modest disclaimer—"The generalizations they suggest are tentative, since they are based on a reading of only about two-thirds of the volumes published in those years [1880 to 1920], all that is at the moment available in Canadian and American libraries"—and we think of those 1,400 volumes by 400 Canadians already mentioned and remember that the nature and quality of most of them was of the sort that these chapters describe, we cannot withhold our sympathy for the suffering the critics must have undergone and our admiration for their diligence.

When we come to the later chapters on modern fiction, we find that the proportion of work of genuine and lasting interest to that of facile mediocrity is much greater. Yet even in these chapters the felt need to mention almost every person who published a work of fiction and to say something, anything almost, about him, means that the good writers are treated less fully than they might have been. The discussions of Grove, of Callaghan, of MacLennan, of Ethel Wilson are generally briefer and less detailed than the introductions to various volumes in the New Canadian Library or articles in *Canadian Literature.*

If some of the lists of very minor writers and their negligible works could have been left to the bibliographers, there might also have been room for a more extended treatment of general and perhaps theoretical problems—problems of identity and definition, such as *are* dealt with in the essays of Professors Bailey, Daniells, and Frye and which make these essays by far the most interesting and valuable in the book.

There would also have been room for more quotation. Quotation, aptly chosen, has the advantage of supplying immediate and striking evidence to illustrate and support judgment and opinion. It is the best way to demonstrate the quality of a style and to relieve your own expository dryness with something to entertain as well as to inform. . . .

When we leave the studies of fiction and belles-lettres and turn to the chapters on the Confederation poets by Roy Daniells, we are in a different world. Professor Daniells has little sympathy for the sociological approach, and he gives us almost the first piece of literary criticism based on general principles since the early chapter by Professor Bailey. It is very refreshing after the blizzards of factual information, copious, accurate, indiscriminating, and blinding, which seemed to cover distinctions and obliterate landmarks.

Daniells offers what amounts to a theory of the primacy of the imagination in providing both motive and justification for the literary artist. The subjective imagination is therefore the proper field of investigation for the literary historian who aims to be more than a mere chronicler. The analysis of political and economic conditions before and after Confederation with which Professor Daniells begins his discussion shows that he is well aware of the importance—secondary though it is—of the non-literary milieu. He boldly affirms, however, the admittedly unfashionable doctrine that "There is no simple correspondence between an objective record of political, social, and economic events, on the one hand, and on the other, a criticism of the arts, whose creation and appreciation are suffused with subjectivity."

Professor Daniells gives us, as might be expected, a sympathetic account of Lighthall's enthusiastic preface to *Songs of the Great Dominion*, an influential anthology published in 1889. This is followed by a scholarly narrative of the part played in the dissemination of culture by some of the literary magazines, such as the *Canadian Monthly*, in the seventies and eighties. Indeed, all the way through these chapters Daniells is careful to show that his critical judgments and evaluations are based on a careful collation of facts. His superiority lies in his willingness, in the face of an accumulation of data, even statistical data, to go on beyond description and become not simply a recorder but a critic whose ultimate task is evaluation and whose essential method is *literary* analysis. This enables him to see the "nature" poets of the Confederation period as they are at their best and most poetic, that is, as poets, and as nature poets—not as social poets or as intellectual poets. When they tried to be those they ceased to be poets. Professor Daniells states this well, implying, I think, that it is a mistake to approach them from a sociological standpoint.

> It has often been noticed that in the decades following Confederation the supreme art in Canada is poetry and that the best poems concern themselves with Canadian natural surroundings. This may be thought incompatible with the kind of Canada First aims that had just previously been discussed, yet . . . we can perhaps concede that the Canadian poets chose with an instinctive wisdom. It is not Lampman alone who, believing profoundly in his country, finds in landscape the intuition of its goodness and greatness. . . . In ways that are not always rationally clear and through channels of expression often far from logically explicit Canadian feeling about the terrain of Canada made itself powerfully felt. Then, as now, the geological, topographical, and lyric features of the Canadian landscape were the fundamental facts of Canadian experience.

This point of view, it will be seen, is closer to the poetry of Pratt and the criticism of Frye than it is to the more mundane and somewhat carping views about the limitations of Lampman and the others expressed in the thirties by W. E. Collin in what is in most respects an extremely valuable essay.

Space demands that I should pass rather quickly over the adequate and thorough but not very inspiring chapters on the novel and poetry of the last thirty or forty years. It is good, however, to note the patient seriousness with which Professor Beattie treats such difficult, original, and very different poets as Margaret Avison, John Glassco, and George Johnston; and to follow Professor Pacey in his painstaking endeavour to do no less than justice by a Callaghan, a Grove, or a Mazo de la Roche. But the finest thing in the fourth section of the book, I think, is the analysis in Professor Kilbourne's account of "The Writing of Canadian History," of the literary art which assures such masterpieces as Donald Creighton's *The Commercial Empire of the St. Lawrence* or *Dominion of the North* of a high and permanent place in our literature. An equal value is assigned to the expression of almost diametrically opposite historical and political views in the brilliant and elegant essays collected in Frank Underhill's *In Search of Canadian Liberalism.* The time is coming, if some of the shorter chapters in this volume are taken seriously, when such works as those by Creighton and Underhill—along with C. N. Cochrane's *Christianity and Classical Culture* and some of the books of Innes, McLuhan, and Frye will be recognized as true classics of our literature, having a greater permanent interest than all but a handful of novels or collections of verse.

It is to Professor Frye's contribution to this book that I must now turn. Frye was given the completed manuscript and entrusted with the task of drawing it all together and of discovering whatever unity there was in its diversity; commenting on the method, style, and significance of the various contributions; and presenting his own conclusions of a synoptic sort. The last part of the job he has accomplished with brilliant success. Once the dutiful part of the critic's task has been taken care of in the more laboured first few pages, stimulating ideas bristle everywhere. Frye has astonished us before with paradoxes which, as he presents them, seem like truisms. Here they have the special advantage of making us go back and read again, and sometimes to question even some of the most impressive things in the book. When, for instance, we read a paragraph like this:

> Civilization in Canada, as elsewhere, has advanced geometrically across the country, throwing down the long parallel lines of the railways, dividing up the farm-lands into chess-boards of square-mile sections and concession-line roads. There is little adaptation to nature: in both architecture and arrangement, Canadian cities and villages express rather an arrogant abstraction, the conquest of nature by an intelligence that does not love it. The word conquest suggests something military, as it should— one thinks of General Braddock preferring to have his army annihilated rather than fight the natural man on his own asymmetrical ground...

we are not only struck by a truth we have overlooked, but we are compelled to re-read Professor Daniell's fine analysis of the nature poets of the Confederation period and, indeed, to modify it slightly in the light of a wider topographical insight.

And when, to give one more illustration, we come upon an analysis of the modern literary situation as pregnant as the following, we realize what we have been missing in the more conventional expositions in the body of the book.

During the last decade or so a kind of social Freudianism has been taking shape, mainly in the United States, as a democratic counterpart of Marxism. Here society is seen as controlled by certain anxieties, real or imaginary, which are designed to repress or sublimate human impulses toward a greater freedom. These impulses include the creative and the sexual, which are closely linked. The enemy of the poet is not the capitalist but the "square," or representative of repressive morality. The advantage of this attitude is that it preserves the position of rebellion against society for the poet, without imposing on him any specific social obligations. This movement has had a rather limited development in Canada, somewhat surprisingly considering how easy a target the square is in Canada.... It ignores the old political alignments: the Communists are usually regarded as Puritanic and repressive equally with the bourgeoisie.... Thus it represents to some extent a return to the undifferentiated radicalism of a century before, though no longer in a political context.

This is new, true, and important, and it is only a sample of the many good things scattered through Professor Frye's conclusion. Unfortunately, as I have suggested, there is less to be satisfied with in the first part of the essay and in the general principles he seems there to have been forced to accept. Anyone who has come this far in the present review will understand the astonishment with which I read the beginning of Frye's second paragraph:

> The book is a tribute to the maturity of Canadian literary scholarship and criticism, whatever one thinks of the literature. Its authors have completely outgrown the view that evaluation is the end of criticism, instead of its incidental by-product. Had evaluation been their guiding principle, this book would, if written at all, have been only a huge debunking project, leaving Canadian literature a poor naked *alouette* plucked of every feather of decency and dignity.

This last sentence is modified a bit—and a little illogically, it seems to me—in the one that follows: "True, the book gives evidence, on practically every one of its eight hundred odd pages, that what is really remarkable is not how little but how much good writing has been produced in Canada."

This, however, is not the main point I wish to question but the more fundamental one of the true function of criticism. I have always believed that evaluation *is* the end, purpose, and *raison d'être* of criticism and that criticism without evaluation would be, if it could be called criticism, the least rewarding of the pastimes available to the dwellers in an ivory tower. It would be limited to classification and the compilation of book lists—a limitation that even the writers on the early novel forget with their oft-repeated epithets "sentimental," "sensational," "third rate," and others even less complimentary.

Professor Frye declares that "the evaluative view is based on the conception of criticism as mainly concerned to define and canonize the genuine classics of literature." But this is both too lofty and too narrow a view. Criticism does, of course, contribute to the slow completion of such a task when there are classics of universal worth to canonize, but when there are not, there is still the job of defining and measuring the good works of local and even national interest and of incomplete perfection. And there is also the imperative need (the condition of our literature being what it is here described) to evaluate the bad works, whether imitative, dull, pretentious, or incompetent—works which are below the level of literature—and to throw them out. For a real critic "standards current in mid-twentieth-century English departments" have more validity than the popular taste for sentimental romance in the eighteen-eighties.

The key word is "literary." Professor Frye is right when he says that in the Canadian context "the conception of what is literary has to be greatly broadened," and points out that in one sense this has been done in the work at hand: "We have asked for chapters on political, historical, religious, scholarly, philosophical, and other non-literary subjects. . . ."

This procedure has gone wrong, I believe, because the distinction between the literary and the non-literary has been based on subject matter and genre rather than on quality. It is to miss some of the truth and most of the significance to say that "The literary in Canada, is often only an incidental quality of writings which, like those of many of the early explorers, are as innocent of literary intention as a mating loon."

It is this very innocence of literary intention (coupled with practical competence) that gives to the writings of a Hearne, a David Thompson or a Dr. Dunlop a quality much more worthy the attention of a true critic than the artifices of a Richardson, a Kirby, or a Carman. This is why the writings of the fur-traders particularly should be granted a high place in the record of our *literary* history. Hearne, Henry, Mackenzie, Thompson, and the rest write with a steady downright competence akin to the skill with which they used the sextant or wielded the paddle, and as a result have become the authors of some of the brightest pages of our literature.

I would broaden the scope of the literary, then, to include in Canada a great deal of the non-bellelettristic work of pioneers and explorers and in modern times that of the historians, biographers, and men of letters who bring the qualities of a literary artist to the expression of practical ideas. But I would narrow it to exclude all those verses and fictions whose quality is not fine enough. They are pseudo-literary or sub-literary, and they should be relegated to bibliographies and dealers' catalogues.

But I do not want to fall into the gravest error of the bad critic—that of condemning a book for failing to be what its authors never intended it to be. It is legitimate, however, to wish that the intention had been a little different and that the philosophy that predominates had had sufficient confidence in our literature to make *quality* alone the criterion for examination and evaluation. The need for such a book as the present is by no means negligible, but it is not so great as it was before the *Check List* of R. E. Watters and the establishment of *Canadian Literature*. What is needed now is a comprehensive "critical history" by a single author who can combine scholarly research with imaginative interpretation and who has enough faith in the literary quality of the best work drawn from all kinds of writing—science, history, travel, biography, and autobiography as well as poetry and fiction—to make evaluation his first business and let the chips fall where they may.

*Impromptu Remarks Spoken at the International Poetry Conference, Man and His World*

*from* Etudes littéraires

I would like to think that I am speaking as a poet to other poets, and that we could, therefore, take some things for granted and that we could perhaps deal with technicalities and problems that touch the poet as poet. But I would also like to feel that the poet speaking to other poets is a man speaking to men. And I would like to emphasize an aspect of the whole human personality that I think is sometimes misunderstood and underestimated, if not by critics, at least by poets, and certainly perhaps by the general public when it thinks about poetry or is instructed about poetry. I would like to suggest that poetry is a human activity and that if it is to be fully relevant, it must speak for the whole man, the whole human being. And I would like to say a word for that despised element of humanity—the intellect, and to emphasize the fact that for me at least intellect has an essential part to play in the creation of every poem, no matter from what depth of anarchic darkness in the mind it originally arises.

In modern American poetry particularly there has been a very healthy revolution against abstraction and what I might call superficial thinking: the reaction is expressed particularly of course, in the dictum of William Carlos Williams; addressing the poet, he says: "Say it; no ideas but in things," and the kind of objective, imagist poetry which came, I suppose, to its triumphant culmination in the work of William Carlos Williams. It began, indeed, much earlier with such imagists as H. D. in the twenties, and, of course, the whole poetic career, technically speaking, of W. B. Yeats has been a move in the direction of concreteness and the sincerity that produces concreteness. You cannot be precise, exact and concrete in the presentation of nature unless you are sincere. "Sincere" is perhaps not quite an o.k. word, but let it pass. The kind of poetry that I think William Carlos Williams wanted and that in his last poems he certainly achieved triumphantly is a poetry that in Milton's words should be "simple, sensuous and passionate." We must not forget, however, that reality is not simple, and that the mind of man is not simple.

And that poetry—even poetry that looks simple—is not, even in its sources, or in its implications. We have heard a great deal about the treason of the intellectuals—*la trahison des clercs*—but there is also the treason of the anti-intellectuals that needs to be spoken against at the present time. The idea that poetry, if it is to reach a large audience, and presumably influence it, must be simple is incomplete. Much popular poetry today is simple and superficial, and sometimes the most superficial poetry is that which moves its audience most vividly and most deeply, and can therefore be extremely dangerous. It becomes a form of advertising, a form of propaganda, a form of public relations. What seems to me therefore to be the task of the serious poet is to practise, study and meet with other poets, to compare notes and talk with them, to read and try to discover how to integrate, how to combine all aspects of the human personality in language. The poet after all is a man of words, words and music, language, and experiments in language and what he is concerned with is an effort to integrate personality. Being a teacher, I do not mind being academic. When we are talking to other poets about these problems that concern us all as poets, I do not think it wrong to mention the names of the kind of poets that seem to me could most usefully help us today—the greatest name of all, of course, is Dante and in some respects his contemporary successor Ezra Pound; the poetry of Lorca, the very last poems of Yeats and of Williams, the *Confucian Odes* in Pound's translation and the poetry of René Char.

In closing, I would also like to mention briefly the concept of poetry as contemplation, as *rêverie*. I was interested to hear Robert Lowell say that he had come to doubt that the best way to be moved and influenced by poetry was to hear poets reading their poetry. It is much better to learn to read for yourself, to read the poem on a printed page in quietude at home, in solitude, in peace, and meditate upon it, and read it many times and in many moods. Just hearing it, without a text before you, and sometimes with the oratory of the reader to add something factitious that is not really in the poem at all, you are sometimes being misled. *Read* poetry rather than listen to it, and write poetry to be read.

Another thing I would say about poetry is that it is not an artificial hallucinatory drug; it is an instrument of search and research. I would like a poetry that avoids the loud, the general, the abstract, a poetry that is music for the inner ear. What good is this quiet intellectual poetry in the age that we live in, this violent wicked age of crises? Well, such poetry nourishes the human soul and encourages, it seems to me, whatever in man is strength to resist tyranny, cruelty and indifference, either in the state or in himself.

*PART SIX*

*A Personal Epilogue*

*from* Canadian Literature, *No. 15*

As a poet I am not the sort unenviously described in the lines beginning

> Though he lift his voice in a great O
> And his arms in a great Y.

When I write a poem I try to know what I am doing—at least with respect to craft. Luck is needed too, of course, and luck is unpredictable. All I know about it is that it has to be earned. Everything beneath the surface of technique remains obscure. It is this subterranean world I shall try to explore in these very tentative notes.

I remember a paradox of the psychology pundits: "How can I know what I think till I see what I say?" To apply this to the poet we need more verbs: *feel, fear, hope, love, hate*—an infinite series whose sum is *am* or *be*; so the question becomes for me "How do I know who I am till I hear what I write?"

> How all men wrongly death to dignify
> Conspire, I tell

sounds differently from "I tell how all men conspire to dignify death wrongly," and expresses (or is) a different person. One can understand, then, that it is with a good deal of trepidation that I look into this handsome volume, as into a magnifying mirror.

Some people may think it presumptuous to call a book of only a hundred short, mainly lyrical pieces of verse *Collected Poems*—but actually that is exactly what it is. Though I have a file full of verses in every stage of gestation from mere spawn to almost finished (that is, nearly *right*) poems, those in the book are all that I want to let out of my hands now, as being beyond my power to improve. Of these hundred, a few were written when I was an undergraduate and published in journals as different as the *McGill Fort-nightly Review* and the *Dial.* And a few were written just the other day. Which is which would be hard to tell. Many of the poems, though started long ago and some of them printed in an unsatisfactory version, were not corrected or really finished (that is, not written) until years later—in one or two cases until I was correcting page proofs last summer. The second to last line of "Far West," for example, as it stands now was a happy afterthought,[1] which not only intensified the accuracy of the experience but got rid of a miserable echo of Cummings that had troubled my conscience ever since the poem was first published in England in the late thirties. The second couplet of the last stanza of "The Fountain" had never seemed quite inevitable, but many hours work-ing over it in proof finally got it right—or at least I think so. Anyway, for bet-ter or worse, it remains, and now the third time round, the poem is written at last.

A really new poem, though made out of some very old sketches, is "The Two Birds." Working on the page proofs, I became dissatisfied with a piece of technically accomplished and rather emotionally enervating word-music that second thoughts told me ought to be dropped. ("The Circle" and "Nightfall" were about all the traffic would bear of that sort.) Almost by chance I came on a batch of old *McGill Fortnightly Reviews* stacked away in the attic. Looking through them I found a long-forgotten poem called "Something Apart." It was awkward, clumsy and undigested. There were some good lines in it but also some very trite phrases and hazy images. There was also one brief bit that had been taken over and worked into "The Lonely Land." But the poem consisted of three stanzas of seven lines each; and that was exactly the dimen-sions of the piece I wanted a substitute for. So I started to work on the redisco-vered sketches. I put a new ribbon in my typewriter, got a batch of typewriting paper and a couple of soft pencils, and started in. Suddenly, my imagination caught fire, and all the vague clichés of the thing began to drop away. I was able to organize it, tighten it, work out a development and bring it to a satisfying and unexpected close. The last lines had been particularly weak and sentimental. They told how the raucous bird was "something apart"—you have guessed it—"from the sorrow in my heart." But now every-thing was changed—the title, which awakens a curiosity which is not satisfied until the last line (though a clue is dropped in the middle line of the middle stanza, "a voice as twisted as mine"); the image of the heart as a second foul bird; the "gold sun's winding stair" of the second stanza; and, last of all to be written, the title and the first word of the poem, *So,* to suggest an antecedent

---

[1] The last two lines of Far West now run thus:

> As the cowboys rode their skintight stallions
> Over the barbarous hills of California.

The change involved only a single epithet—the substitution of "skintight" for "girl-smooth."

unspecified source of the bitterness, remorse, and self-disgust that the complete poem finally expresses. Unspecified, of course, because irrelevant—"another story," hinted at perhaps in the "Who is that bitter king? It is not I" of the first poem in the book and the reference to "this savory fatness" in "On Knowing 'Nothing'," one of the last. And here perhaps, with luck, will be the source of poems yet to be written.

You will see from all this that I do not believe in progress in the ordinary sense of the word. The more recent poems in this collection are neither "better" nor "worse" than the earlier, and what differences there are depend on the genre or the occasion, not on the time of writing. Such development as has occurred took place before the poem was printed. If the development was not marked enough then the piece remains in the notebook or file. The different voices and different modes called for by the different occasions should not obscure the underlying unity pervading even the most apparently different poems. "Ballade un peu Banale" is in one tone, "Good Friday" and "Canticle of St. John" are in another; but each is equally serious, and each modifies the others. The same is true of, say, "The Offices of the First and the Second Hour" and "Song Made in Lieu of Many Ornaments," the first a programme of asceticism and the second a playful but not frivolous treatment of the Pauline doctrine of holy matrimony. I agree with Geoffrey Grigson that there is no essential difference between an epic and a limerick. "You cannot suppose a divine or an inspired origin for one against a secular or rational origin for the other." Each must be equally well written; each must be as good as its author can make it. That is the function of the poet with respect to his poems. He is a craftsman, and for a great part of the time he is a conscious craftsman. It is only in the essential climactic moment (or hour) that the muse takes over and the work goes on one cannot say how or why.

My poems are not autobiographical, subjective, or personal in the obvious and perhaps superficial sense. None of them is reverie, confession or direct self-expression. They are fiction, drama, art; sometimes pastiche, sometimes burlesque, and sometimes respectful parody; pictures of possible attitudes explored in turn; butterflies, moths or beetles pinned wriggling—some of them, I hope—on the page or screen for your, and my, inspection. The "I" of the poem, the protagonist of its tragedy or the clown of its pantomime, is not me. As Rimbaud said, *Je est un autre,* I is another.

"Indeed?" I can hear you exclaim: "Then who *is* this collector of butterflies and bugs you have been describing? Your emblem ought to be the chameleon or mole, not the phoenix or swan."

You have a point all right. And it is an important one. It goes to the heart of the general problem of the role of personality, conscious and unconscious, in artistic creation—the problem, indeed, of personal responsibility. As a poet (no philosopher or moralist) I can only touch upon it lightly and indirectly—as in the poem "Poor Innocent":

> It is a gentle natural (is it I?) who
> Visits timidly the big world of
> The heart, . . .

The question is answered (or not answered) in the denouement of the little metaphysical comedy that is so well suited to the dynamics of the Italian sonnet:

> Back to your kennel, varlet! Fool, you rave!
> Unbind that seaweed, throw away that shell!

The controlling mind, the critical shaping faculty of the rational consciousness sends the tremulous instinctive and sensuous fancy packing.

It is this rather bossy intelligence which chooses what is to be expressed, considers how, and judges the final outcome. But what a lot escapes it—or cajoles it, or fools it. It did not choose the images, the metaphors, the sensations, or the sounds that chime and clash in the consonants and vowels—though it did eventually approve them. What or who was it, indeed, that suffered a sea-change so it could breathe in a world

> Where salt translucency's green branches bear
> This sea-rose, a lost mermaid, whose cold cave,
> Left lightless now, the lapping seatides lave
> At base of Okeanos' twisted stair

or watched

> What time the seamew sets
> Her course by stars among the smoky tides
> Entangled?

I do not know. Where *do* the images of a writer come from? From experience, I suppose. But not—in my case at least—from experience as emotion, and not remembered (that is, not *consciously* remembered) in tranquillity or otherwise. When, for instance, did I look up at an "icicle-sharp kaleidoscopic white sky" or see "birds like dark starlight twinkle in the sky"? When did I gaze on "the gold sun's winding stair" in the deep pinewoods or see "the green hills caked with ice" under a bloodshot moon? I do not know when, but I must have, waking or in dream, and the experience sank into the depths of the self to be dredged up heaven knows how long afterwards.

I do remember—not any one specific moment, but as in a dream many times, always at evening or in the early morning, the swallows skimming over the rapids by the old mill at Laval-sur-le-Lac near Saint Eustache where we used to go for the summer when I was a child. I remember 4 August 1914 there, and I remember helping to search for the body of a young man drowned in the rapids. And so the swallows, associated with loneliness and death by water, swerve into one or two of the more intimate of the poems and become a source of simile and metaphor. But why *crisp* should seem to be an obsessive word and *love* more than once evoke stinging whips I do not know.

Let us return to the known world of the consciousness. Irony and wit are intentional, and I note that there is one device of irony that I have seemed to find particularly congenial. This is ironic understatement or anti-climax, the intentional and rather insulting drop into bathos. This can be dangerous when turned upon oneself; ironic self-depreciation can be too easily taken by others as sober literal truth. But when turned against the knaves and fools who are the traditional targets of classical satire it can be very effective. I find a number of instances of it, however, whose intention or effect is less certain. I will try to take one or two of them apart to see how they work. This may perhaps help the reader to know why he thinks them good or bad.

In the following lines from "Bird and Flower" the destructive criticism is concentrated in the bathos of the last word:

> Some holy men so love their cells they make
> Their four gray walls the whole damned stinking world
> And God comes in and fills it *easily*.

The paradox here is in the statement that God should find anything easy or (by implication therefore) hard. What we have actually is an inverted hyperbole calculated to emphasize how small and mean is the monastic world of the "holy" men who blaspheme the world of natural love. Only for them, not for the poet and the particular woman he is writing about, is the world a damned and stinking world.

There is a similar paradoxical misapplication of a limiting adverbial idea to the infinity of God in the comic poem "Ballade un peu Banale" where in order to take the virgin cow to heaven Christ is described as having to make use of "some miraculous device." This sort of thing is found, without irony, in many primitive Christian paintings. I find another application (this time without pejorative intention) of a similarly incongruous or limiting epithet in the lines "To Henry Vaughan"

> Lifting the rapt soul out of Time
> Into a *long* Eternity.

As applied to the infinite duration of eternity *long* is understatement and bathos. Its purpose, however, is not to be ironic at the expense of the naiveté of Henry Vaughan. Far from it. The poem is a genuine tribute to a wholly admirable poet and seer. The purpose of the figure is to convey as sharply as possible the identification of time and eternity (see also "The Two Sides of a Drum") in the mind of Vaughan as a mystic,

> Where Heaven is now, and still to be.

I think this gets across for the reader who is sympathetic to Vaughan or to Christian or platonic ideas. For one who is not (and the present writer is sometimes one such reader and sometimes the other) the effect of irony does come through after all, and gently indicates the noble futility of Vaughan's magnificent piety.

A couple of other instances of this device will emphasize how characteristic it seems to be. From "Noctambule":

> Reality at two removes, and mouse and moon
> *Successful.*

Merely successful, not triumphant or victorious or right or good, so that even mouse and moon (as well as lion and sun) suffer from the deprivation that it is the main business of the poem to lament.

And in "The Common Man":

> At first he thought this helped him when he tried
> To tell who told the truth, who plainly lied.

The hyperbole in the idea that it is a matter of great difficulty to tell who *plainly* lied is the concisest way of suggesting the confusion of values in the modern world of political propaganda, mass media brainwashing, and cold-war bilge. Though this poem was written in the mid-forties it has got truer every decade and is another version of the ironic series of events outlined in the angry political poems on the threat of nuclear suicide.

It is obvious that there is much here that is consciously contrived; much too whose author, a greater poet might say, is in eternity. How good either is, it is not for me to say. I hope every reader of this piece will buy the book and judge for himself.

1964 | *The Poetic Process*

On the Making of Poems

*Fifth Annual* Centennial Review Lecture,
*Michigan State University*

As a professor of literature and a student of criticism, I find the mechanics of
motivation and the workings of the intellect and the emotions in poetic creation afford material for speculation that is of absorbing interest; but insofar
as I am a poet it has been my habit to treasure the finished composition alone,
and to hide, forget, and discard the preliminary sketches, the abortive or tentative drafts and all the messy paraphernalia of notes, hints, guesses, and
errors—even though most of them were as necessary to the construction of the
work as scaffolding to the building of a tower. The *finished work* rather than
the work of finishing is what I have valued most. Indeed, if the poem produced is not more interesting than the account of *how* it was produced, one
would be hard put to it to write a defense of poetry.

I suppose I am what is called an academic poet; but I accept the epithet
only if it is cleansed of its opprobrious implications, its suggestions of
pedantry, mere bookishness, pure formalism, and timid conventionality. I
prefer to think the term an honourable one. It implies (or should imply) an
awareness of tradition and an understanding of the forces that bring about
change, development, progress, and growth. I think of the act of a poet as the
antithesis of a naive or primitive surrender to chance or impulse and equally
the antithesis of any sophisticated and calculating abandonment of control
or consciousness.

The poet who is more than an occasional dabbler or a mere self-expres-
sionist knows that poetry is an art and a craft; and he seeks, by study, practice, imitation, and discipleship, to master it, and later, if he is successful, to
develop it, to extend its limits, and push forward to new discoveries. But this
most difficult of all tasks must wait upon mastery and maturity. A few poets
of genius (for example Pope and Rimbaud) attain this mastery early; others,

like Yeats, win to it after half a lifetime of patient devotion. As I think of the term, not only Yeats and Pound but William Carlos Williams as well are academic poets.

I name these poets particularly, for these are the poets who have formed me—and my generation. These are our "bards triumphant," and all of us, even the meanest of their sons need not be afraid to testify (in the words of Pope) that he: "Glows while he reads, but trembles as he writes." Wordsworth, it is sometimes forgotten, recognized as clearly as Pope that nature (that is, truth and reality) was to be found in Homer as well as in hills, meadows, brooks, and fountains. The poet, he writes in "The Prelude," receives in peculiar measure

> enduring touches of deep joy
> From the great Nature that exists in works
> Of mighty Poets.

A writer of verse who, like myself and so many poets today, is also a teacher has the advantage of being compelled to expound, explicate, and reconcile different and apparently incompatible theories of poetry. This makes it impossible for him not to be aware of what he is doing or trying to do. In the experience of other poets in other times he has a series of touchstones that help him understand and evaluate his own practice.

One may begin by asking: Why are poems written? What are the motives that induce or compel a poet to write? "Fame is the spur," said Milton—and added "That last infirmity of noble minds:" Donne had another explanation, and perhaps a better one—*to find relief:*

> I thought, if I could draw my paines,
> Through Rimes vexation, I should them allay,
> Griefe brought to numbers cannot be so fierce,
> For he tames it, that fetters it in verse.

In these lines it is relief from the pangs of unrequited love; but more generally the relief that the poet seeks in the hard work of "turning his verses" is relief from the pain of an unborn poem swelling in the womb of the mind. Certain emotions and certain as yet inarticulate ideas are seeking rhythms, cadences, and words; until they find them the mind is painfully agitated. There is a nagging, teasing unrest (akin to the feeling of mental distress when a name you know perfectly well has slipped from the memory and defies all your efforts to make it come back—until later when you have given up trying some chance association suddenly restores it).

I think this analogy expresses very clearly what happens when a poem-subject is just beginning to push up out of the unconscious (or at least out of the wordless) into the articulate. Paul Valéry has described the situation with exemplary precision.

> The poet awakes within a man at an unexpected event, an outward or an inward incident: a tree, a face, a "subject," an emotion, a word. Sometimes it is the will to expression that starts the game, a need to translate what one feels; another time, on the contrary, it is an element of form, the outline of an expression which seeks its origin, seeks a meaning within the space of my mind.... Note this possible duality in ways of getting started: either something wants to express itself, or some means of expression wants to be used.

This experience (triggered by "an unexpected event") has an affinity with Joyce's epiphanies, Eliot's "objective correlative," and the effect of the taste of the madeleine dipped in tea upon Marcel Proust. Valéry goes on to say that sometimes for him a rhythm or a metrical pattern was the only seed of a poem, which later took words and structure simply to express that rhythm. This is his explanation of the origin of one of his greatest masterpieces, "Le Cimetière marin."

Not many poets, I imagine, are as pure as this, but perhaps if we could push our scrutiny back far enough into the pre-natal life of poems we might find a connection here with the fact that Coleridge liked to compose while walking over rough ground. I must confess that I myself am not enough of a poet ever to have found the source of a poem in a pre-conceived musical structure.

In my case, the nagging thought that such and such a "subject" ought to become a poem grows more and more insistent. When this feeling (it is hardly a thought) first came into being I do not know, but after a time it begins to limit itself, to become more specific, clearer, sharper, and at the same time more intense. When this has gone on for a considerable time—weeks or even months perhaps—there is suddenly and unexpectedly, through the operation of I know not what fortuitous catalyst, a sudden breakthrough. It may be a line, a phrase or two, or a cadence that comes into the mind. But whatever it is, the period of gestation is over. The actual birth-pangs are beginning and the conscious mind, in the role of midwife, is ready to start working.

Now the sheer hard unromantic brainwork begins. What happens is very like what happens when you are working out a crossword puzzle or trying to solve a chess problem. I do not find, however, that this sort of activity alone will carry a poem through to the end. Conscious calculation is a secondary, revising, and controlling activity. Soon the mind will have shaped all the material (emotion-idea, cadence-image, picture-word, resonance-word—I am trying to invent names for the as yet unsounded or unarticulated bits of the coming poem)—the mind will have shaped all the material that invention has so far brought into view. Perforce the poet stops. He sits bowed over the typewriter like a devotee at the shrine of some cruel deity. His mind is blank; there is an almost trance-like concentration until, if he is lucky, imagination begins to clothe itself in words again.

At these points of hesitation and crisis I have to stop, take a rest, put a new sheet of paper in the typewriter, and start all over again from the beginning. My own experience (I can speak for no other writer here) is that I cannot go on to a third stanza, say, until stanzas one and two are finished and seem, at the moment anyway, perfect. Conscious progression, I find, has to stop and wait for a return of the subjective excitement felt at the beginning when the idea of the poem began (in John Donne's phrase) to take on limbs of flesh and blood.

Conscious awareness, as distinct from emotional excitement, does begin sooner, I think, and goes deeper than is generally realized. "As much consciousness as possible" is the rule that Valéry gives, and he advises the poet in the act of writing to "try by conscious will to achieve a few results similar to those interesting or usable ones which come to us (out of a hundred thousand random events) from mental chance."

Such remarks as these—if I may be allowed a digression, which is not, however, altogether irrelevant—belong to a tradition of thinking about the creative process in poetry that stems from Baudelaire and through him from Poe. This effort is the work mainly of poets—Baudelaire, Mallarmé, Rimbaud, Yeats, Valéry, and the surrealists. These extreme romantics plunge into the depths of personality and seek to isolate a unique essence, fished out of the unconscious and discovered not as thought or emotion, not as picture or music, but as poetry and nothing but poetry.

Rimbaud sought this through the systematic distortion of the senses—and failed, though he wrote two immensely significant poetic documents, *Une Saison en Enfer* and *Les Illuminations,* before renouncing the art of poetry completely. Mallarmé, fascinated with the idea of purity, potentiality, and Nothingness, came to think of the creative act as a progressive paring away of the outer shell of reality until nothing is left but a tiny kernel of essential being. Choice after choice is refused, because *any* choice destroys the rich potentialities and possibilities in the sum of all the others. The ideal poem for Mallarmé is the one which continuously and most closely approaches an absolute, an infinite series whose final term, were it ever reached, would be zero. This is metaphysical poetry with a vengeance, and in speaking about it one is driven to use the language of mathematics.

The effect of this kind of thinking is to throw the emphasis on poetry as a process rather than on a poem as a thing, and this has been the result also of the criticism of Mallarmé's greatest disciple, Paul Valéry, to whose essays and discourses I could not possibly conceal my indebtedness. It is Valéry who has made the most cogent attempt of any modern poet to isolate and define the unique emotion of poetry and to describe—at least insofar as he himself has experienced it—the nature of the poet's work as maker.

I would like to quote a rather long passage from a lecture Valéry delivered in 1927 entitled "Propos sur la poésie" ("Remarks on Poetry"). I introduce it here because it has made me aware of what I believe, and perhaps have experienced, without actually knowing it or being able to put it into words. Valéry is embarked on the project of isolating and defining a unique emotion, which he calls the *poetic* emotion. He goes about it in this way:

> You know what most men feel, more or less strongly and purely, when faced with an impressive natural spectacle. We are moved by sunsets, moonlight, forests, and the sea. Great events, critical moments of the affective life, the pains of love, and the evocation of death are so many occasions for, or immediate causes of, inner reverberations more or less intense and more or less conscious.
>
> This type of emotion is distinguishable from all other human emotions. How is it so? This is what we must now discover. We must contrast as clearly as possible poetic emotion with ordinary emotion. This is a delicate operation to perform, for it is never accomplished in fact. One always finds tenderness, sadness, fury, fear, or hope intermingled with the essential poetic emotion; and the particular interests and affections of an individual never fail to combine with that *sense of a universe* which is characteristic of poetry.
>
> The poetic state or emotion seems to me to consist in a dawning perception, a tendency toward perceiving a *world,* or complete system of relations, in which beings, things, events, and acts, although they may resemble, *each to each,* those which fill and form the tangible world—the immediate world from which they are borrowed—stand, however, in an indefinable, but wonderfully accurate relationship to the modes and laws of our general sensibility. So, the value of these well-known objects and beings is in some way altered. They respond to each other and combine quite otherwise than in ordinary conditions. They become—if you will allow the expression—*musicalized,* somehow commensurable, echoing each other. The poetic universe defined in this way bears a strong analogy to the universe of dream.

After disavowing in his own thought the romantic confusion of poetry with dream—("figures formed by chance are only by chance harmonious figures")—Valéry goes on to point out a real and useful affinity between the world of poetry and the world of dream:

> a dream makes us see by a common and frequent experience how our consciousness can be invaded, filled, [and] made up by an assembly of

productions remarkably different from the mind's ordinary reactions and perceptions. It gives us the familiar example of a *closed world* where all real things can be represented, but where everything appears and is modified solely by the fluctuations of our deepest sensibility.

In very much the same way the poetic state begins, develops, and dissolves within us. That is, it is wholly irregular, inconstant, involuntary, fragile, and we lose it, as we acquire it, by accident. There are times in our life when this emotion and these precious formations do not appear. We do not even think them possible. Chance gives them and chance takes them away.

Valéry calls it chance. I prefer to call it luck, and to affirm that when it comes, it comes to the deserving. After it comes, then consciousness begins, and judgment and technical manipulation are brought into play. This happens, it seems to me, when will and desire have reached such a pitch of excitement that they spill over into images or rhythms, which perforce can only find expression in words. The form or shape, in its widest sense, that this mental activity tends to adopt as it becomes objectified determines the form that the poem itself will take. Whether the poem will develop as something new and unique or, what is much more likely, grow into a traditional and well established pattern is an early and crucial decision in which both the unconscious and the conscious mind play a part.

Such a decision is the result of a crystallization in the mind, a sort of irradiation of light or warmth that surrounds the "subject" of the poem and begins to delimit it. This is the ultimate source of the poem's form. Where this light or warmth is, there is the poem. The place where dark and cold begin marks the edge or formal frontier of the poem. This is the shape of the content, and this determines what might be called the "amount of the subject matter"—for only enough to fill out the form can be admitted.

Such forms have often been strict, intricate, and difficult. But they present a challenge, a challenge that is not a hindrance but a stimulus to creativity. The greater the challenge the greater the response, until in the case of a mature and experienced poet—W. H. Auden is a good example—the formal, the artificial, and modifications of the conventional become a second nature.

Strict, intricate, and difficult forms are not, of course, a departure from nature or a violation of nature. The artist, as Jacques Maritain has put it, steals from nature its own secrets of poetry. The forms I think of in nature as strict and intricate are such forms as the snowflake, the crystal, the butterfly wing, or the chain of carbon atoms. The poet can rarely hope to equal these—perhaps only Pope in *The Rape of the Lock* and Shakespeare in *A Midsummer Night's Dream* ever did it; but there is nothing contemptible in aspiring to formal perfection, even on the smallest scale.

But it is time to be more specific. Let me draw these general remarks together by a concrete illustration of how one particular poem came to be written. It is a short poem of two stanzas, and its general subject is the very common one of death.

The general idea of death or nothingness as a vague but yet disturbing and, if concentrated on, frightening concept has been hanging over my sensibility for longer than I can remember. (I call "nothingness" an idea or concept, but that is hardly accurate—how can you give a name to non-being, what Donne called "dull privation and lean emptiness . . . absence, darkness, death, things which are not"?) In the state of discomfort and frustration caused, I suppose, by an imaginative realization of the inescapable and unpleasant *fact* of death and the seeming impossibility of controlling it in any way—even to the extent of finding a *name* (not the glib conventional meaningless word or sign) for it, there came (Valéry's chance; my luck) an image or a picture of an arrow winging its flight through an empty sky—to what end? into what heart or target? The image gave no clue. Into darkness? into nothingness? Or was the flight infinite? Something in the picture, I cannot tell what—perhaps a slight downward inclination of the arrow's tip—made that impossible. My arrow was to be no symbol of immortality—of that at least I was certain. Shelley's phrase "into the intense inane" came into my mind, but brought no light. Then I thought of Longfellow's lines, memorized in grade school:

> I shot an arrow into the air
> It fell to earth I knew not where.

The laws of association are not made for snobs, and unfashionable poems (indeed bad poems) are often as memorable as good ones. But Longfellow's couplet gave me the answer I had been unconsciously avoiding. It was the phrase "to earth." I do not know whether the idea, the picture, or the line came into my awareness first: the idea of life as a speeding arrow; the picture, not logically or rationally consistent, of the statuesque figure of a mighty archer; and the line "Bend back thy bow, O Archer, till the string. . . ."

The line is incomplete as picture or statement, but metrically it was quite satisfactory—and indeed mandatory. It was an iambic pentameter, and it ended with a word that was a fairly easy rhyme. Though it was too early to tell yet, it looked as if this might be the start of a sonnet. The heavy break in the line after *bow,* followed by the rhyming vowel *O,* followed in its turn by the pause demanded by the beginning vowel of *Archer*—the whole cadence suggesting effort and demanding force from the lungs of the reader to overcome the sequence of stresses and heavy pauses—all this gave promise of a sound-and-sense identity that is one of the hallmarks of the classical sonnet.

I said the line was an iambic pentameter. It is a very abnormal and eccentric one, of course, made up mostly of spondees:

> Bend back/thy bow,/O Arch/er &c.

so that it would be more accurate to say perhaps that it was an exceptional line, metrically speaking, which would, however, fit easily into a regular sequence of iambic pentameters. The desired effect of effort and strain is reinforced further by the alliteration of the three *b's* followed by the two vowel sounds *O* and *Ah.* So we are started on what may turn out to be a sonnet. The general theme is suggested as metaphor, analogy, or symbol; and we have an opening cadence and the beginning of a statement. To bring the statement to a completion is not hard. Indeed, the sentence practically writes itself:

> Bend back thy bow, O Archer, till the string
> Is level with thine ear.

One other property of the poem has now already been decided, and, it seems, without any conscious act of will on my part. The presence—the quite natural and inevitable presence of *thy* and *thine* has indicated that the poem is to be formal, dignified, and traditional. And this imposes a real burden. It is very hard today to write in this mode without becoming imitative and stuffy. But if the rhythm can convey the movement of a real and intense feeling, truly and vividly, all will be well.

I will not tire you with a minute and detailed account of the slow progress of what indeed did turn out to be an Italian sonnet. By moving from cadence to cadence and sentence to sentence—and from rhyme to rhyme—controlled now quite consciously, I was able to get the discourse under way. Draft after draft (to the number of twenty or more), each effecting some slight step forward or small clarification, brought the first part of the poem near to completion. It came out like this:

> Bend back thy bow, O Archer, till the string
> Is level with thine ear, thy body taut,
> Its nature art, thyself thy statue wrought
> Of marble blood, thy weapon the poised wing
> Of coiled and aquiline Fate.

There is a full stop here; we are just over half way through the octave of an Italian sonnet. But here the mind is pulled up sharp. It must halt and take stock. Where to go next? and how?

So far all has been static. The bow is drawn back; the archer is poised in a statuesque tension; the arrow is aimed. Now the coiled spring must be released and the arrow take its flight. In the next strophe, therefore, the movement of the verse must be fast, not slow; there must be no resistance; the sentences must run on without a break or pause. In the first four and a half lines the reader has been impeded by commas and little blocks of phrases; now he must be made breathless by the uninterrupted and unflagging continuity.

In the actual writing, the momentum of what had gone before and the guidance afforded by the rhymes made the course easy. The next strophe came quickly and almost effortlessly, though when I began to write the one sentence it is made up of, I did not know how it would end. . . .

> Bend back thy bow, O Archer, till the string
> Is level with thine ear, thy body taut,
> Its nature art, thyself thy statue wrought
> Of marble blood, thy weapon the poised wing
> Of coiled and aquiline Fate. Then, loosening, fling
> The hissing arrow like a burning thought
> Into the empty sky that smokes as the hot
> Shaft plunges to the bullseye's quenching ring.

The "inspiration" of the final phrase *the bullseye's quenching ring* was made easy, if not inevitable, by the necessity for a rhyme—indeed, after *string, wing, fling,* what is there but *ring?* But it is the word *quenching* that is best of all—the final anticlimactic word to follow *hissing, burning,* and *smokes* and to prepare for the identification at the very end of the poem of the bullseye with the grave, the "earthen lake" of Anglo-Saxon poetry.

But as yet the sonnet is only half finished; the sestet remains to be written. This is a more pressing and difficult new start, for the "turn" (the emotional and rhetorical change that occurs at the point between the octave and the sestet of the Italian sonnet) is as much a part of its traditional "form" as the rhymes or the metre. How well the poet can make the emotional, ideational, and tonal contrast or comparison between the two parts is a measure of his skill. Clearly one of the reasons why poems are written is that they present an intriguing technical problem crying out to be solved and a challenge or test of one's credentials as a poet. It is very hard, however, to draw a sharp distinction between what is conscious and what is unconscious in the work. The form demands conscious effort and a knowledge of the laws of poetic architecture, but the seed of its inception is sown in darkness though it is nurtured in the light of cerebration. Yet when the finished stanza or completed poem comes to be examined, it may well turn out that the best strokes of all got in when the conscious mind was not looking and that the most praiseworthy strokes surprise the author as well as delight the reader.

But to return to "The Archer." By the end of the octave, the bow has been loosed, and the arrow is in flight. It is moving fast—but we have six lines to go before it plunges to earth. How shall the poem proceed? Meditation and prolonged thought do not provide the answer here, or if they do, it is indirectly—by tiring the mind and lulling it into an almost trance-like state of receptivity in which by chance or luck the answer sometimes comes.

In this particular instance, the answer was to personalize and individualize the poem by introducing the pronoun *I*, and thus to identify the archer with the writer himself (not literally, of course, but anagogically) as well as with man and/or death. This I found involved a return to the stasis of the beginning in an attempt to seize imaginatively the moment just before the decision is taken to loose the bow and let the arrow fly—which means, I suppose, the acceptance by the intellect (though not necessarily by the will) of the idea of death.

By now the *plot* of the poem has become clear. It remains only to fit the developing theme into the pattern imposed by its traditional form and draw it to some kind of climax in the final line—a climax that is not yet certain, but I am reasonably sure now will develop out of the discourse as we go along.

All the thought expended on the problem and the emotion experienced and, so far, mastered, now begin to bear fruit. The sestet got under way and moved forward quickly, with only two or three pauses and revisions. Its first four lines were these:

> So for a moment, motionless, serene,
> Fixed between time and time, I aim and wait:
> Nothing remains for breath now but to waive
> His prior claim and let the barb fly clean. . . .

Halted at this point, just before the end of a sentence and the end of the poem (with just two lines remaining in which to rear up for the final climactic blow) I noted with a certain satisfaction the amount of assonance, alliteration, and internal rhyme that, quite without being consciously sought for, had come into these four lines—good-character witnesses, I think, testifying at least to the genuineness and intensity of the emotion. The unexpected concatenation of *serene-between; aim-wait-remain-claim-clean* and *waive* indicated that my Muse at last had taken over. Best of all was the fact that the rhymes suggested (indeed practically dictated) the last two lines—*wait* called for *hate,* and *waive* demanded *grave* (the final aspect of earth as the arrow's goal) and kept, as the strongest of these words, for its place at the very end. The poem came to its close, then, like this:

> Nothing remains for breath now but to waive
> His prior claim and let the barb fly clean
> Into the heart of what I know and hate—
> That central black, the ringed and targeted grave.

It was only after this poem was finished and I was coming back to it (as I always do) as a stranger reading something written by somebody else, that I noticed how significant was its Freudian imagery—so that the poem may very well be a betrayal of the guilty knowledge hidden in the unconscious self of the identity of love and death—a knowledge revealed also in Keats' last sonnet and in his "Ode to a Nightingale," as well as in the Elizabethan and Restoration meaning of *to die*.

Perhaps after all our careful planning, it is the unconscious that triumphs after all.

The account I have given here of the composition of a sonnet may help you to understand that it is not generally more difficult to write in a strict form than in a free one. Usually it is easier. When Robert Frost said that he would no more write free verse than he would play tennis without a net, he meant that without rules and conventions there is no game and therefore no fun—in other words, no poem at all, not a work of art, only a hunk of raw expression. Good free verse, of course, (as composed by Walt Whitman and the seventeenth-century translators of the Bible) is not free at all, but its laws are uncodified and elastic and demand a great deal of tact, taste, and intuition. The unpracticed and unaccomplished beginner is doubly wrong when he thinks that free verse is easy and the stricter forms are hard. The tennis net and the chalk boundary lines are only impediments to the novice. For those who have learnt how to play the game, they are guide lines and supports.

When we come to the question of language, however, it is impossible to go by any hard and fast rule. Here anything goes—*suitability* to the theme, *relevance* to the situation, *appropriateness* to the poem—loose enough restrictions, heaven knows!—are all we can postulate—these, and the greatest possible variety the traffic will bear. In "The Archer" that was not much. There the diction had to be consistently precise, elegant, and even exalted. It sought a level midway between the bookish and the colloquial.

"The Archer" is not the only poem that the ambivalent and very oppressive feelings about death (and especially about my own death) led, or rather forced, me to write; but it is the only one that was traditional or academic in form and diction. It found a style for the expression of universal and somewhat majestic reflections on a traditional theme. More often, however, in my experience, a more personal, particular, peculiar—and therefore more limited—cluster of feelings is what begin to take shape and push up into the awakened mind. To illustrate this more usual experience, let me quote a sentence or two from another poem on the same theme as the sonnet we have been discussing.

They are from some irregular and rather casually rhymed verses called "On Knowing 'Nothing'." This poem was produced out of a troubled and uncomfortable fascination with unconsciousness or non-being, a brief or prolonged form of death that is experienced under anaesthetics or at the climactic moment of love, and which *might,* but does not, bring a reconciliation with the idea of death. This, as I state it here, strikes me as the kind of subject particularly suited to poetry. Music or painting are not quite specific (or verbal) enough to deal with it fully; but the poetry that could deal with it best would be a poetry that goes as far as possible in the direction of painting or music—a poetry in which idea, sensation, and emotion have become one. I do not pretend to have written such poetry, and ought not even think it necessary to say so. Dante is the only poet who consistently writes on that level.

The feelings and ideas, however, clustered about the concept *nothing* like lines of force about a magnetic point are, I repeat, poetic in their very nature, and their natural expression is verse. There is no possibility of artifice and convention here. The words are as simple and straightforward as the feeling is immediate and personal.

These feelings had been lacerating my mind for a long time, but the chance-born catalytic incitement had not come. One evening I was sitting quietly, alone in the house, reading Camus' *The Plague.* The book is filled with images of death and descriptions of dying, but when I came upon a sentence that tells of a mortally stricken woman lifting herself from the bed with one last cry—the single word *Never!*—I was seized with a sudden and unexpected thrill. I dropped the book, grasped a pad of paper and a pencil, and began to write, almost without stopping, these lines:

> Others have seen men die
> Or heard a woman scream
> One last word *Never!*
> How do *I* know the horror
> That breaks the dream,
> Hateful, yet clung to
> As the image hugs the mirror
> With such a silver shiver
> As chills and almost kills?

The rest of the poem—two similar but not identical stanzas—came very quickly, within two days and with not more than half-a-dozen drafts of each stanza. I will quote the last one only because it comes round specifically to the theme I have described and has a conclusion almost identical with that of "The Archer"—ending on the same last word *grave.*

> The surgeon's jab, a woman's thigh
> Give blank surcease
> For short or long.
> I cannot let the hollow
> Interval alone,

> But pick it like a scab
> To probe the wound within—
> As deep, as nothing, as the grave.

If you read what the great poets have written about the nature of poetry, the motives for writing it, and the way it gets written you will find that every man's description—as everyone's *must* be—is an *apologia pro poemate sua,* an account of the kind of poetry he himself writes.

From Dryden, who wrote with genius what his public wanted—public poetry, didactic, witty, and satirical, you will learn that:

> The composition of all poems is, or ought to be of wit; and wit in the poet, or Wit-writing . . . is no other than the faculty of imagination in the writer, which, like a nimble spaniel beats over and ranges the quarry it hunted after. . . . Wit-written is that which is well defined, the happy result of thought or product of the imagination.

From Wordsworth you will hear—in words that every schoolboy knows, or ought to know—that

> Poetry is the spontaneous overflow of powerful feelings: it takes its origin from emotion recollected in tranquillity: the emotion is contemplated till, by a species of reaction, the tranquillity gradually disappears, and an emotion, kindred to that which was before the subject of contemplation, is gradually produced, and does itself actually exist in the mind.

Then you may turn to a modern critic and read in T. S. Eliot's *Tradition and the Individual Talent* (an essay quite as fruitful as Wordsworth's famous *Preface)* that we must believe

> "emotion recollected in tranquillity" is an inexact formula. For it is neither emotion nor recollection, nor, without distortion of meaning, tranquillity. It is a concentration, and a new thing resulting from the concentration, of a very great number of experiences which to the practical and active person would not seem to be experiences at all; it is a concentration which does not happen consciously or of deliberation.

One other passage, a little earlier in Eliot's essay, clarifies these ideas with the aid of a brilliant image—that of the catalyst, which brings on a chemical reaction without itself being affected by it. The instance he cites is that of a filament of platinum which when introduced into a mixture of certain gases causes them instantly to unite in chemical combination, but is itself unaltered.

The mind of the poet is the shred of platinum. It may partly or exclusively operate upon the experience of the man himself; but, the more perfect the artist, the more completely separate in him will be the man who suffers and the mind which creates; the more perfectly will the mind digest and transmute the passions which are its material.

Nothing, I think, than the juxtaposition of these passages by Wordsworth and by Eliot could more clearly define the distinction between the romantic and the classical point of view with respect to poetic creation. For Eliot, and for the modern poet generally, poetry is not an expression but a distillation of experience; passion is transmuted; and suffering (if a physiological or medical term may be permitted) is digested.

After all, Aristotle spoke of *catharsis*. But in the writing of a poem, it is the poet himself who first of all is purged of the dross of experience, and finds relief. If you think this image undignified, let me offer you an alternative one—a sentence by Santayana that covers the poet and philosopher alike with the gently ironic praise that might be offered to a peacock or a nightingale:

Every animal has his festive and ceremonious moments, when he poses, or plumes himself, or thinks; sometimes he even sings and flies aloft in a sort of ecstasy.